We Never Learn

The Gunk Punk Undergut, 1988-2001

Eric Davidson

Backbeat
Books

An Imprint of Hal Leonard Corporation
New York

Published in 2010 by Backbeat Books
An Imprint of Hal Leonard Corporation
7777 West Bluemound Road
Milwaukee, WI 53213

Trade Book Division Editorial Offices
19 West 21st Street, New York, NY 10010

All images are from the author's personal collection except where otherwise specified.

Grateful acknowledgment is made to the following for permission to reprint lyrics from the songs indicated: Paul Cafaro for "Fuck 'em All," "Drugstore," "Let's Fuck," "Motherfucker," "Dominator," "Saturday Night," "Back Seat of My Car," and "Anybody Out There" (p. 52); and Ned Hayden for "I'm Sick" (p. 89).

Printed in the United States of America

Book design by Michael Kellner
Interior titles hand lettered by Cliff Mott

Library of Congress Cataloging-in-Publication Data is available upon request.

Davidson, Eric, singer.
  We never learn : the gunk punk undergut, 1988-2001 / Eric Davidson.
    p. cm.
  Includes index.
  ISBN 978-0-87930-972-5
  1. Punk rock music—United States—History and criticism. I. Title.
  ML3534.3.D38 2010
  781.66—dc22
                        2010013011
www.backbeatbooks.com

For New Bomb Turks

We've always been of the mind that it's easier to ask forgiveness than to ask for permission.

—EDDIE SPAGHETTI

CONTENTS

FOREWORD
THE INEFFABLE WHATSIS

Eric Davidson has set himself a formidable task with the writing of *We Never Learn*. He is attempting to name, codify, and delineate the history of a scene that existed nameless and in the shadows of various parallel movements within the general drool of underground punk rock during the latter half of the 1980s and the bulk of the 1990s. As an active participant in the scene (as a member of the New Bomb Turks) he has solid knowledge that some kind of scene did, in fact, exist. But what do you call it? It wasn't grunge, wasn't scum-rock, wasn't paisley-revisionism, wasn't post-core-thud, wasn't a whole goddamn lotta things.

The term Davidson chooses to use is gunk punk, a phrase as simultaneously useful and useless as any other, but one that he uses as vessel into which he pours meaning and definition by rigorous expostulation of examples of the ineffable whatsis for which he grasps.

Because Davidson uses his own experiences as a template and a failsafe bullshit detector, the book offers certain biases, especially canted toward Ohio bands and various maniacs associated with the Crypt Records universe. But that is hardly a problem. The history of Ohio's rich raunch heritage and the massive aesthetic vortex whirling around Crypt's Tim Warren are suitable peaks from which to try and make sense of it all.

The story is a patchwork, told in bits and pieces by various voices that were involved in creating the massive huzz of the bands. There are shards of Fred Cole's pre–Dead Moon story that reach back to the mid-'60s. Billy Childish's saga starts with the Pop Rivets in 1977. Billy Miller and Miriam Linna founded *Kicks* fanzine in 1978. The Lazy Cowgirls formed in L.A. in 1982. Death of Samantha's first

Cleveland gig was in 1983. Tim Warren released the first *Back from the Grave* compilation in 1984. That's the pre-history.

The rest of the story unfolds as a kind of great drunken brawl among record collectors, label guys, fanzine editors, musicians, promoters, and anyone else who was interested in pursuing certain questionable lifestyle choices. It's quite impressive that Davidson got as many of these gumps to talk to him as he did. They are a notoriously prickly and self-serving bunch. But they are also a cavalcade of bigger-than-life characters who don't seem averse to telling stories that present themselves in an unflattering but highly entertaining light.

Tales about New York's Raunch Hands, Chicago's Dwarves and Spain's Pleasure Fuckers are especially pleasant, but the whole book is really a good ride. By pounding home the three main motifs of the book—drunk, loud, and funny—Davidson manages to create a sense of how these aggressive, anarchic vanloads of fools managed to create something congruent in emotional terms, even if stylistic holism wasn't even worth considering.

The book's latter part is an interesting discussion of the dissipation of the scene's energy, brought on by the encroachment of major label politics, smarmy managers, and the illusion that there was money to be made in the wake of Nirvana's fantabulous season of shit.

There are a lot of testimonials to bad decisions made by one young drunk or another, but the most savage recapitulation is the saga of the White Stripes and their original mentor, Long Gone John of Sympathy for the Record Industry.

But that reminds me of a story that's not in here about one time Nate Young (aka Wolf Eyes) had a gig but no amp, and he asked Jack if he could borrow his. The deal was effected, but Nate, being Nate, managed to blow out Jack's speaker during the course of the evening. He got the amp back home, and he and John Olson were trying to figure out what to do. Finally, Nate remembered that he had some little radio speaker back in a box somewhere, so he hauled that out, they cut out the old speaker and soldered this tiny little one in its place. Nate gave the amp back to Jack and never heard any more about it. "But right after that," Nate recalls, "the band started getting a lot more popular and everyone was saying what a cool guitar sound Jack had. I don't really know, but Jack may owe me some royalties."

Anyway, Jack White or no Jack White, this is a very solid read and a fairly rousing argument for a scene you may have sensed existed, but which has never been really documented 'til now. And if Eric Davidson wants to call it gunk punk, so be it. The man has done his homework.

—Byron Coley
Deerfield, MA, 2010

Prologue

SONIC REDUCER

S O, YOU GUYS are *punk*, right?"
"Uh, yeah, I guess."
"But I saw some pictures of you, and you were wearing *sweater-vests*."
"Well, I guess it was cold."

This exchange is from a fanzine interview with me from the early days of my band, New Bomb Turks. While sitting in the beige backstage of a long-abandoned VFW hall somewhere in the Midwest, I had to explain that while it was true we liked our three-chord crap real fast, we just wanted to play rock 'n' roll and get the crowd wrapped up with us like fingers balling into a fist raised against that wall of approaching adulthood drab.

"But, like, *preppies* wear sweater-vests."

THESE WERE THE sorts of heated debates that raged amongst punk bands and their pimply chroniclers back then. And while having to defend the donning of a sweater-vest may seem fucking ridiculous today, you may want to check the distance from your high horse to the pavement. The topic is still apparently intriguing enough—see recent tomes like *Our Band Could Be Your Life*, *My So-Called Punk*, *Babylon's Burning*, *American Hardcore*, the endless literary and filmic CBGB laments, BBC and VH1 alternative rock specials, and the documentary flick *Punk: Attitude*. Yet those chronicles continually frame punk's story from the late '70s heyday into very early '80s hardcore, then straight to Nirvana and Green Day as household names, basically skipping an entire decade of underground rock.

Even in the early '90s, where it's generally assumed that Nirvana,

R.E.M., Marilyn Manson, and the Offspring brought "edgy" to the mainstream, there was a fringe on the fringe, an exponentially growing gaggle of low-rent rockers who, owing to their innate retrograde preferences, were never fashioned into a marketable movement by a *Spin* article or an *Entertainment Weekly* sidebar. And even if some critics lazily tagged these bands as "just" more punk, that helped little since by the early '90s "punk" mostly meant leftover, unsmiling hardcore or candy-coated skate-punk. As the Billboard charts were becoming increasingly dominated by hip-hop, which had entered its golden age, and rock was reeling from goofball hair metal and grunge's morose mirrored response, it seemed that ass-shake rock 'n' roll was about to be washed away into history's moldy basement—which is, of course, as good a place as any to start a party.

This particular soiree kicked off in the mid-'80s with bands like the Cynics, Lazy Cowgirls, Thee Mighty Caesars, Raunch Hands, Union Carbide Productions, and more, rocking around with a ragged revamp that seemed to have completely dismissed hardcore and gazed through beer goggles back to lost '60s garage rock (Sonics, Seeds) and/or early-'70s proto-punks (Stooges, MC5, Dictators, New York Dolls, Flamin' Groovies, Cramps). Oddly influential were feverish reissue labels that crawled out of the early '80s, like Norton and Crypt Records, which were initially just following fanboy impulses to reissue lost midcentury weirdos, but ultimately created a new canon of crazy for the kookier kids. By the ass-end of the decade, new black sheep were being birthed in herds, also dismissing hardcore and making it okay again for punk bands to get loaded and scream about screwing. Goon squads like the Dwarves, Didjits, Devil Dogs, Pussy Galore, the Gories, Cheater Slicks, Dead Moon, and more unknowingly reestablished punk rock as—surprise, surprise—fast, funny, and furiously fucked-up rock 'n' roll. Just in time for the emotional polar opposite: grunge.

Slapping these new sicko sounds onto vinyl slabs were indie imprints like Sympathy for the Record Industry, Crypt, Empty, Estrus, and even soon-to-be behemoth Sub Pop, Seattle's automatic-drip ground zero of grunge.

Considering there were no major wars going on, the economy was doing all right, and there was a well-spoken lover boy in the Oval Office, it's not really clear why grunge's whining was so appealing. Though it did seem like yet another extension of the post–*Sgt. Pepper's* misjudgment that "important" rock music must be overproduced, midtempo, and certainly never silly fun. So for that you got Seven Mary Three and Matchbox 20. Well, the medication the Dwarves and more were taking was not packaged by Pfizer. And their mood was anything but dour. In fact, a kind of coke-fueled, borscht belt humor ran rampant through these groups.

While "lo-fi" is a term that's tossed out like VHS copies of *Forrest Gump* these days, it's easy to forget that it was these drunken, pun-pushing punks who really kicked that recording style into gear. Nastier, noisier bands like the Mummies, the Supersuckers, New Bomb Turks, Oblivians, Teengenerate, the Rip Offs, and more started releasing increasingly crunchy 7" slabs of vinyl just as the lo-fi pop of Guided by Voices and Pavement caught the ears of college radio. Not art-wrangled enough for that crowd nor manicured enough for mainstream radio play, these bands chugged along in the music industry equivalent of trailer parks, micro-imprints like Bag of Hammers, In the Red, and Datapanik.

By the mid-'90s, all indie rock labels were forged from the DIY ("do it yourself") spirit of the '80s (so well documented in Michael Azerrad's book, *Our Band Could Be Your Life*). Originators like SST, Touch and Go, Homestead, and Amphetamine Reptile were great templates of how to avoid major-label traps of bad contracts, wasted dough, and overextended rosters. But their sounds were mostly of a more angular, serious, post-hardcore punk. These new '90s raw rock labels laid those wizened lessons learned over their wiseass bands, which added to an eruption of independent labels in the '90s, though distribution was still inefficient, contracts still wobbly. For the time being, a workable success was possible for indie bands, if they kept their expectations low. Touring bands were benefiting from access to nontraditional venues (UAW/VFW halls, forgotten urban dives, abandoned warehouses, university student unions, house shows). But the traditional tour maladies remained: busted vans, asshole sound guys, shady club owners, drug problems, stolen equipment, finding a place to crash—all dealt with during the last moment of pre–cell phone/easily accessible Internet technology. If a band had a Wednesday night show get canceled on a Monday morning, there was no MySpace bulletin to be thrown out from a laptop, no quick cell phone call from the van while stranded on a Montana highway, and no GPS once the engine sputtered up again.

And when/if the band got back home, studio technology was at its priciest yet, a negative effect of the whizzing dollar signs of the alternative rock boom. A four-track cassette recorder or even old boom boxes in cramped practice holes usually sufficed for "studio time."

You know what else gets you up a couple more rungs on the mainstream ladder? An identifiable and marketable genre name. And for that, whatever these bands herein were doing, it ain't been coined. "Punk 'n' roll," "lo-fi punk," and "beer punk" are just some of the somewhat appropriate if instantly gag-inducing terms that have been offered. "Gunk punk"? Sure, or whatever, in the parlance of the times. Such denunciations are never the bother for bands of this ilk, of course. The concentration is on action, and for that, these acts ultimately released an intensely impressive mountain of music, toured like mad with a perseverance and revived desire to entertain (in the face of hardcore punk's serious scowl), and engendered the kind of slobbering fan loyalty usually reserved for Kennedy assassination aficionados. But for those who need dollar signs as proof, know that these bands formed the rugged outback from which sprung the pop-pruned emergence of the White Stripes, Hives, and basically the whole neo-garage rock movement of the early '00s.

1.

BASTARDS OF YOUNG

I T'S BEEN A foregone grumble that the 1980s were the worst decade for rock 'n' roll. Fact is, there was just as much crappy, one-hit wonder, Top 40 pap in any other decade; it's just that our increasingly moola-centric society and its technological tools were getting much quicker at forcing said pap into our craws.

Time has faded some of the Delorean decade's Day-Glo, so can we let gleaming dogs lie? (The kids will walk those dogs again against all protestations anyway, as history has always taught us.) Apocalyptic targets of the end of "authentic" music back in the day—tripe like Milli Vanilli, Paul Young, or Winger—didn't really have that much power after all, did they? Today, you're as likely to hear Foreigner right next to the Cure on "oldies" radio stations or laundry detergent commercials. And for the preteen iPodders coming up—scrolling to "random" ten times as often as we pushed the "play" button on the Walkman—the relativity of music history is now a given. Or, as Richard Hell supposed, "Time sublimely silences the whys."

Since the Velvet Underground appeared in the late '60s, the most inventive rock music had become increasingly minimal and messy. Popular rock, though, like jazz and classical before it, was settling into genre, replete with strictly defined earmarks, so anything that went in new directions was considered "fringe." Soon you had dying industrial town misfits like the Stooges, MC5, and the Electric Eels recording raw rants about suburban dullsville, fascism, race riots, and hopped-up and horny runaways to an audience of few; while Jethro Tull, Yes, Pink Floyd, etc. were readying the mass music–buying hordes for eleven-minute suites about gnomes. Now really, which one sounds more intriguing?

So flash just past the original late-'70s punk rock explosion, and all that post-Velvets invention had ground down to chintzy British synth-pop and some burgeoning jangly college rock, both understandable re-actions to '80s hair metal's clowning. Bands like New Order, R.E.M., and Echo & the Bunnymen were actually selling fairly well (especially in England) and today just sound like classic pop to most who'd barely blink if their tunes popped up in a Volvo ad. But at the time, due to their ef-feminate stance and asymmetrical hairdos, they were in stark contrast to the classic rock canon. Hence the biz condescendingly slotted the lot un-der "modern rock" (as if conceding that "real" rock could not be modern anymore) and relegated their output to late-night college radio playlists.

"Relegated" isn't the right word exactly, since in general, college ra-dio has always been a far superior choice. But suffice it to say, these acts were mostly sequestered from gaining the larger following that would later come for some. For example: You know how everyone now has to endure drunken uncles babbling "Blister in the Sun" by the Vio-lent Femmes at weddings? The debut album that song came from was in medium rotation even on college radio's radar the year of its re-lease. There was actually a time when housewives didn't like the B-52s. R.E.M. weren't deemed worthy of a big Warner Brothers deal until they'd had four albums that sold in the hundreds of thousands each. (Today, records open at No. 1 on Billboard's Top 40 chart with sales of fewer than eighty thousand.)

Press was a far different proposition back then too. Today, if bands/fans want to find a review they essentially agree with, they can trawl umpteen blogs until they find it. Hence among music fans and the pub-lic in general, there's been a decreasing sense of "authoritative voice," just like us anti-authoritarian punks always wanted. Oops. Watch what you wish for. . . . But in the later '80s, local weeklies were thicker, and there were loads of national music magazines: *Rolling Stone*, *Spin*, *Rock Scene*, *Musician*, *Crawdaddy*, *Creem*, *Star Hits*, etc., plus such brainier, underground-propping periodicals as *Forced Exposure*, *Option*, *Thrasher*, *Trouser Press*, *Maximumrocknroll*, *Flipside*, and many more. Lots to read, but not a numbing blur like the infinite, quarter-hourly one-upping music sites that bloat Google today. Hence, print press still had some promotional heft, and their writers held onto quickly fading notions that record reviews—then usually around eight hundred words (today two hundred at best, and dwindling)—could convey something more substantial than "buy it/skip it."

Add all that up, and the Hunters & Collectors and the Alarms of the world could skate by in the '80s even without Top 40 hits or prime-time MTV play. Many of these acts garnered hits in England or Europe and dominated college radio here. So their labels made just enough dough to pony up for publicists.

From the perspective of the bands in this book, though, and the shoestring labels we were on, the use of a publicist was either economically out of the question, or like grabbing a magazine from under the sink when the toilet paper runs out midpinch: a last resort. At a time slightly less saturated with the clatter of constant hawking, it was possible to believe some word of mouth down at the mom 'n' pop shop and a few well-placed flyers at a girls' dorm would draw enough bodies to a gig.

It could be noticed right around when Reagan was packing his bags that slowly but surely, the old rock guard was beginning to dry up. I mean Phil Collins can't live forever, right? *Right?!* Also, corporate conglomeration was beginning to homogenize local commercial radio stations, but even in that lurked a bronze lining. Anyone with a more than passing fancy for music was, hopefully, gravitating toward college radio, where hard-slogging, fresh rock 'n' roll bands like the Dream Syndicate, Hüsker Dü, the Leaving Trains, the Replacements, X, and many other potentially accessible but still somewhat angsty acts were getting airplay. The burgeoning DIY record label and tour structures were spreading and converting a generation of musicians to new notions of success. And live music clubs were becoming more amenable to bands that played originals.

I'M OFFERING UP this somewhat rosy picture from the vantage point of a lad who lapped up his first few Pabsts in Cleveland, Ohio. Contrary to the coastals who harbor moldy notions that Ohio is a place that has always brimmed with white picket fence–ensconced fundamentalists, let it be known that northeast Ohio at the end of the century was anything but. It was still a largely Democratic, union-heavy region (when blue-collar workers worried more about economic stability and cold beer than gay marriage and "Moos-lums"), with a creaky skeleton of diverse, old-world-immigrant quirk. Dennis Kucinich, an avowed atheist, was mayor of Cleveland for a while in the late '70s, while the near-west side suburb of Lakewood housed the third-highest concentration of homosexuals in the States *and* the head office of the American Nazi

Party. That office is thankfully long gone, but the joy-boys stuck it out and made Lakewood a model of the broken-down, urban neighborhood spruced up and gone hip, and the epicenter of North Coast alt rock by the late '80s.

Musically, northeast Ohio was, until the early '90s, one of the top ten radio markets in the country. DJ Bill Randle brought Elvis Presley to town for his first shows north of Memphis; Alan Freed had thrown his infamous Moon Dog Ball in Cleveland in 1952. The Mad Daddy and Ghoulardi spewed koo-koo with their late-'50s/early-'60s slop-art radio and TV shows, respectively. And the Alarm Clocks and the Choir were just some of the garage rock oil streaks that seeped from the Cleveland suburbs.

New York and Boston were the only towns that hosted more Velvet Underground gigs than Cleveland. Other hallowed alt-rock heroes, such as David Bowie and Roxy Music, and such sturdy classic rockers as Bruce Springsteen and Todd Rundgren had the biggest crowds of their early days down at the Agora Ballroom. In 1972, the town's sooty skies coughed up the first American punk band, the Electric Eels. (Admittedly, the vast majority of Clevelanders never noticed.) And within two more years, down in "the Flats"—by the ashen, trash-strewn, sputtering-factory-filled shores of Lake Erie—glue-huffing, Beat-reading weirdos like Rocket from the Tombs, Pere Ubu, Frankenstein (later the Dead Boys), Peter Laughner, the Mirrors, and the Pagans, among others, basically created the American underground bent-rock blueprint for the next twenty years. Blue Ash and the Raspberries helped usher in power pop early in the decade. And I can name three important acts from nearby Akron alone—the Cramps, Devo, and Chrissie Hynde—that trump the rock music contributions of the entire state of Florida.

And I have not even traveled a hundred miles toward Columbus, home of Ohio State University, the country's second-largest university and one of the nation's most sizable gay populations; or 250 miles down to Cincinnati, where James Brown made all his early records. Even drab Dayton dumped out three of the most influential bands of the early indie rock era: Guided by Voices, the Breeders, and Brainiac. The most U.S. presidents and serial killers came from Ohio, as did Phyllis Diller, Harvey Pekar, Jim Jarmusch, Joel Grey, Bone Thugs-n-Harmony, LeBron James, Gloria Steinem, Albert Ayler, Wes Craven, Toni Morrison, Don King, Cy Young, *and* Dean Martin. So please, enough with the Buckeye bashing already.

As far as free-form college radio access in the late '80s, there may not have been a more saturated city than Cleveland. There were no fewer than five college stations that one could tune into, given the right weather and reception. The commercial stations sucked, of course—a load of calcified classic rock stations, some straggling AM oldies outlets, and even a new wave station for a year. The mishmash of these made for a distinctly rust-belted result of encrypting, in the most music-minded citizenry, an encyclopedic knowledge of crusty classic rock, along with an attendant disregard for those old dinosaurs that waddled defiantly through our DNA.

Cleveland spewed out an incredibly active underground rock scene, but the local bands themselves were suffused with little belief that anyone beyond I-71 would ever give a fuck. Hence most of the bands—the morosely beautiful My Dad Is Dead, jangle mods the Reactions; hardcore fearmongers the Dark; garage-rocking Anne Frank obsessives New Salem Witch Hunters; goth-metallers Shadow of Fear; melodimoodsters Terrible Parade; the Baudelaires of barroom punk, Prisonshake; and perhaps the greatest lost pop band of the '80s, the Mice—could never get their collective stool softened enough to slide out of town often and let the rest of the world in on the joke.

Robert Griffin, longtime leader of Prisonshake and Scat Records head honcho, recalls the extent of Cleveland's own ignorance of the new noise going on around it throughout the end of the century: "I was always reminded of the scene's insignificance while growing up, just in everyday ways. You went to the 'import' section to buy Pere Ubu albums, even if they were domestic pressings, never mind them being a local band! I went to a pretty massive high school, but no one there had even heard of the Dead Boys, even though they were on a major label. The Electric Eels' first 45 came out four years after they broke up, and on a British label. It doesn't give you much hope of making an impact. It's easier to say it's hopeless. I suppose the thinking would be along the lines of, 'Hey if you're going to fail at least you won't look stupid for it, because it wasn't like you were *trying* to be successful.'"

2.

STRUNG OUT ON JARGON

M OST PUNK BANDS get their start playing some beer-soaked dive in front of people in black leather. We got ours playing next to a popcorn machine, on chicken wing night, in front of a bunch of people in acid-washed jeans, in August 1983, at a Ground Round restaurant in Parma, Ohio." So says John Petkovic, singer/guitarist for the best bawdy bards of Cleveland's late-'80s scene, Death of Samantha.

To this day, Petkovic is a whirlwind: longtime leader of the glam-rock band Cobra Verde, staff writer for the *Cleveland Plain Dealer*, and working on two books, a side project with J Mascis, and another side project with a guy from Fucked Up.

"I was working as a janitor there at the time, and the manager was on vacation. The place would have these urban cowboy–casual guys do acoustic guitar strum-alongs of Eagles and America songs. So I told the guy who was running the place while the manager was on vacation that this group I had was going to do a show and that everything was legit. Into the second song, customers started complaining and the waitresses started yelling at me to get off the stage because their customers were leaving, their steak–baked potato dinners untouched and unpaid [for]. Then the cooks came out and started banging the popcorn machine, turning the lights on and off, and throwing chicken wings at one another and us. So the guy in charge of the place turned off the power, and I got fired."

That initial scam at the Ground Round was the first of many subversive pranks Death of Samantha regularly doled out like chicken wings at a suburban family restaurant. An Elvis funeral on stage, clarinet solos, feather boas—none of it was party to anything increasingly serious alternative musicians were *supposed* to be doing in the late '80s.

"I think the soot and pollution emitted from LTV Steel and the auto plants had the same effect on everyone's brains who created music in Cleveland," says Death of Samantha guitarist Doug Gillard. Gillard has since gone on to form his own unique pop band, Gem; he gained notoriety as lead guitarist for Guided by Voices from 1995 to 2006, and has still a busy solo career. But when I first saw him onstage a few months after he joined DoS in 1985, he looked like a Kandinsky doodle

Plain Dealer Magazine, Cleveland, 1987.

of Johnny Thunders (fishnet armbands, glitter platforms), a Weimar-era prostitute (black stockings, lace), and a suburban punk (guitar slash shards and greeeezy hair). Which basically summarizes DoS's musical means, an alley stumble 'n' run getaway from everything the members obviously enjoyed about the Stones, Stooges, New York Dolls, Pere Ubu, Roxy Music, the Birthday Party, and the Sex Pistols.

"I just loved rock 'n' roll," says Petkovic. "I always thought irony was a literary device, not an aesthetic sensibility. In the late '80s, a kind of critical take on music you liked was a good idea. And now irony is an assumed first response for people who don't know what they like, because they need a stamp of approval from others, and need to hedge their bets somehow. Otherwise, they might commit the biggest faux pas: looking foolish."

That was never a concern for Death of Samantha. Their comically cynical attitude was also a natural reaction in a town as beat down as Cleveland was. "It's weird, but Cleveland has always had a connection to the past, the previous generation of bands, more than the present," Petkovic claims. "The city is a former metropolis that lost its population. And as such, it always seems to be looking back to this previous time, like a small Eastern European country that was once part of a great empire. You see it in the music too. Even the first wave of bands— Rocket from the Tombs, Pere Ubu, Dead Boys—were very conscious of the city's glorious past, both economically and musically."

Cleveland's Crock-Pot was also spiced with a burgeoning sense that the town was an important cog in rock's history, only bolstered further, if inconclusively, when it "won" the Rock and Roll Hall of Fame and Museum in the late '80s (though the building itself didn't open until 1995). Then dump in the inversely proud effect of Cleveland's deeply depressing history of economic decline and abject sports failure. As much as the heps loved to sit around and make fun of the town's sad-sack shtick, they were clearly oddly inspired by it, as the best local bands were usually a stormy skewer of some classic rock subgenres.

"The Easter Monkeys, Electric Eels, and X-X were all unique in their sounds," Gillard recalls. "Spike in Vain was around then, a kind of cool mixed bag of punk, jazz, country, and no wave. But except for the Dead Boys, there was no straight-ahead 'punk' identity to feel you had to carry on. Back then, a lot of people hungry for 'alternative' forms of music in Cleveland had wide nets when it came to what they would go see and listen to. I know a lot of folks who saw the Dead Kennedys, then were at the Laurie Anderson show the week after. Tastes weren't put into that many compartments then. People were just happy to be able to see this kind of stuff that wasn't classic rock or disco."

When New Bomb Turks later traveled to places like San Francisco or Washington, DC, I was often regaled with the fact that "the kids" could cuddle themselves into various all-ages house shows and only see the bands they preferred, never afforded the opportunity to spew hate at lame goth, metal, or country bands that might've slipped onto the bill had they been forced to use their guile and sneak into bars. I usually had to make it through Brownstown's latest attempt at new wave or a hardcore band that, while waiting to go on, sneered at Death of Samantha's lace gloves and smoking jackets. It was a cornucopia of incongruity, and I loved it.

Admittedly, my beaming reaction to DoS was not mimicked in the heads of every scenester in Cleveland. In fact, the extremely sarcastic, foofy, then suddenly screeching stage demeanor the band flaunted—and Petkovic's indignant lounge lizard persona—bent many the wrong way. Especially heated was the Jesus & Mary Chain show in 1986 at the still-standing Phantasy Theater in Lakewood, Ohio. At the time—given the intense press hype J&M Chain was getting (*NME* called their debut "the most important record since *Never Mind the Bollocks Here's the Sex Pistols*")—this was the biggest opening slot DoS had landed so far, much to the consternation of just about every alt act in town. So what did DoS do? Well, they leaned heavily into their infrequent but infuriating drone and drag-out bag of pricks, while Petkovic chimed in with jumbled barbs about J&M Chain's rider that could be seen flying over the heads of the crowd. To this day it was one of the most "punk rock" performances I've ever seen unleashed on an unsuspecting audience. Even I was a little disappointed, if gut-sore from laughter. The J&M Chain were great that night. But DoS were confoundingly funny and absurdly abrasive. I then knew which path I preferred.

"When I first hung out at punk rock shows," says Petkovic, "I saw everyone dressed so much alike, when I thought I would find all this individuality. I realized that fitting in was over for me. A friend told me that there once was a time when you'd see someone in a Misfits T-shirt and want to talk with them. Now you see someone in a Misfits T-shirt and want to run away from them."

After only releasing one 7", DoS were signed to Gerard Cosloy's Homestead Records, long before he formed the highly influential Matador label. (Homestead had also signed '80s Clevo locals the Reactions and My Dad Is Dead.) They had some well-received NYC gigs. Nirvana and Smashing Pumpkins opened for them. And Chuck Eddy raved about DoS in *Spin* and subsequently in his book *Stairway to Hell: The 500 Best Heavy Metal Albums in the Universe*, calling them, suitably, "Roxy from the Tombs."

One attribute DoS shared with many Ohio bands to this day is an inability or lack of desire to consistently tour, beyond quickie East Coast jaunts. Partially, that was due to economics. Most bands from the rust belt do not have trust funds and platinum credit cards to pick up the tow tab should the van transmission conk out. And most restaurant jobs aren't too keen on you taking four weeks off. So best to stick close to home. Death of Samantha added a layer of frustrating-to-surreal situations to their doomed tours.

Witness one of only two brief attempts to head west, a California tour in 1989. Petkovic recalls, "We flew out there, and as usual, our drummer Steve-O packed his 'costumes' (like a multicolored coat made out of shag rug) not in suitcases, but in large garbage bags. You could do that back then. When we went to baggage claim at LAX airport, his stuff eventually rolled out, strewn all over the carousel. We ended up getting to our first show late, at a bar called Nightmoves in Orange County. Not only did the promoter hate it and not want to pay me, but he hit me over the head with a gun, then pointed it at me and told me to 'get the fuck out!'"

Many in the Cleveland club scene didn't appreciate that Death of Samantha would think of rock 'n' roll as vaudevillian either—which of course by 1986 was the most honest assessment. "Part of the problem was people thinking they live in 'The Rock 'n' Roll Capital of the World,'" says Petkovic. "So they saw irreverence as a threat to that 'status.' They just thought we were noisy jerks." But for all the sarcastic stylistic wink-winks, DoS absolutely slayed onstage. On their best nights, the sheer force of their guitar and grin slinging could not be denied, best represented on *Where the Women Wear the Glory and the Men Wear the Pants* (Homestead, 1988). Considering Petkovic's charisma and ever-evolving songwriting, Gillard's lead guitar prowess, and the band's ability to craft a truly unique personality, there had to be some A&R guys sniffing around, right?

Well, bands in DoS's position at the time lived in an odd music-biz purgatory. Listen back to the canonized first wave of '70s punks like the Dictators, Patti Smith, Television, Richard Hell, and Blondie (all major inspirations to DoS and many of their peers). Even though the media chatter back then was about all this "weird, violent new wave," those bands' albums are actually fairly clean productions (if still raw compared to radio rock of the time). Sire Records even paid Phil Spector to produce the fifth Ramones record. Even into the early '80s, you had Ray Manzarek of the Doors producing early X albums. There was still an assumption that this was the next round of rock acts that would populate mainstream radio for a while, and they were signed and recorded as such.

But by the late '80s, bands like DoS that basically fit into the traditional model of guitar/bass/drums/front man were working within an increasingly suspicious and economically depleted major label industry, on top of the usual mainstream musical trend shifts. So the indies that were forming under the new DIY rules (Homestead, Twin/Tone, Touch and Go, Caroline, Restless) were now snatching up groups that the majors might've taken a chance on previously (Dinosaur Jr., the Replacements, Soul Asylum, the Long Ryders, the Three O'Clock, Green on Red, and many more). Hence the bands themselves could harbor just enough ambition to allow for the stripped-down production and stage demeanor they gleaned from the hardcore era—or "pre-grunge," as it's usually dubbed now.

"We'd basically been broken up when a country label called Curb Records approached us in '91," says Petkovic. "They were looking to revive Wayne Newton's career by getting him to do 'alternative rock,' and they wanted a band that would be willing to back up Wayne on a record of glam covers—Roxy Music, New York Dolls, David Bowie, etc. They even had this storyboard for a video: Wayne playing a Vegas casino with him and Sammy Davis—also on Curb then—tap-dancing with these strippers and us backing them up. It sounded like a great idea until Wayne filed for bankruptcy, and then Sammy Davis died, and the deal was off. For good."

JUST AS ROCK 'N' roll had become "rock," punk rock had become "hardcore." Genre stereotypes have a way of worming their way around and into to the heads of the very crowds that derided them at the start. So by the late '80s, punk was firmly framed as a nut-grabbing, scowling, flip-side frat house soundtrack. It's obvious that for easy-to-grasp, consumerist, and generally sucky reasons, the tenets of hardcore from the mid-'80s—the jocky mosh pit armlocking, asshole family histories, desperate faux liberal politics (mistaking conformity for community) that masked sometimes racist shades, and most especially the exceedingly fast if increasingly tinny and rootless musicality—have sadly held sway. To this day, "the kids" think Bad Religion, at best, is punk ground zero. More likely it's post-hardcore suburban solipsism like that of Rites of Spring, which gets us into emo, which gets really depressing and bland. I heap most of the blame on AIDS, Ritalin, "to the extreme" marketing, and other cans of beans that shall remain unopened. . . .

So in through a punk back door of the late '80s walked some pretty funny, sexy shit. For me it was Death of Samantha. And through the squinty eyes that result from frequent laughing and/or confronting abrasive affronts to assumed rock doctrine could be seen in the distance a load of loons similar in attitude, if not exactly sound, to DoS, who bounded about with the facetious fury of the Ramones, Sex Pistols, Dead Boys, the Damned, the Weirdos, et al.—bands that had only a few years earlier (though it felt like eons) slapped rock out of its stadium tedium—only to have already settled back into whatever the hell everyone complains about when discussing '80s rock.

3.

TAPPING THE SOURCE

WITH BANDS LIKE the Cynics, Lazy Cowgirls, Raunch Hands, and more scattering around the end of the decade, it felt like there were in fact many abnormally annoyed cats out there who liked playing fast and furious, but who seemed to have been able to completely ignore hardcore's dogmatic scowl and stick to figuring out what to do with girls, empty pockets, fear of death, and weekends—the timeless stuff. Rather than breathlessly waiting for the next Dischord 7", these bands peered back to not only the whole '77 explosion but to Lenny Kaye's *Nuggets* compilation, Stooges/MC5 thug-boogie, the Rolling Stones at their nastiest, '60s garage greats like the Sonics and the Count Five, the hillbilliest of '50s rockabilly, and Russ Meyer movies. Too loosey-goosey for hardcore, owning nowhere near enough Beatles boots for the cartoon '60s revivalists, and not steeped in enough Derrida theory or Americana posturing to hobnob within more serious college radio fare, these bands were the carnies of college rock.

The Cynics were the house band for the Pittsburgh, Pennsylvania–based Get Hip Records, one of the best of the garage revival labels that arose in the mid-'80s. Singer Michael Kastelic was cofounder of the label, along with guitarist Gregg Kostelich. At first, the Cynics fell into the category of those retroid bands like the Fuzztones, Marshmallow Overcoat, etc., that had perfect black bobs, vintage organs, paisley button-ups, pointy boots, and a set of mostly covers.

"By the time I started singing with the Cynics, the Pittsburgh scene was totally uninteresting to me," says Kastelic, speaking while on tour in Spain, where they remain rock deities. "The punk heyday of the late '70s had given way to a bunch of clueless college boys playing really

**Michael Kastelic (Cynics) lets loose at Stache's, Columbus, OH, 1991.
(Photo by Jay Brown)**

loud stuff that I didn't understand. It seemed as if they had lost a sense of humor and artistic bent that the real punk bands had. So we just played with out-of-town luminaries like the Fleshtones, Lyres, etc., and that's partly because Gregg was the one bringing them to town."

Kastelic, a longtime record store manager, was, ahem, hip to the impossibilities of getting a ride on the major label train, and so put forth the idea of the band's own label. "Bill von Hagen, our first drummer, and I chipped in money," Kostelich says, "and Get Hip was born." To this day, Get Hip remains one of the most active labels and distributors of the large lake of garage sounds.

The Cynics, in the thick of the East Coast retro shtick, had a different clue about making the guitars at least as loud as the Farfisa. "We were really excited about bands like the Lyres, the Long Ryders, Rain Parade, and the Leaving Trains," says Kastelic. "My faves at the time were Thee Mighty Caesars and the *Back from the Grave* comps. They sounded like my all-time fave band, the Fall. But before finally recording, we were still more [like some of those jangly retro bands]."

Few of the janglier Whatevertones of the era unleashed as deep and dreaded a chorus-ending scream as Kastelic. He dragged the band along with it—and by their third album, 1989's *Rock 'n' Roll*, they'd become harbingers of a more abrasive spirit. Cheeky psychedelic side trips were cut to a minimum; the guitar crunch was upped; and everything rocked with a more torrid tempo. And no more keyboardist, which was an essential sonic move at the time. "We never looked at garage punk as being 'retro,'" Kastelic surmises. "To me, it was a logical forward progression back into primitivism. . . . What was the Firesign Theatre line? 'Forward into the past.' Or is that *The Great Gatsby*?"

Kastelic's searing scream—not to mention his androgynous, long-curls head explosion, bony frame, and propensity to simultaneously bait and goo-goo-eye the audience—made him one of the most intriguing front men I've ever seen. He was hilarious, prancing about just milliseconds before unleashing that screech; then, after the show, pinching either gender's hindquarters and mincing pickup lines like a young Truman Capote in pleather. "I got serious shit in middle school, and in high school bands," says Kastelic. "I had my daytime life of hell, and my nighttime life of punk rock kids that accepted me the way I was. Being in a band was a refuge against that sort of criticism. If you sing in a band, then you get a free pass to be 'prancey.'"

Considering the band and label have stayed active through a couple more garage waves, do they feel the Cynics had any impact? "I am touched and honored to think that bands were even aware of us," says Kastelic. "I was really doing a lot of drugs at that time, eventually landing in jail and a mental hospital in 1995. I'm sure I would have had a more personal connection if I wasn't so fucked up. . . . As anyone who has ever been in my presence knows, I usually swear I'm going to quit several times a day. But I just can't stop yet. There is another town, another chance, another drink, another dance. . . . Oh, now I remember: 'So we beat on, boats against the current, borne back ceaselessly into the past.' F. Scott Fitzgerald, *The Great Gatsby*."

PAT TODD IS, in time and soul, a few years older than everyone else in this book. He was probably grumbling about "the kids" before he hit legal drinking age. But somewhere down in Todd still beats the ticker of a teen. His roots-wrangling gang, the Lazy Cowgirls, are the stuff of bar stool boo-hoos over the injustice of this goddamn world. If you hanker for the purest distillation of Americana rock 'n' roll (as if Hank Williams were Hanky Ramone), then Todd has been ladling out your lunch for nearly three decades. He's just been too honest and too bald to ever get the inches in *Entertainment Weekly*.

After kicking around the un-scene of his hometown, Vincennes, Indiana, a teen Todd got a few fledgling Cowgirls to eventually join him in a move to L.A. in 1981, and he's still there, working as a production assistant for a special effects studio that's worked on the *Jurassic Park* and *Indiana Jones* franchises, *Iron Man*, *Terminator*, etc.

———

PAT TODD: The Lazy Cowgirls were formed in L.A. in 1982. I had bands in Indiana first, but there was no place for us to play because we played originals and a few weird covers. This was all before the DIY thing that now exists where you can go from city to city and there are brethren bands and clubs. . . . So we knew some people in L.A.; that's why we moved there.

ERIC DAVIDSON: *Is this one of those stories with, "Ooooh, the big city lights," and stumbling into bars where the Weirdos were playing? . . .*

PT: Not at all. To be honest with you, I have no connection to L.A. punk. I don't know anything about it, and I didn't care about it once I did. And I was never into the hardcore thing. I was more into songs and that kind of thing. I didn't really know too much about those bands, though slowly I tried, but it just wasn't for me.

ED: Most of the bands I've talked to for this book feel like they didn't fit into some scene.

PT: We definitely didn't. Even [on] our second album there is "Heartache" by Jim Reeves, "Yakety Yak" by the Coasters, "Justine" by the Don & Dewey. Those [early albums] are probably louder and faster than we really wanted to be. It was kind of the thing to do. I was never dishonest, but I think the all the way through the first five or six albums, really until *Ragged Soul*, well it wasn't fake, but it really wasn't me. I was still searching. We were swept up too, I guess. I'm sure everyone during that era had to play really fast and hard, and you can't have melodies and all that. Our songs were always more personal. They were not about "the kids." We played with a few hardcore bands, but we didn't really want to. We didn't want to play under-twenty-one shows most of the time. . . .

ED: Because you wanted to be able to drink?

PT: Not even that. I grew up on rock 'n' roll. Punk was great when it happened, and probably in the long run. But when you really look at it, there isn't a whole lot of good music there. To me, I still play *Exile on Main St.* all the time. . . . Anyway, then [famed alt-rock critic] Byron Coley said he'd like to come check us out. He brought along [Flesh Eaters singer] Chris D., who was an A&R guy for Slash Records at the time, we thought, but he had already been let go from that job. He sold that first album to Restless. . . . That record is a little slicker than we were.

ED: I found that record out in Ohio, probably a couple years after it came out, and it sounded like it came out of nowhere. Faster and meaner than the Blasters, Long Ryders, or any of the few bands from that era doing that kind of roots thing, besides maybe Tex & the Horseheads . . .

PT: It came out in '85. If you look at the first album and then the second album, God, you can see it was so reactionary. We went with a crappy-looking black-and-white cover. We did it ourselves—we didn't know what we were doing. There were too many cooks, and no money from Bomp! at all. We started touring just after that album came out, to nobody all over America. And we also did that *Third Time's the Charm* record with Dave Laing from Dog Meat Records [from Australia]. Then Sympathy [for the Record Industry] comes into the picture after that. Yeah, we were the reason why Long Gone John started that label. . . . John never did anything but what he said he would do. I can't say he ever told me anything that was a lie or went back on anything he promised.

ED: I have to say that when How It Looks—How It Is *came out (Sympathy, 1990) it was much more blazing. . . .*

PT: That band was unbelievably, what is the word, dysfunctional! To me, all those early albums are missed chances. . . . I would say '88 to '90 were all pretty bad years. I'm sure you know this yourself that the best art of any kind happens when people come together and are having fun—but also when you have a lot of frustration. That album is a perfect example, our Sub Pop single is a perfect example. . . .

ED: Was there ever any talk of Sub Pop wanting to sign you guys?

PT: No. In fact, I don't know what happened with that Sub Pop thing, but it was not a good experience. Those [singles] were in the stores but we didn't have any; I had to call just to get a few. So then we toured from '87 through '90. And overall it was pretty good because, even though the band couldn't get along and there were bad things that happened, it was still a good education. Got to see lots of things, went all over.

ED: When I first started going to shows and listening to college radio, it just seemed like there were these bands—Raunch Hands, the Cynics, you guys—that sometimes people would say, "Oh, they're retro, you like retro bands." I just didn't get what they meant, y'know?

PT: When someone uses words like *retro* or *old school*, to me, they're a conformist. I am not very big on slang and jargon because to me it cheapens human thought. It's an easy way out of a discussion. Anyone who is inspired, telling their truth, entertaining, not cliché, and not repeating some party line, they're always the latest thing, whether they're a hundred years old or five.

ED: How'd you get together with Crypt Records?

PT: We did a four-song demo with songs that ended up being on *Ragged Soul*. We just did it quickly, as we'd been playing out full tilt since '93 with the new lineup. . . . We did two records and a single with Crypt, and Tim Warren treated me nothing but good the couple years we were on the label. I know a lot of people don't like him, but for us he followed through with everything he said he was going to do. We went to Europe a couple times too then. It worked out really good.

ED: So at this time, touring Europe, hearing about Nine Pound Hammer, the Devil Dogs, and probably us and the Supersuckers . . . new bands that clearly loved the Cowgirls.

Lazy Cowgirls leader Pat Todd ponders the punch line at a bus stop, L.A., 1994. (Photo by Bill McCarter)

PT: Well, we're one of those bands—and I hope this doesn't sound bigheaded—but it seems like someone in every band liked us. We'd go to places and play to fifty people at the most, and half of those fifty would be in bands. But then later on they'd open up for us and get to be a lot more popular than us.

ED: You recently started your own label, Rankoutsider Records. Why?

PT: Well, when you look at what it costs to make/press records, really, you can do it yourself. If there is a hundred dollars to be made, you might as well make it yourself.

ED: Why did you change the band name to Pat Todd & the Rankoutsiders?

PT: I just thought it was time for a change. I didn't want to be the band that does the same ten songs over and over. We don't do any Cowgirl tunes. None. We already have a double album out with twenty-eight songs and a new album with twenty songs.

ED: It's amazing that you have really kept going, because a lot of musicians get disillusioned really quickly.

PT: I came to this realization it's nobody's fault but your own. When people run out of the juice and become a drag, that's when you move on. That is why I've had so many people in and out of the band. I will no longer be anyone's babysitter. And I will make it happen on my own because I still have the hunger and the inspiration to do it. . . . I'm not jaded at all. I get more out of it than I ever did.

ED: Sometimes people just do it for a while because they were the awkward kid at school who didn't fit in, and then they found the crowd that would accept them. . . .

PT: And later on, the people with the Mohawks who slit their wrists are selling insurance. I like music for the way it made me feel from the time I was little kid, and I still feel that way! I feel like if people get to hear our new records with an open mind and open heart, they'll like them. But it's hard to get people's minds and hearts open. I can understand why. There is just so much stuff at every turn. . . . Right now everything is so fast and there's no journey anymore. Everything is at your fingertips. Everyone is sophisticated and witty, and those are fine qualities, don't get me wrong. But that doesn't make you wise just because you know everything. . . . Sometimes you don't want to, but you have to change that flat tire. There is something to be said for that, the physical and mental thing. It seems to be leaving. I don't know, everything is too easy . . . even for me.

THIS GURGLING GARAGE upchuck was not confined to the continental

U.S. But who would've thought that some of the most guttural growls of this whole late-'80s under-whatever would've come from that seemingly satisfied state of blonde babes and cradle-to-grave health insurance, Sweden.

Since the early 2000s' rise of spark-pop like the Hives, Hellacopters, and the Sounds, and the more recent every-week blog-bumping of another Swedish indie electro-pop outfit, we've become accustomed to the fact that a small, serene country that heretofore offered up only ABBA and "adult" art house flicks and was rumored to be the Nazis' hiding place of stolen paintings has become so musically active. But that wasn't the custom in the late '80s.

Over the past decade, Ebbot Lundberg has become moderately famous as the shamanistic front man for Swedish epic-rockers the Soundtrack of Our Lives. After a minor spike of popularity in America (one of their songs was even used on NFL broadcasts back in 2003), they've retained star status in Europe, and continue as one of the survivors of that prolific "neo-garage" trend of the turn of the century. But before that, Lundberg was the svelte, hyena-eyed teen yalper for the amazing end-of-the-'80s apes Union Carbide Productions.

Number one on my personal list of "Bands I Could've Maybe Seen But Never Did" (No. 2, Nation of Ulysses), Union Carbide were notorious for their incendiary, audience-baiting, and often bloody shows which contrasted with a hilarious blue-blooded bent—press photos of the band hanging with their grannies or decked out in dapper new suits, leaning against a Rolls-Royce—that confused and contrasted well with the decidedly un-haughty, animalistic power of their early records.

The first two Union Carbide albums stand as testaments to what impish punks like my then twenty-something self assumed the MC5 must've been like in their most pharm-fetched state, and had they switched singers with their Stooges chums. Union Carbide upped the ante on that famed Detroit sound by playing just that much faster, shoving in Stones swagger, psychedelic edges, fearsomely loud production, and—within all that massive energy and dual-guitar knife-fighting—Lundberg snuck in some of the smartest, hippie-baiting lyrics imaginable. While Union Carbide seemed like some odd anomaly from the land of the lovelies, to me they made for a perfect corollary to Death of Samantha's sarcastic glam-bamboozle. Lundberg, though, felt like the anomaly.

"Very much so," says the singer. "But that was the whole idea, to be honest. The music just helped to get us through at the time. But that combination sometimes made things worse, pushing too hard for the magic moments along with our young egos. Anybody who has the patience for the whole band constellation thing knows that for sure."

Ah yes, the patience for the whole band constellation. It's worth telling those who still harbor notions that being in a band is a mythical endless weekend that the kind of keep-your-mouth-shut-or-get-fired fears of the nine-to-five world translate in their own ways to the rock band existence.

There is an unspoken understanding that the three to six of us stuffed in the van for hours at a time will usually turn a deaf ear to the shitty stupid stuff that comes out of our mouths periodically—all for the good of finishing off the next show. I'm not saying that on the eve of the second decent practice, band members lock arms and make a pact that "it is heretofore all for the music, gentlemen!" But kind of, if you're going to survive. Those days when your drummer thinks it's funny to put pubic hair in your sandwich when you're not looking, the desire to walk into the proverbial boss's office and scream "I quit!" is not an option, lest ye want to walk home from Mississippi midtour. We can, though, settle for a quick half-hug and an "Ah, ya asshole, I love ya." I would not suggest you try that with your boss.

Again like Death of Samantha, Union Carbide's offbeat contemporary musical inspirations were not of the ubiquitous mosh manner. "We listened to Green on Red, Hüsker Dü, Kilslug, Hoodoo Gurus, and the Cosmic Psychos," says Lundberg. "But we were also into Prince and George Michael." Dropping names like that while urinating in the general direction of the crowd has a way of alienating large swaths of the audience who don't appreciate such stylistic eccentricities.

"The absence of humor is the worst kind of thing when it comes to certain bands," says Lundberg. "In the late '80s, people became— probably as a reaction to hair metal—too intellectual, and [mostly had] a dorky, pretentious attitude, wearing silly dropout costumes." As opposed to Union Carbide, who onstage often dispensed with clothing altogether. "We mostly shared bills with strange avant-garde acts or mainstream dance acts," Lundberg recalls. "I was too self-absorbed to notice if people didn't 'get it.' I remember one of our first shows playing in a restaurant, and the owner tried to grab my short hair and drag me off the stage because I was puking in front of the guests during a solo. He failed and couldn't stop it because people went berserk, of course. But the best show was in Germany where there were about fifteen different dogs in the audience trying to poke each other right when we started to play. Come to think of it, maybe the dogs were the only ones who ever really did 'get it.'"

This is not to imply that Union Carbide were just clowning their way through the awkward phase. Their records and live experience attest to an energy and fury that would cause most hardcore punk fans to take a step back. "Well, considering the fury and energy, I would blame that on too much masturbation," says Lundberg. "That's probably the real reason why the Dischord bands painted an *X* on their right hand[s]. Straight edge, indeed!"

Supposedly enlightened Americans like to pooh-pooh U.S. culture in contrast to Europe's longer cultural history. It's a good bet most of them have not spent more than a few days in an Amsterdam coffee shop, because if they did, and watched some TV and listened to the radio over there, it's apparent that really crappy pop culture dominates everywhere. "It was a nightmare living in Sweden listening to the radio in the late '80s," Lundberg explains. "And I think that was the same all over Europe as far as I recall. I would say there were maybe two or three independent stations doing that sort of [fucked-up new music] thing once a month."

Writer, editor and all-around ug-music arbiter Johan Kugelberg was best chums and tour roadrunner with Union Carbide from the get-go. And he's claimed that by the third Union Carbide record, "they wanted to be Led Zeppelin," which is of course one of the most cutting putdowns one could lay on anyone involved with this scene. I'd argue they were just veering toward a melodically enhanced formation of a Euro *Exile on Main St.* with their brilliantly expansive third album, *From Influence to Ignorance* (Radium, 1991). And the misguided mewl of their last record, *Swing* (Puppet, 1992), had as much to do with the always compression-heavy production of Steve Albini as it did with the band simply running out of gas.

"The reason [we used Albini]," claims Lundberg, "was that the record company knew he was going to produce Nirvana. I was not interested in what he had produced, except the Pixies maybe. I really hated the wagon-jump that was going on when grunge arrived. Apart from Nirvana, Mudhoney, and Tad, grunge was basically another name for bad metal. And at least Mr. Albini had the same opinion about this. . . . But going to Chicago in 1992 made the whole thing worse. The only positive thing I remember [is] listening to the original Cheap Trick

Live at Budokan tapes in the studio with Steve. And the live shows we did together with Laibach and Jesus Lizard. The rest was totally crap."

The band's only other trip to the U.S. was for a brief, more enjoyable East Coast jaunt in April 1988, which included a CBGB show at the behest of underground filmmaker Richard Kern (whose skuzzy urbanabilly band, the Black Snakes, also played) The sparse crowd included noisesters Jim Thirlwell, Lydia Lunch, and members of Sonic Youth and Pussy Galore, plus Michael Weldon (*Psychotronic* magazine) and Jello Biafra (Dead Kennedys).

Union Carbide Productions broke up not long after *Swing* was released, which of course was the first UCP record to get decent distribution in the U.S.

"Same as always," laments Lundberg. "You want to go in different directions, and we slowly did. Some of us had serious drug problems, and the communication did not work so well. So we canceled the big U.S. tour we were supposed to do and decided to do a farewell tour [in Europe] by the end of 1993, just to pay the huge bills for the tour bus."

TOUR BUSES WEREN'T in the cards for the Raunch Hands. These boozy R&B foot-stompers started out circa 1984 pawing toward big label straws but would soon be kicking out Crypt Records releases full of slavish pining for poon and moonshine, with a demented '50s heartburn. Little did I know when I first heard them on the 1986 Coyote Records compilation *Luxury Condos Coming to Your Neighborhood Soon* that guitarist Mike Mariconda would be recording New Bomb Turks' debut six years later.

November 2008—Mariconda, Michael Chandler (howling front man), Mike "Sharky" Edison (drummer and putative editor of this book), longtime Crypt art-doer, Cliff Mott, and Crypt honcho Tim Warren—had a fuzzy family reunion at the vintage East Village joint Great Jones Café. The gab began with an update on Pete Linzell, the sax man for most of the Raunch Hands existence, who'd decided to move to Columbus, Ohio, a few years ago to dry out.

———

MIKE EDISON: Ah, Pete was great. You know when you watch the Nature Channel, and you slow it down to see how an animal's legs work—that's how Pete moves. But he blows great!

MIKE MARICONDA: He's the kind of guy on a European tour who purchases a hat in Paris with an Eiffel Tower on it.

ME: We were in Spain touring a lot, and he didn't know any Spanish at all. So we're at this bar, and Pete says, "Hey Sharky, I really like this bartender, she's really cute. I wanna ask her really politely for a beer. How do I say it?" So I taught him how to say, in perfect Spanish, "Give me a beer or I'll fuck you up the ass." So he practices it for half an hour, and says it to her, you know, really proud that he was speaking Spanish, and she jumped over the bar and punched him in the head. But man, he said it perfectly!

MICHAEL CHANDLER: Before the Raunch Hands I was working at Club 57, doing stand-up and putting on shows. Me, Ann Magnuson, burlesque dancers, Steve Buscemi was performing there . . . but my stand-up was not funny. Like concept stuff, Beatnik poetry about living in suburbia.

TIM WARREN: *Oooh yeah, margaritas sound good!*

MC: So anyway, I was riding home on the bus and trying to think—what can I do to make my comedy better? I know, I'll do music! I'll write novelty country songs. . . .

TW: Yeah, you took on a persona of this truck driver!

MC: Yeah, this misogynist, hates women, beats his wife . . . Back in the early '80s, that was funny.

CLIFF MOTT: That was the novelty of it, no one else was doing it—everyone else was playing Jackson Browne.

MC: So I called this guy Michael Chang who I worked with and got him to learn this old song, "Long Tall Texan." Chang got frustrated and said, "Why don't we write our own song?" All right! And I wrote "Never Comin' Home," the first Raunch Hands song. Then "Man Needs a Woman," "Spit It on the Floor," "The Wild Man of Wall St.," "Black Jack"—the Hives eventually covered that, one of my stand-up numbers. So that was as a duo then, just guitar and vocals, Chang and Chandler. It started to go over well; we started playing at the Pyramid Club. . . .

TW: More margaritas!

MC: Anyway, then the Outta Place needed a singer. They had a whole set rehearsed, something we could never do. . . .

TW: *We need the oysters! The gumbo! We'll take the gumbo! Gum-bo!*

MC: The Outta Place was getting gigs, so I went with them for about a year and a half. People I respected, like Tim Warren, couldn't stand the Outta Place, couldn't stand that retro scene at the Strip club. . . .

TW: No, wait, I liked Outta Place okay, but I didn't like the people in the band. Too Fuzztones retro. And the guy that ran Midnight Records, he has a heart of gold. He's a dick, but he has a heart of gold.

MC: We had records come out, we got shows, we got pussy, I got to get drunk all the time. . . .

MM: The first show I saw of that Chang and Chandler stuff was the first show they played before I got in the group. And Chang and Chandler played Tim Warren's wedding in Jersey. . . .

TW: Yaaass! My first wedding. The first of many!

MM: We used to just play at

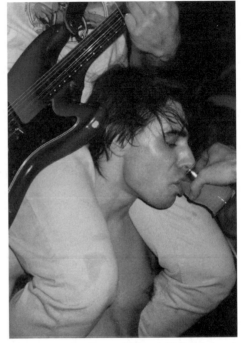

A fan lends the Raunch Hands' Michael Chandler a hand, 1990. (Photo courtesy of Raunch Hands)

No Sé No, this completely illegal after-hours joint. We couldn't get booked anywhere because we didn't have a demo.

TW: These oysters are amazing! The oysters are crazy, right?

MM: Yeah, Tim, fucking great . . .

TW: It was March of 1984 that I saw Raunch Hands at CBGB. . . . I was like, Jesus, these are the same guys that played my wedding?! I was freaking out. What the fuck?! So that's when I was putting together *Back from the Grave III*, and I just said, "Hey, you guys wanna cut a record?" And we put it on that *Grave III*. (*Back from the Grave* is the title of a series of highly influential Crypt compilations of rare, wild '60s garage rock singles; the Raunch Hands are the only modern band to ever, secretly, slip onto a *Grave* comp.)

ME: Before that Mariconda and I had this group, the Empire State Combo, just this pickup garage band. This jock frat house at NYU needed a band for a party, and we didn't have tape, so I made a tape of the first Sonics record, and I just gave them that. And they said, "Great! When do you wanna play?"

MM: Yeah, we hadn't even rehearsed, made three hundred bucks, and never played again.

ME: We played "Louie Louie," "Wooly Bully," "Double Shot of My Baby's Love," "Psycho." Nothing terribly obscure or weirdo like the *Back from the Grave* comps, but no one was doing that stuff then. Anyway, we wore out our welcome quick at that frat house. Our friends made a fuckin' mess of that place. Drunk punks versus asshole jocks.

MC: When the Raunch Hands started, we played about once a week at No Sé No. We played right on top of the bar and we stuck the amps back where the liquor shelf normally is. That lasted about two or three months, and we got a good following of our friends. Our friends were very heavy drinkers, and every nightclub loves that. After that we played everywhere in NYC. Peppermint Lounge, Danceteria . . .

TW: There was good money for bands back then. . . .

MC: We did that for about six or eight months and started to figure, if we keep doing this, people are gonna get sick of seeing us. So by then, we had enough money to get a van, and we started getting shows out of town.

MM: Our real first big gig was opening up for the Replacements at Maxwell's in Hoboken, and we were real excited, right after *Let It Be* came out. And after our set, I walked outside, and I noticed that their van had a big window busted. There was glass all inside the van, on their sleeping bags, everywhere. I ran back in the club and told their manager, Peter Jesperson, "Hey Peter, man, I hate to be the one to break the bad news to you, but someone just busted into your van, and there's glass all over the place." And he said, "Yeah, that happened a week ago. We haven't had the time to fix it." They were sleeping in it!

ERIC DAVIDSON: Did you like them?

MM: No, not really, but—

TW: THEY SUCKED! The only good song they did was that Monkees song.

MM: Yeah, it was one of those shows where they'd do thirty seconds of "Iron Man," then tune up forever, then go to the bar.

MC: We could drink twice as much as they did and still finish our songs!

ED: Speaking of which, did you hear the Stooges' van just got stolen? Someone jumped in the van and took the whole thing.

TW: That's what you get for recording fucking *Zombie Birdhouse*, Iggy!

MC: Oh wait, how about the time Tim fucked a disco square!

TW: I fucked her on top of a van in a parking lot . . .

MC: . . . on Independence Day in Switzerland. We thought Rolf [Euro tour manager] was going to kill Tim because he was so disappointed. The great Tim Warren fucked a disco square.

TW: I didn't know she was a disco square! It was good pussy, that's all I knew.

MM: Our van had gotten busted into, and I'd blown two amplifiers and eaten a piece of hash this big. Then got in a fight with Chandler onstage.

MC: I don't remember, I was pretty drunk. So, it was Independence Day, and we went to this unbelievable party afterwards where they were having fireworks . . . typical debauchery . . .

MM: But hold on. . . . So after I busted the second amp, I'd eaten a chunk of hash like this that someone gave me. Then I went to the van to change my shirt, and the van had been broken into. So I went fucking completely apeshit. I went back in and started throwing shit, walking around all covered in sweat, threatening people with a screwdriver, "Where's the fuck is my Walkman!" So they took me back to the hotel to chill out, and Tim was missing. He was fucking the disco square.

TW: On the roof of a car. A Fiat!!

ED: *How'd you know she was a disco square? I mean, was she singing "I Love the Nightlife" while you were fucking her? Did she say anything while you were fucking her that tipped you off to the fact that she was a disco square?*

TW: Yes, she did—"Oh, ahhhh, oooo, ohh, ooohhh . . ."

MM: Yeah, the band was fucking chewing me out 'cause I was so high, but there's Tim fucking a disco square.

TW: Can we get more hot sauce over here?! So we finally abandoned the disco girl and headed to this party. Rolf, the Swedish manager and '60s punk fanboy supreme, was utterly aghast at my having boned a disco girl and was hitting the bottle. He kept saying, "Tim Warren, I hate you! You fucked a disco square!" Mariconda and I crashed in the VW van, and Rolf came in and thought he punched me, but his fist hit Mariconda right in the head! So Mariconda hauls off and clocks Rolf real hard in the jaw, Rolf tumbles down and vomits up a torrent, then passes out. Rolf tells me she was a square. Ha! A guy who never got laid in his entire life, and he says she's a square, so I shouldn't fuck her! Jesus Christ, this is hot hot sauce!

ED: That's around when I first met you guys.

MC: We went from drummer to drummer to drummer. Then we got Sharky.

ME: They'd asked me a few times, but I was always busy. I had my band Sharky's Machine, and I was playing with GG Allin, and then I got a legit job editing porn mags.

MC: He'd always been our friend. He was a human ball of fire.

ED: It's funny, because hanging out with you guys tonight, it's the least I've ever heard him talk.

MC: Yeah, well, it's Tim, he's scaring him.

TIM: Sharky! We need more drinks—marrrrgarrrritaaaasss!!

ED: What'd you guys think of the other new Crypt bands?

MM: Loved 'em. I'm the one that got the Gories signed 'cause I was the first guy in the whole New York area to see them. I hipped Tim to 'em, because I loved them.

ED: I guess we benefited from you guys and Nine Pound Hammer going over there first, because Crypt was a big shit deal already and—

MC: —and it wasn't like that at all when we first went over! Oh, you gotta know about our very first Crypt tour of Europe, in 1989. We went there for like five weeks, with only eight or ten shows booked. We had to pay the tax on shipping the equipment, which was like eight hundred dollars more than we probably paid for buying and shipping all the equipment. Then Tim bought the van, and we're trying to modify the van to sleep in, in the middle of August, in Madrid, with the Pleasure Fuckers feeding us cocaine, hashish, and beer. . . . We went there in August thinking, Hey, no bands are over there in August, so we'll be the only game in town. Of course then when you get there you realize that every town is a ghost town, except by the beaches. So we'd drive all over Europe, show-ing up in some small town and saying, "Hey, we're the Raunch Hands from the United States! Can we play in your club?"

MM: And back then, we had to book everything by telephone, so we're still waiting for a lot of calls. We had a gig set in Switzerland, and all of a sudden the Paradiso club in Amsterdam calls us, and Tim's like, "Oh, you've gotta play the Paradiso!" We had to drive from Switzerland to Amsterdam, then back down to Switzerland. That was a three-nighter.

MC: And we stayed in Berlin with no gigs, no money, for like ten days. It was everything I could do to stay drunk.

MM: But that's when Tim met his first Micha, 'cause the van broke down.

MC: Tim Warren traveled with us all over Europe, drove us to so many shows, and never saw a single Raunch Hands show the entire time we were on Crypt Records.

TW: Naaaahhhh, I saw, uh, I at least saw one. . . .

MC: He'd drive us to the show, disappear, then we'd wake him up after the show, and he'd drive us to the next show. We were playing Hamburg, the world headquarters of Crypt, stayed at his house for three days, and the gig was at this club he's been trying to book us in for a while, a big deal. So we're about halfway through the set, and I realize that there's a song I don't have the right harmonica for; it's backstage. So I run backstage, and here's Micha standing over Tim, he's in front of the sink—"I'm sorry, I didn't see your show, I'm sorry. . . ." He never saw us play. Signed us sight unseen 'cause he heard we were so great. But never saw a show . . .

MM: How about the Vera show [club in the Netherlands] where he had a Hitler mustache drawn on his face and blood all over his clothes. I remember seeing him in the audience from the stage, so I guess he saw that show.

ME: Yeah, he'd been pounding a beer bottle against the stage trying to get us to go back on, and it smashed and he was covered in blood. . . . I saw him right after backstage, and he's standing there all drunk and bloody, and with speed dripping out of his nose, and someone had drawn a Hitler mustache on him with a Magic Marker. And he's raving, "Hey Sharky, good show huh?!"

MC: Then later, Tim was parked illegally. He went to the hotel to shower, and a cop came by the room. . . .

TW: Ahh, *fuck*! Yeah, here's "Mr. Rock 'n' Roll" that morning, moving the goddamn van so we didn't get a ticket. So I ran to the bank first because I only had Belgian money, and I needed Dutch guilders for the goddamn meter. Then I get to the van, and the fucking meter is broken! I shoved some money in and figured, Hey, I fuckin' tried. Get back to the hotel, have some eggs and coffee in the hotel restaurant. Then I go up to my room, look in the mirror, and I've got a fucking Magic Marker Hitler mustache on me! And every inch of me coated in dried blood! I jump in the shower, then *boom! boom!* at the door. Throw on a towel, and it's a policewoman, and they haul me off to jail for two fucking hours! I had no idea what I did 'cause I was blacked out. So in the end, they accuse me of breaking into a parking meter. *What?! Are you fucking kidding me?!* You tore my hotel room apart, I had five thousand in Belgian money in my motherfucking wallet—*why would I break into a parking meter for five fucking guilders?!* I was just tapping the meter. I'm a fucking gentleman. But I guess some fucking yuppie saw a Hitler guy covered in blood. . . .

MM: That was the scariest fucking thing I've ever seen in my life. But y'know, everyone was just kind of fucking laughing at it. Looks like he's getting close to that tonight. . . .

TW: Ahhhhhhh, fucking yuppies . . . goddamn . . .uhhh . . .

————————

IN 1975—WHEN most people's visions of the 1950s were primarily defined by *Happy Days* or TV commercial parodies of that supposedly "bland" white-bread era—the Cramps effortlessly and obsessively dug through their pile of junk store finds (when the very notion of "vintage Americana" was just forming) and saw a time only around fifteen years past teeming with sleazy B flicks, repressed sexuality, the cold war nuclear shakes, and oodles of forgotten wild-ass rockabilly, garage, and novelty singles. They swirled it about with LSD and wrapped it in fashion shards that were still considered über-tacky (and this was in the '70s!), and remade the '50s (with some help from John Waters) into a psychotically simultaneous high/low point of American values and design that informs pop culture to this day.

Billy Childish, though, is not so enthralled: "Mark Perry [Alternative Television singer] gave me a copy of the first Cramps album in '79 when it came out," Childish told me. "I chucked it in a trash bin. I never had a second Cramps LP."

If the Cramps are the raft in the sewer we're hurtling down here, Childish is the raft's grizzled captain. Starting with the neo-Merseybeat Pop Rivets in 1977, Childish has slash-skiffled his way through a number of groups and solo shots on literally countless records, stalwartly sticking to no more chords than would get you through one side of a Sonics album, eventually becoming the Bo Diddley for this generation of garage adherents. His aesthetic stamp has landed on the ass of bands from Mudhoney to the Mummies to the White Stripes.

Along the way his novel and poetry writing has been nearly as prolific, his paintings and woodcuts even more so. He spawned a book imprint/record label, Hangman, that gave a number of other artists, including singer Holly Golightly, their start. To this day, he has consis-

Billy Childish and Tim Warren at Childish's pad, Chatham, UK, 1991.
(Photo by Michaela Warren)

tently upheld all the often quickly discarded beliefs of the DIY artistic existence. No matter how hard UK culture has tried to shove him to the corners of the isle, he has become a British institution while also being one of the few raw rock acts who flip the script by being somewhat more popular in the States than overseas. In general, another example of that Velvet Underground adage: Not many people saw the Velvet Underground, but everyone who did formed a band. Whether Childish likes any of the bands he inspired was one of many topics covered as he called from his hometown of Chatham, England, one sunny Sunday afternoon. . . .

ERIC DAVIDSON: An old friend told me some stories of hanging out with you and Tim Warren in New York.
BILLY CHILDISH: Well, it is possible, because Tim asked us to play

the Bad Music Seminar [in November 1988; Warren's infamous, one-night party parody of the now-defunct New Music Seminar music biz conference]. We went to New York for that at the tail end of my group, Thee Mighty Caesars. Tim rang me up and said, "I run this label, Crypt Records," which I had never heard of. . . .

ED: *How was that Bad Music Seminar?*

BC: It was rubbish. It was everything it said it was. Ha! I think we played three hours late, and we were jet-lagged, and woken up in the middle of the night, and put on the stage with a lot of borrowed equipment, which wasn't what we asked for. So basically, nothing sounded like what we wanted it to. Most people involved in music don't care what things sound like, which is not something I can quite understand. It's like painting pictures and not caring what colors you use. So it's just that music for us is a complete bore and headache.

ED: *Even back then you were already feeling that way?*

BC: It was worse! The '80s was like the worst period in the history of music. And now it's only slightly alleviated, because now you have garage rock groups that have the idea that maybe it's possible that some of the music should be left to sound exciting. But that is only a maybe.

ED: *When Tim asked you to be on Crypt, I guess he thought he had some contemporary bands that were in the same ballpark. . . .*

BC: He didn't ask us to be on Crypt. He asked to release a couple of records. Look, I find it very odd that the questions are based around Crypt. I mean, I'd been playing music ten years before Crypt. My music career doesn't begin with the great Tim Warren.

ED: *Of course, I was just starting with Tim because Crypt started around the beginning of the era of the bands that will be covered in this book. And I'm going to be talking to him too.*

BC: Well, that is going to be a lot of bullshit. I like Tim, but it's just a lot of shouting and not actually understanding anything. . . . Like that big spat with the Mummies. The Mummies and possibly the Gories were the only groups that had a sound that I would say understood anything that Thee Mighty Caesars were trying to do. But obviously I didn't hear everything. I have not gone out to see groups since 1977. I gave up engaging with music. After '77, I thought it was a pointless waste of time because nobody did what we tried to with punk rock. They got rid of the punk and just stuck with the rock.

ED: *Okay, so about the Pop Rivets—*

Bad Music Seminar flyer, NYC, 1988: "It was everything it said it was," according to Billy Childish. (Courtesy of Cliff Mott)

BC: The Pop Rivets played their first show in September 1977. We were from Chatham. We refused to play London, but played Germany a lot, and made what I think was one of the first completely independently recorded and released records, hand-colored sleeves and hand-stamped labels.

ED: What were you listening to at the time?

BC: Well, when I was little I heard the Beatles, Rolling Stones, the Kinks, Bob Dylan, and then Jimi Hendrix. In '67, when I was about seven, I heard Jimi Hendrix and I liked that in the beginning. A lot of the English punk groups listened to glam music and liked David Bowie. I didn't. I listened to the Andrews Sisters and early Rolling Stones, early Beatles, Buddy Holly, Bill Haley & His Comets. And I thought new music had nothing to offer me because it's all so boring. Then I heard "Anarchy in the U.K." and some of the early punk rock groups. My favorite was the Clash—the show with Richard Hell supporting at the Pier in Hastings was good. The Damned, X-Ray Spex, Johnny Moped, Generation X. And I actually liked the Sex Pistols, but even that was too "rock," really. We'd formed a group in the meantime and were playing "Hippy Hippy Shake" and some of the older rock 'n' roll stuff I liked, and writing some songs. . . . Then we decided to release an LP ourselves, which we did. We borrowed some money off somebody who got a social security back payment. And then we did some tours in Germany, made a second album. We were listening to Link Wray, John Lee Hooker, and Bo Diddley around that time. We were trying, but we couldn't understand why our records sounded so dull when we went into the studio.

ED: Where were you recording at the time?

BC: Just at studios, and we did some home recording, some demos. So we split up the Pop Rivets around 1980. The roadie, Mickey [Hampshire], had Mickey & the Milkshakes. We started to form a rock 'n' roll group and I learned how to play guitar—because I'd just been the singer in the Pop Rivets. Oh, I forget to mention Alternative TV as being one of my faves! Anyway, we were really big on the Beatles' Star Club record. That's the best; *Sgt. Pepper's* was the worst. But the punk rock groups were going up their ass and turning into David Bowie freaks again. But we were rock 'n' roll and listening to Link Wray . . . and we realized we needed drums with all skins on it and small amps turned up loud. Not big amps, small amps. We tried to get what we thought was an exciting sound.

ED: It's always said in those rock documentaries that the only thing British kids were listening to mid-'70s was T. Rex.

BC: That's true, but I thought it was useless. I probably don't think it's as bad now as I did then, and I can appreciate that David Bowie was okay when he was sort of ripping off R&B music. But that is no excuse for a grandfather thinking he was from Mars. I hate middle-aged people trying to be teenagers. I hate teenage society. I think all the people who thought rock 'n' roll would undermine society and ruin all values were right. People who smashed "Be-Bop-A-Lula," who said this music was going to ruin everything—they were correct.

ED: But you stuck with it.

BC: Well yeah, I stuck with rock 'n' roll, but I still think we would be better off without it.

ED: So by the early '80s, you've got the Milkshakes going, right?

BC: Yes. The Milkshakes were getting quite successful, but the other guitarist decided to leave. So I formed Thee Mighty Caesars, which was just a more stripped-down version, the one Nirvana and the all the Yanks picked up on, but no one in England liked.

ED: At the time in America in the mid-'80s, there was the Fuzztones and stuff like that. . . .

BC: Oh, that terrible stuff. Yeah, I hated all that.

ED: I love the Cramps, but those kind of retro bands really picked up on only the dress-up end of the Cramps, I guess. . . . But the Gories certainly picked up on the Cramps sound.

BC: The thing that makes the Gories work is that they have a good girl drummer. I hated the Velvet Underground, but they had a good girl drummer. The Gories had a good girl drummer. And Mick sang like John Lee Hooker and is a bluesy player. That is what made them good. And they were naked; it was so stripped-down, it sounded vaguely dangerous.

ED: What did you think of what you were trying to do?

BC: We were trying to make what wasn't there. Basically we were the antidote to New Romanticism, glam, rock music, and the rock 'n' roll "lifestyle." None of us had earrings, none of us took drugs, we were terrible drinkers. We never hung out at rock star parties and tried to get signed. We didn't have a producer. And we never, ever did anything we didn't want to do. We thought anyone who did was a twat. We were a failure on our terms.

ED: By the time of Thee Mighty Caesars, you were already in some back-and-forths with New Musical Express, right?

BC: Not yet. We just got completely ignored. What went on with *NME* was very simple. Steve Turner [Mudhoney bassist] came over to England when he was fifteen to see Thee Mighty Caesars play. Then in 1990 Mudhoney came over, and they got us a record on Sub Pop. The band was Thee Headcoats by then. The *NME* wanted to interview me because Mudhoney told them I was a genius. So I said okay. But is this interview being done on the basis that I have done independent rock 'n' roll music for the *past* fifteen years, or because I just got asked to do an album with Sub Pop? But I said I'd do an interview, if I can edit it. And they said that was totally out of the question. And that is how the fun started. I don't like it now, but I was very idealistic, I thought it should be done on merit. So that was that, and shortly after that is when we did the "I Hate the *NME*" single. I thought it was witty. I was one of the greatest rock 'n' roll lyricists going, and no one ever mentions it. It's very rude.

ED: Some of your stuff has extremely brutal, personal lyrics. . . .

BC: I do write some personal things, like "Every Bit of Me," by Thee

Headcoats. That was before child abuse was cool. I was the pioneer! I was sexually abused when I was nine, and that song is all about that, about Norman. I had a photograph of him playing the guitar because he was a friend of the family. So we put it on the front of the record sleeve. I wanted to find his address so I could mail it to him so he would have to try and explain it to his wife. Ha! Fucking whatever. God fucking damn.

ED: *Any idea if he's alive?*

BC: No. I know his daughter was in a psychiatric hospital, but that is most I could find out. But I like getting some personal lyrics in, political stuff, things like that.

ED: *Often with the press, if the music is trashy or not "properly produced" and a little fast, they do not even bother to look at lyrics.*

BC: I think we have lots of very well recorded songs. We worked very hard at it. I am not really somebody who thinks things through very well with what they call rock music or rock journalism or rock lifestyle or doing what someone else thinks is cool. I have zero ambition in any areas because my ambition is far greater. . . . We aren't trying to produce rock music that sounds like it's something that takes six months to squat out. Well, we are actually shitting each morning, and sometimes it goes quite well and sometimes it's a bit constipated, and sometimes it, you know. . . .

ED: *It flows.*

BC: Yes, pebble dashing! Generally we are trying to have good health, do a good shit.

ED: *How did Thee Mighty Caesars morph into Thee Headcoats?*

BC: The Caesars had ground to a halt. I think I just got fed up with Graham, our drummer, who was being a cook or working for Mr. Defense and couldn't do the gigs. Then we got the wrong date for our last show. It was our first sold-out show, and we were at home in bed! Then we just decided with [drummer] Bruce [Brand] to form a Downliners Sect (raw' 60s Beat band) kind of R&B group. We felt there was a need for recognition of the Downliners Sect, which was one of the greatest British rock 'n' roll groups.

ED: *So you said there wasn't that much ambition, but can I assume when you were doing Thee Headcoats and the double-CD comp with Sub Pop, you were dealing with contracts?*

BC: They did ask me to sign a contract, and I asked, What is a contract? Can you eat it? We never saw it after that. We got $2,500 to do the first album, and we did another for $2,000. Sub Pop then got $25 million from Warner and offered me $6,000 for a six-LP world deal. And we said that didn't seem right. So we politely declined that. They were long-haired rocker gentlemen—but I don't allow others people's taste in music to get in the way of working with gentlemen. We get a few dollars from royalties occasionally.

ED: When did you start Hangman Records?

BC: I think 1985–'86, just to be able to release things I thought were good without any commercial restrictions. We had a production/ distribution deal with Revolver. I told them, I will never take any money from this label, as long as you never tell me what I can and cannot release. They sent me a check a couple times by accident, and I returned them to them.

ED: Really?

BC: Well, I said I couldn't take any money from this label because then I have to figure out who it belongs to, and I can't because I can't add

Billy Childish points out the restrooms; Thee Mighty Caesars reunion gig at the Las Vegas Grind festival, Las Vegas, 1999.
(Photo by Mark "icki" Murrmann)

up. So then they said we had to do CDs, and I said, CDs are the biggest rip-off that has ever happened in the music industry since vinyl.

ED: *Does Hangman still exist?*

BC: It sort of exists. We sort of got into some trouble. A friend of mine gave me some unreleased Link Wray records that we swapped, He had swapped them for an answering machine. And then the person who originally had the recordings subsequently hung themselves. Then someone else said they owned the recordings, and that I owed them some money. And I said the label doesn't have any money. We only made a thousand copies. And the label was going down at that time, and another friend of mine from Germany took a lot of records and never paid the distributor. Which was the final death of the label. And we had major issues with Crypt because we never got paid, because I guess the distributors never paid.

ED: *So this is around the latter '90s. Were you personally starting to focus more on your writing and painting?*

BC: No, no, I was mainly a painter all along. And I wrote all the time as a poet, and wrote my first novel in the early '80s running a small press—because don't forget, Hangman Records was named after Hangman Books, which started in '79. . . . I still don't own a house. I never made money off music. I live a little bit by painting, a little bit by music. I still write poetry and novels and do readings, but you can't really make a living doing that stuff. I do three different things so I don't have to do anything I don't want to in any one of them. We do turn down tours. We were just asked to tour with the Hives in Europe, which I think is highly insulting, especially since no one wants to pay us anyway. And this group the Black Keys just asked us to tour with them. And we don't have an agent, and we don't have management, so we just turned it down. It's insulting—not the Hives personally. It's funny, these groups think I am going to do a support, like we are teenagers, and they pay us two hundred pounds a night. I mean, I've been playing for thirty years. It's like they think we are old black bluesmen and they can fuck with us. There isn't a great deal of respect. It's kind of like me saying to Bo Diddley, "Okay, you can do a support. . . ." We don't want to anyway because we've got lives. We are not interested in the rock 'n' roll lifestyle. I don't think loud music is cool. I think it is a pain in the arse.

ED: *You haven't really done a lot of proper tours in America.*

BC: Any tours we had in America were with groups who liked us and would lend us their equipment, and without an agent. So usually our tours in America were six shows. And we said, the audience needs to come see us, because we weren't going to go see them. If we weren't playing their town they could drive six hours to see us, because we had just flown ten hours to find them.

ED: I remember you toured with the Makers in 1997, and that's when we played together on that bill in Columbus, Ohio.

BC: Yeah, we did some thing with you in some godforsaken club. This is the other thing. New Bomb Turks were quite heavy, and what happens is you do these gigs with people and you are playing to sweaty men. We are not interested in drunken men. That is another sort of cabaret, not mine. I can put up with confusion, but I just can't put up with jostling and heaving groups of drunken, um, what do you call them—"jocks" are they? It's not my cup of tea.

ED: What kind of crowd reception do you enjoy?

BC: I like 50 percent girls/50 percent boys, and quite the mayhem. But I don't need the girls to like us. They can be there with their boyfriends, which is even better because you get some kind of hormonal balance, and people start to think politeness is a swell thing to have.

ED: Well, most loud bands run into "sausage parties" eventually. But hey, those dudes paid their two bits to get in too.

Thee Headcoats make the 1998 Wild Weekend fest in London a lot more suave. (Photo courtesy of Damaged Goods)

BC: True, and I don't mind that, but I don't have to be there for it. It was quite funny when we were doing the Seattle shows because people started asking what it's like to come from England and play shows to next to no one. Well, like when we played to three people on Vancouver Island with the Mummies, I think there were three people. I don't mind three people because they can't really set the agenda. It is up to us. They do what they are told—they deal with that.

ED: *So how did things go sour with the White Stripes? Jack White was a big fan of yours, and name-dropped you when the hype on them hit. . . .*

BC: I mean, in my eyes, Jack's [estimation] would seem like, "Well, two million people think I am great, and nobody knows who the fuck you are." So my answer would be, "Then why do you care?" Ah, that is just not my cup a tea, what they call "garage rock." We did this song called "Bugger the Buffs," kind of taking the piss out of the groups that have been fans of ours . . . because we had a name for all those groups, which had components of all their names—the Strokes, the White Stripes, the Hives—we called them the Strives! People need to develop a sense a humor. A lot of people identify themselves by what they do, and that is kind of an immature thing to do.

ED: *What do you identify yourself by?*

BC: By knowing myself. By the feeling of continuity that you are awake in the world and you can laugh and respond to things in the world. Like, I enjoy a cup a tea, but I do not think I am a cup of tea. I don't stop and think, "I am a rock musician," "I am a painter." I mean, sometimes we do things that are good, but I don't identify myself by my achievements. I'm only trying to put out what I think is missing in the world, and have a sense of humor about it

ED: *So with Jack White . . .*

BC: Just a different type of humor there. I talked to Jack and we got along fine. He asked me to do things with him, tried to be friendly and inclusive. I just don't think he gets it.

ED: *And what is "it"?*

BC: Well, Jack obviously wants to be liked and wants to do things that he thinks people will think are cool. So *GQ* in America did a big article on me. They asked to speak to Jack too, but Jack refused. So they decided to get at him, I think. So they asked me what I thought about [the White Stripes], and like an idiot I said, "Well, it doesn't seem so charismatic." And I don't think it is. They wanted people to think that there is some kind of similarity between he and I, but there is not. We are trying to close fifteen yards between the audience and us; and the White Stripes want that fifteen yards. And Jack got very upset with me and wrote this thing about me on the Internet saying that I was a plagiarist, and that he felt sorry for me because I was a bitter garage rocker. That was in the *NME* and *Melody Maker*. I wrote a reply for the press and sent it to them saying that I undoubtedly angered Jack because his former admiration for me wasn't reciprocated. I said, It smacks of jealousy to me. I have fully blistering guitar sounds and a developed sense of humor. I said, I follow stringent music industry standards and only plagiarize 50 percent of my music. Ha! When that went out, I e-mailed Jack immediately after and said, I am sorry if you are offended by anything I said. This is just stuff people write down in the press and it is nothing personal; it's just I am not really into the music. And he didn't reply to that. Also, you need to put in the fact that if I was Jack, I would think, "Two million people know who I am, and no one even knows who you are." Isn't two million enough?! Why do I have to like it as well?

ED: *Why do you think you even responded in the first place?*

BC: I thought it was funny. I wrote a really good laugh. If you can do that with humor, and say what you want to get said, it's worth it. If you are going to get serious and get caught up in things, then it's not. You know, the world needs entertainment.

4.
BLOOD, GUTS + PUSSY

MANY HAVE LAID claim to the title "Greatest Rock 'n' roll Band in the World." They can all eat shit.

At the height (about 1989–'93) of their staunch stance as the un-repentant, Babel tower–high middle finger to all that is proprietary in this hideously hypocritical world, the Dwarves laid waste to all punk comers. Kooky kill-tune conquistadors, they truly evoked the "blender" metaphor, pureeing all grease-rock tenets into one-minute hilarious heaves to the head via an unholy trinity of trash classics and the most crazed live performance of the era. If some losers wimpily declare that the Dwarves—who slay still—have long entered the pantheon of dead-horse beaters, you lose again, as savagely flailing away on an ex-equine would be an inviting tune topic for these Bay Area bozos.

Since their 1983 birth in Chicago as twisted '60s graveyard-garage revivalists to their subsequent Mr. Hyde dive in San Francisco as trash-thrash gods, they've already covered murder, familial sex, lesbian nuns, drug overdose as ambition, underage deflowering, bug fucking, and some really crazy shit too. And yeah, they smash bottles and mic stands on audience members' heads, piss onstage, play too-short sets, etc.

What is constantly lost in all the dirty-laundry listing is just how damn good a songwriter and producer Dwarves' mastermind Blag Jesus really is. Fine, you don't have to go see them live if you can't deal. But at least sit at home and listen to any of the Dwarves' releases and pay some attention! True, the point of punk rock is anything but reflection, and surely the Dwarves canon is reliable for quick fixes of riot ignition. But that's what makes all the sidesplitting samples, crisscrossing hooks that stick like napalm, racquetball bass, Jim-Thompson-meets-

Bushwick-Bill-chewing-Bazooka-Joe lyrics, and sonic layering of it all that much more impressive. It's easy enough to nod through slow, six-minute Radiohead amoebas or ambling Animal Collective jams and stumble across nice melodies, eventually, maybe. What is flippantly ig-nored by naysayers is that it actually takes a lot more dedication, atten-tion, and energy to get past the speedy thrust of a Dwarves record to fully swallow the endless gobs of ideas spraying you in the face.

While I chatted on the phone with singer/mastermind Blag Jesus (squatting in his San Francisco crib) for about two hours one balmy night, gazing across the courtyard at the other group of brownstones, a woman in an apartment directly across from me, who was apparently drinking a lot, must've thought the lighting in her bathroom was as weak as her bladder. The curtains were wide open, and she continued to pass through the can, dropping her drawers and peeing right there at the window the whole time Blag and I conversed. Fitting to the point of tears . . .

———————

BLAG JESUS: My brother bought me my first single, "Brandy, You're a Fine Girl," and then he got me my second single, which was Stevie Wonder's "Living in the City," which I still have. AM radio used to play black songs and white songs together. Unfortunately, radio has become really weird and segregated again, but when I was a kid you could hear great shit. I would listen to AM radio in Chicago and you could hear the Banana Splits and then the O'Jays. It was great!

ERIC DAVIDSON: What came first—the cherry-popping or the band?

BJ: The band! I always had the band so I could hopefully get my cherry popped. Guess it worked!

ED: When did either happen?

BJ: I think I got laid when I was a junior in high school, when I was sixteen or seventeen years old. I had the band before that. The very first show I ever did was in a band called Sexually Deprived Youth. Nineteen eighty-three, "Focus on the Arts Day" at Highland Park High School, Highland Park, Illinois, tenth grade. The songs were "Problems" by the Sex Pistols, "Mongoloid" by Devo, "Camarillo Brillo" by [Frank] Zappa, "99th Floor" by the Moving Sidewalks, "You're Gonna Miss Me" by the 13th Floor Elevators, "Are You Gonna Be There (at the Love-In)" by Chocolate Watchband, and "I Found That Essence Rare" by Gang of Four. My brother got me going on shit like Zappa, Monty Python, and jazz records. That's always been the basic thing in the Dwarves, weird influences from across the board. . . . Oh wait, hold on, my drug dealer is here. . . . *(Sounds of a door opening, mumble greetings, etc. . . . SLAM.)* Hey, you just witnessed a crime! Anyway, we'd come into Chicago from the suburbs with our miniskirts and minibob haircuts, and they fucking hated us. I loved punk rock music and bands like Black Flag and the Misfits, but we never fit in with that crowd. That's kind of the Dwarves, uh, aesthetic is that we never do the right thing at the right time. You know, I could've gotten in some real shit in Chicago. I used to buy drugs off these El Rucan gangbangers on the west side. Now that's where everyone hangs out. But back then there was nothing but Mexican and Puerto Rican gang dudes there. I would drive down there in my parents' station wagon with a thousand dollars cash in my pockets and crack jokes with dealers and buy a bunch of weed. I don't know what the fuck I was thinking. I guess they were so amused by me they didn't just fuck me up and take my money. When I finally got arrested I had bare feet, but fortunately I also had cash for bail!

ED: *Where did you get a thousand dollars at the time?*

BJ: From selling other drugs! I was a teenage drug dealer. I wasn't greedy, I just liked to get fucked up and have girls call me up on the phone. . . . So then eleventh grade I was in a band called Suburban Nightmare. We even did a record, *Hard Day's Nightmare.*

ED: *A number of people I interviewed for this book who don't like the faster Dwarves stuff said they like the kind of weird recording and dark feel of that Suburban Nightmare record. It doesn't sound down with the '60s retro bands of the '80s.*

BJ: Yeah, that was the whole thing! I would go see those revival bands, and I saw them all. They were always kind of polite and lame. They had the original, vintage guitars and vests, but it didn't feel like the energy of the Black Flag shows. However, I liked that music better than hardcore bands. So I was looking for something that had that excitement, but was still rock 'n' roll and sexual and fun. We were a punk band trapped in the rotting corpse of a '60s garage band. . . . Midnight Records put out the Suburban Nightmare record, and it was the worst back cover in history. We changed the band name out of embarrassment. So we recorded the Dwarves *Horror Stories* album [Bomp!/Voxx, 1986] in Champagne, Illinois, where Adrian Belew had a studio. It was all done in two days, recorded and mixed. And it sounds like it! Then we started playing with garage bands and realized they were even more generic than the punk bands, but with a huge dose of tedious, by-the-book nostalgia thrown in.

ED: Was the Dwarves' batty behavior already in effect?

BJ: Oh yeah. I remember taking acid at one show and then trying to drive home. I was heading right for the guardrail fifty feet over the Edens Expressway. Fortunately, my drummer wrenched the wheel away and saved us from being premature legends.

ED: So when did you move to San Francisco?

BJ: Well, I had lived in New York City and Boston and thought rock music was dead on the East Coast. I wanted to move to L.A., but Saltpeter [bassist] wanted to go to San Francisco. And that's where the Dwarves moved, in 1985. I'm glad we did, because when you move to L.A. you burn brightly for five minutes, and then you're replaced. No one in either town cared much about us until they thought we were from Seattle several years later when we were on Sub Pop. It took us a few years to get our bearings, but when we did we realized that these locals are so obsessed with this town that they won't even go to L.A. to play, let alone anywhere else. So we just fucking crossed

Blag Jesus (Dwarves) dictates the terms of the pit, Seattle, 1992.
(Photo by Charles Peterson)

the country. We worked shit day jobs and then we'd just fucking go. I worked in a T-shirt factory, making screens. It's funny, there're all these working-class-guy bands, though the Dwarves were never considered that, but that's what we are, Midwestern working guys. We hated that life, it made us sick. I'm not going to sit around and celebrate working for a living. I fucking hated work. We were born to rock 'n' roll.

ED: When you were in San Francisco then there must have been a lot of rich kids playing pop punk and things like that who didn't dig what you were doing.

BJ: Pop punk wasn't popular yet—if it was, it might have been a different story, but the popular genre then was pussy fucking hair metal. That stuff was huge in the Bay Area, guys who wanted to be from L.A. Punk had died, there were no all-ages venues. People don't associate the Dwarves with the DIY scene that was just starting to go on there. We just don't fit into things. We fucked with people's expectations. We would hang out and drink and fuck girls in San Francisco, and people would say, "Why don't you play at Gilman Street?" And I said that I liked having kids at shows, and think

The Dwarves lay waste to Stache's, Columbus, OH, 1992.
(Photo by Jay Brown)

kids should do their own shows, and I believe in punk rock. But all
the people who thought at first that we were teenage kids from
Berkeley didn't want to hang out with a bunch of weird fucking
dudes in their midtwenties scamming on their girlfriends, on acid,
freaking out. . . . We were in Seattle, playing with Nirvana, part of
the grunge thing. But we were too punk, too fast. We went to Gilman Street, but we were too decadent and weird, so that was that.
We like poppy things, but we like to have a little dirt on it. . . . I was
always fucking high, I would have a real bad temper. I'd get mad at
the audience even if they did like us. . . . I just wanted rock 'n' roll! I
wanted it to be people really getting the experience of "Bam—that
just knocked my ass off!" We had all this shit on our records about
sex and violence and being crazy—and people were always testing
us on it. I guess I didn't get the memo that said you can only write
about what you actually believe in. We did crazy shit and you read
reviews about how we were misogynist and weird—and we were!
But we didn't think we were those things. I just wrote songs I thought
people would find amusing. . . . The best era of punk to me—and
I think it applies to anything—is that era when it's young and you
can do anything you want. If you look at CBGB and that kind of
shit, there is no blueprint. All the bands were different. Then punk
became a blueprint. But in the early days you had Black Flag, the
Misfits, Minor Threat, just different bands who were really good
at what they were doing. I felt we were part of that tradition, an
American folk tradition of being a unique, weird little entity. . . .
Then the phenomenon called "alternative" took hold, and it gave
people a safe little cheap out, they didn't have to say they were punk.
It was like new wave, people who wanted to have a little bit of punk
aesthetic but were really making pop records. In the late '80s, that
spawned the modern indie scene, which I think is really boring and
there's little to recommend from it.

ED: *How did the Dwarves end up at Sub Pop?*

BJ: They were a mess from the get-go for sure, and I absolutely didn't
think it was going to go anywhere. We wanted a record deal. I didn't
know where it was going to come from, or why. Sub Pop got a lot
of people to do singles. So we went up to record for a single and we
ended up with enough for an album. So we sort of hard-worked
our way into it. I like the aesthetic of the people up there, I liked
Nirvana, I liked Soundgarden, I liked Mudhoney. The people who

profited the most from that scene though were not the Dwarves, who got there in 1989; it was the people who were there after Nirvana hit, 1992, 1993, that's when all those wack bands got signed. A lot of people forgot about the Dwarves. We made three albums for them. People just said, "Fuck those guys."

ED: Can you tell me more about that first Sub Pop album, Blood, Guts & Pussy *[1990]? Obviously it was a big sound change from the* Horror Stories *album (though two sleazy 7" EPs in the interim—*Lucifer's Crank *[No. 6 Records, 1987] and* Toolin' for a Warm Teabag *[Nasty Gash, 1988]—hinted at things to cum . . .)*

BJ: We started to morph into my harder influences. We turned into something that was more Motörhead, whatever. It was the genre that took over my songwriting for a couple of years.

ED: There wasn't a magical drug or a maniac ex involved?

BJ: The girl who I went out with in high school was just a real nutcase and we finally exploded by then. We slugged it out. But yeah, that's when I wrote "Skin Poppin' Slut" and things like that. It was absolutely some female trauma, sinking heavier into drugs, and watching people get over heroin and different shit—a very strange era. There was never much hope of getting a big record deal. Then, after Nirvana, we thought we were all going to get big record deals, but by then the Dwarves had kind of run their course. What came next was when bands like Green Day and Offspring got big, and I said, "I know I can do that, I happen to know all these bands." We played with Green Day early on, we played with NOFX too— but by the time they got big they weren't anxious to tour with the Dwarves. . . . But see, there are these different levels. Some people can only think about partying and beer. The next level are people with a little education, the people who are kind of bright or kind of hip. These are the people who recognized that the Iraq war was a farce. Then there is the vast majority of the people who came around several years later who could admit things weren't working. Then they look at us like we're idiots 'cause all we want is sex and drugs. I go home and read *Harper's* or the *New Yorker* and make up my mind about some political shit, but that has nothing to do with my rock 'n' roll. You come off seeming smarter when you're in there with your half-baked political ideas. We already knew more about that stuff than people who thought we were dumb.

A SAMPLING OF CHOICE BLAG JESUS COUPLETS

"Seems like ballin' bitches is all I ever do.
You better watch your ass, I'll fuck that too!"

("Fuck 'em All")

"I killed my mother and my dad did not approve.
How come they always try to tell me what to do?"

("Drugstore")

"Old enough to bleed, old enough to breed,
old enough to pee then she's old enough for me."

("Let's Fuck")

"My dad was outta town, my sister was at school,
and I ain't been inside that bitch since 1962."

("Motherfucker")

"I am the dominator, leader of the pack.
Two tons of steel that's hanging from my sack.
I take the cake and then I take it back and attack,
Yeah, because you lack, Jack!"

("Dominator")

"It's a shame the kind of pain that I inflict. It's sick.
But you know deep down low you're loving it."

("Saturday Night")

"I wanna get fucked fucked fucked fucked fucked fucked fucked
in the back seat of my car."

("Back Seat of My Car")

"Is there anybody out there?
I am so horny, I'm so lonely."

("Anybody Out There")

ED: *And people assume that if the music is fast, it's dumb, though it takes so much more energy and concentration to absorb everything in a song when it's flying past you. . . .*

BJ: Tempos change with time. If you listen to original rock 'n' roll, kids danced to it, it wasn't that fast. When the Ramones did that, it was past the time of people dancing to things, so it was way faster. Music moved forward in terms of speed. The speeds we were playing at in the early '90s, people thought it was hardcore. Twenty years later it doesn't sound that fast.

ED: And the lyrics!

BJ: What people didn't get about my lyrics is that they worked on two different levels. Take a song like "Back Seat of My Car." It's not exactly Shakespeare, but to me the subtext is you get this aggressive punk sound that's saying, "I live in the backseat of my car"—that's level A. Level B of it is that I'm trying and I'm hopeful, but I'm poor so I'm living in the backseat of my car. I want something, but all I can hope for is to get fucked. . . . It's funny because most of my phrases come from things that really happened. HeWhoCannotBe-Named [guitarist] lived for a summer in the back of his car, so I just wrote a song about it. It tells you something about America, about who has what.

ED: Musically, you guys had fat bass lines, the guitars were crunchier, your voice had some gravel in it . . . whereas Operation Ivy, Screeching Weasel, and some other lame West Coast pop-punk bands some might have lumped you in with, the actual music was really fucking thin sounding, for supposedly "tough street punks."

BJ: One thing that happened to me in the mid-'90s is that I met Eric Valentine who's a real good producer. Most punk is recorded badly and sounds thin and shitty. It doesn't sound like an old Ramones or Sex Pistols album, which was the regular production of those times. It's bad punk production. People want to convince themselves it's better because it sounded more homemade, so they said it was good. I just call that putting up with bad circumstances.

ED: The sound effects, samples, voice-overs, etc. that you use are pretty inventive. What was the inspiration for that stuff?

BJ: To me that stuff is part of the music, and one big failing of critics—both those who hate us and those who love us—is they failed to see that in the punk realm we were the first to systematically use sound effects and later drum programming way before it was common.

ED: You've told me before that you were hired to write songs for well-known pop-punk bands.

BJ: Eric Valentine and I have done some of that, and I believe in that kind of music too, it's very interesting. I remember five, six years ago Good Charlotte were complaining about how bad Britney [Spears] and Christina [Aguilera] are—but at least they can sing and dance! These rock bands are a bunch of phony shits where producers are writing and playing the stuff for them, and they can't even play it themselves. I respect the world of having a great song, a great producer, and a great performer. To me that doesn't contradict punk rock. To me a great record is a great record. To me the limitation of most punkers is they can't write a great song. . . . I was on that last Good Charlotte record, helping them write songs. I didn't get credited, but they paid me. But there were others. . . . It's interesting to see the corporate machine in full effect. Yet still these little tools act with disdain, weak-ass tenth-generation punk people look down on people who can actually sing or dance, when they can't do anything. The only thing they have going for them is that they're supposed to be this cool punk band.

ED: *Can you talk about the whole "HeWhoCannotBeNamed is dead" thing? [Circa 1993, the Dwarves leaked rumors that their masked, ever-in-skivvies guitarist, HeWhoCannotBeNamed, had died, and that the band would be no more. Such dark clowning around didn't sit too well with Sub Pop, who took it seriously for a few days, even sending out an obituary press release before sussing the gag; then sending out another more incensed press release, announcing that the band had been summarily dropped from the label. Neither fans or industry insiders were sure if the joke was all on them.]*

BJ: Well, HeWho transcended life and death, he is a great figure, and he fucking dies for your sins. I told them that at Sub Pop. How was I supposed to know that he would rematerialize? Meanwhile, they had no sense of humor about it. My record deal with them was over anyway.

ED: *And didn't Sub Pop send out an angry press release about it later?*

BJ: Indeed they did. First they did the obit press release, then they did the famous "We were hoaxed!" press release. It even showed up in *Harper's* magazine, of all places! Then later they tried to say it was all their way of playing an elaborate joke on us. In all cases, they were lying.

ED: *Another nut in your band, Vadge Moore. When did you figure he was the right guy for the job?*

BJ: Vadge was born a Dwarf. He was always fucked up and would sleep with anything that moved. Unless she was unconscious, in which case . . . she didn't move! Vadge is in a class by himself for decadence. His antics were so much worse than mine, he made me look like a Girl Scout. You know all that crazy shit we yell about in Dwarves songs? Well, Vadge would actually do those things. He'd come in all excited about finding a girl who sucked his dick while he took a shit. Or one time he came running into practice all excited saying he had a ménage à trois with his girlfriend. And I asked who was the other chick, and he said it was a guy! That's not a ménage à trois! He was the best. Today he makes these weird noise records and lives in Georgia.

ED: I assume being a Dwarf is a challenging career move. You've gone through more musicians than speed. Can you give me a member roll call?

BJ: The Dwarves on tour can be a high-stress proposition, especially the early days where violence and poverty were our closest companions. Most quit for school or work, and a very few hated my guts. For the most part, though, we operate like the Wu-Tang Clan of punk—people come in, go out, return, appear on certain songs and at certain shows. It's like a big happy dysfunctional family. Part of my thing is being more of a ringleader than being the main focus. I took the most lumps because I spent the most time in the crowd and was the most provocative.

Okay, the roll call: Blag Jesus (aka Blag Dahlia, Julius Seizure, Junior High, Blag History Month, Paint It Blag, Blag Tuesday, Blag the Ripper), HeWhoCannotBeNamed, Sgt. Saltpeter, Vadge Moore, the Fresh Prince of Darkness, Gregory Pecker, Clint Torres, Rex Everything, Royce Cracker, Marz, Wreck Tom, Thrusty Otis, Black Josh Freese, Marky DeSade, Crash Landon (Michael Landon's illegitimate son), Chip Fracture, Tazzie Bushweed, and more!

ED: So what was the most fucked-up thing you did to an audience member?

BJ: This guy threw a full bottle of water at me, and it hurt! So I took my mic, lashed out, completely missed him, and just bashed some chick right in the head. I saw a fountain of blood come up. The guy just disappeared. But then, there have been plenty of those. I got my throat cut in Canada. I broke a bottle that was in some guy's hand, and he got mad and raked me across my neck. There was blood everywhere. I finished the show though.

ED: You've done bluegrass and rap side projects and worked on Top 40 pop-punk records. There must've been some sniffing from major labels.

BJ: If anyone would have recognized how good we were, we would have gladly made commercial records. When *The Dwarves Must Die* came out [Sympathy for the Record Industry, 2004] it almost happened. I had some meetings with people. They thought it was some brand-new band, but I walk in and I'm forty years old. They didn't know how they could market that. I'm reminded of when Bowie was broke and still taking limos so it looked like he was rich. And that's what major labels are—just a bunch of douchebags bleeding money. You wind up meeting people like Lemmy [Kilmister, of Motörhead], who we played a bunch with. I hated him, not because he wasn't a cool dude, but just because of all the people around him. There were a bunch of hangers-on from the '80s sucking on what little dick he had left. It was fucking sad. That's rock 'n' roll—people hiring people to be their cheerleaders and carry their cases for them.

————————

THE COVER SHOT of the Cosmic Psychos' debut LP, *Go the Hack* (Sub Pop, 1990)—sporting three burly blokes standing atop some kind of megatractor, and, uh, whatever the hell "go the hack" meant—made it apparent these guys weren't down on the Iowa farm tip. Once the needle dropped, this metronomically pummeling, economically comical booger-woogie shit definitely did not come from of the minds of guys I knew growing up who'd dig extended wah-wah solos and reference Van Halen. It came instead from some Dumpster behind a pub in Australia.

Finding that Dumpster, or wherever singer/bassist Ross Knight was currently residing, was no easy task. He currently lives a leisurely life of hard-ass farming out in the country. When I finally heard back from him, he asked of the interview questions, "Hey mate, could you dumb it down a bit? I'm just a simple farmer." As if I'd asked him for a complete history of the aborigines. But the thing is, the Cosmic Psychos were men of action, of course—blunt, barreling, beer-braised action. "Mate! I can only just now use a mobile phone, and I don't own a computer," says Knight. "But I'm sure some people find that stuff real handy for talking about themselves and stuff."

Australia has always had an incredibly inspired music scene, and the late '80s/early '90s were no different. Bands like the Birthday Party, the Lime Spiders and Celibate Rifles had reestablished raw rock cred for the post–Saints/Radio Birdman era down under. Thanks to '90s Aussie imprints like Au Go Go, Dog Meat, Giant Claw, and Rubber, some new wild sounds were making it over. "Yeah," Knight recalls, "we liked bands that had fun, rocked hard, and didn't mind a beer, could take and give shit without crying and running home to mum and dad. Mudhoney, Tad, New Bomb Turks, Raunch Hands, Nine Pound Hammer, Fluid. Aussie bands like Bored, Poppin' Mommas, Meanies, and the list goes on."

To hear the Psychos' songs at first can be a battering blur of buzz-riff, often hair-dragged out by two-chord jammish midsections. But when lyrical bons mots about Elle Macpherson and dead kangaroos

Cosmic Psychos' Robbie Watts pours on the charm, Stache's, Columbus, OH, 1993. (Photo by Jay Brown)

come shouting out of their rusty-battering-ram rush, their pummeling one-two combo turns into a chortling ass-slap.

Once regional attention came, the Cosmic Psychos were landing gigs like opening for Pearl Jam. Knight exclaims, "Fuck me, where do I start! Supporting Pearl Jam in front of forty-five thousand people, fair to say they didn't get it. Ed [Vedder] came out and sung a song with us, crowd goes nuts, I'm thinking, We're okay now! Ed leaves the stage, and forty-five thousand people want us dead again. At the end of our set they all got to see my shit hole! Basically, it was all about getting drunk for free. I didn't give a fuck, and still don't."

Sub Pop did, and unleashed the band's best records from 1989 to '92, smack-dab in the eye of the alt-rock storm. "Sure, it was good being on Sub Pop with all those bands," Knight says, "'cause I got free CDs and T-shirts and some of the best music of all time came out of that 'explosion of alternative rock.' Do I think the Psychos had anything to do with it all? No. Being on the same label as some of my favorite bands was cool! But did it help the band? Dunno. We were just stumbling along doing what we always had done—drink."

Amazing original guitarist Robbie Watts sadly passed away in July 2006. The Psychos still sporadically play, though they rarely record. "If the individuals within the band can still self-destruct, you will always have the music left," says Knight. "The music scene over here now seems very serious and totally up itself. It don't hurt none to have a fuckin' good laugh at yourself sometimes, in fact all of the time, and kick a few fuckwits in the balls as you stagger past as well!"

As WELL DOCUMENTED, the rainy skies and proximity to the Asian drug trade made Seattle and its most famous record label, Sub Pop, a perfect breeding ground for that most morose rock subgenre, grunge. So it's worth noting that the two decidedly nonmorose bands just covered— the Dwarves and Cosmic Psychos—were both on Sub Pop while in their very-early-'90s prime.

But at first, Sub Pop was just another late-'80s, SST-emulating, cassette-only, post-hardcore label before it and its hometown became grunge icons. Gas Huffer—think the Raunch Hands as reburped by that smart-aleck kid who's always kicking the flowers out of the crazy lady's garden down the street—seemed attitudinally opposite from their mostly surly Seattle scene. Drummer Joe Newton peels off that bumper sticker.

"The early scene in Seattle was pretty fantastic," says Newton. "There were new wave bands, hardcore bands, avant-garde noise, and free-jazz horn ensembles—all sorts of things. And there were a couple of art galleries, most notably those run by Larry Reid. He later went on to help found CoCA [Center on Contemporary Art]. Larry was one of the first to recognize underground comics and car culture as an art form. CoCA hosted concerts, and featured the 'Misfit Lit' show with lots of Fantagraphics stuff. He also did the 'Kustom Kulture' show that featured Robert Williams, Von Dutch, Ed 'Big Daddy' Roth—before all this 'lowbrow art' stuff made its way into the mainstream too."

"Sure," adds singer Matt Wright, "a lot of the attention was focused on The Grunge, but there was a great garage punk scene happening too. Bands like the Fall-Outs, Nights and Days (later the Night Kings), Girl Trouble, the Derelicts, to name just a few."

"And of course, the Fallout Records store," says Newton, "another *really* key part of the early Seattle scene. It connected the whole music, skateboard, and comic book scene. Bruce Pavitt worked there when it was Bombshelter Records; then it moved and turned into Fallout, after Bruce left to cofound Sub Pop."

"So many people hung out at Fallout," says longtime owner/manager Tim Hayes, who worked at seemingly every important record store of the '90s. "Big Black had their last show in Seattle, and they hung out at Fallout for a solid week. I remember Psychic TV hanging out, and some guy came up and wanted to invite them to his private dick-piercing party. I kicked Jello Biafra out numerous times—in a loving way, of course. It'd be five minutes before closing, and he'd want to play this huge stack of singles. "Uh, Jello, it's time to go. Jello!" That happened at Fallout, Wax Trax in Chicago, Sound Exchange in Austin. . . .

As Norton and Crypt were at first utilizing grave-robbed reissues to reveal that the midcentury wasn't all Elvis and the Beatles, new indie labels like Sub Pop, PCP, and Amphetamine Reptile embraced their late '70s basement 'n' bong, heavy metal teendom.

Amphetamine Reptile (or "AmRep," as most devotees end up calling it), began in 1984, eventually becoming was one of the more active indie labels of the '90s. As grunge took hardcore's DIY aesthetic to the bigger halls, AmRep ground surly mosh-ish conventions through the kind of metal shop most of its fans spent their high school time skipping out of to go do whippets. Extremely irascible and musically regimented bands like Tar, God Bullies, Hammerhead, and Janitor Joe were major daddy-issue destructors who took the heaviest of SST's post-core pound and further jackhammered it into a pulp. In other words, powerful, sometimes scary, often laborious, but not very sexy or fun.

AmRep head Tom Hazelmyer's band, Halo of Flies, was the best crew on AmRep. Their whiplash trash offered a modicum of the mussy rush of the garage punk that was gurgling up, with guitar sounds that had more spastic edges than the gear-grinds of most AmReppers. "A G&L guitar, a solid-state Ampeg head, and a used speaker cabinet of dubious origin I bought off Soul Asylum for $150," Hazelmyer reports. Most startling was Hazelmyer's insane wiry/gravelly voice that furiously darted around their flailing sound. And their tunes usually killed it in under two minutes, which set them firmly in the punk playbook.

"I've been influenced by a lot of the same sounds as the most hardline 'garage' bands," he says. "But I was open to anything and everything along the raw-power end of the sphere. I even followed a lot of early speed metal at the time, Slayer, Metallica, etc."

A perceived right-wing bent was another reason for most mealy slackers to often disavow Hazelmyer and his label. "Well, 'right wing' in an ardent libertarian sense," says Hazelmyer. "But I've also lived and worked deep in the bowels of the hard-left arts community. So, unlike most of my friends and associates who preach tolerance, I've had to actually learn to practice it, or I could've never existed in that world." Further, Hazelmyer was once a marine, and he probably didn't run into too many of those at indie rock concerts. "One thing I could usually count on was, despite it 'not being cool' by any stretch of the hipster code of ethics, most of the folks were wise enough to keep their opinions to themselves lest they prompt a response from the babykiller. Ha ha."

Hazelmyer was also not reticent about releasing 7" singles—another connection to the garage trash scene that would soon be pumping out singles with the veracity of a Beijing sperm clinic. The usually limited press runs on AmRep singles frustrated many fans while exciting those who turned AmRep and the similarly sneaky Sub Pop singles into instant collectors' items. "I knew our initial pressing of two hundred singles was lame but decided to use it," Hazelmyer admits. "The 'limited edition'—that bogus stance that we indeed could have made thousands of these things, but we've chosen to just deal with an elite few. Ha! But it also really helped the business initially, as we were able to not get bogged down with trying to keep titles in print when the working budget was for about two singles at a time anyhow."

NORTON AND CRYPT were based in New York; AmRep in Minneapolis; Sympathy in L.A.; and Sub Pop in Seattle—historically consistent musical territories all. No one expected much action from Denver, Colorado. But an aimless and violent hardcore scene that sputtered around there mid-decade eventually birthed the Fluid in 1985. Their sashaying slam was more proof that there was some kind of loosey-goosey Stooges oogling going on out there somewhere, separate from the flannel-framed form going on up Northwest way.

Guitarist Rick Kulwicki and bassist Matt Bischoff had been in the Frantix, who kicked around the Denver hardcore scene in the early '80s (offering the world one of the best slob-punk songs ever, "My Dad's a Fuckin' Alcoholic"). After joining with drummer Garrett Shavlik and guitarist James Clower (who were in a similar hardcore crew, White Trash), to form the short-lived Madhouse, they soon roped in the younger John Robinson, a handsome cad who was never above diving face-first into crowds, and the Fluid were flowing.

"We started playing a hybrid version of what we were all listening to at the time: the Stones, Stooges, and the *Pebbles* series," says Kulwicki. "We were and still are musicians first," says Kulwicki, "not poster children for some sort of 'scene.' There were a handful of bands in Denver, but also a really bad skinhead problem, and we tried to alienate those people as much as possible. There was still the potential for anything to happen, though, because we played real loud and our shows could get chaotic."

As I sat with the whole band cramped up in the basement backstage of Maxwell's in Hoboken in the fall of 2008, it still felt like they were working to extricate themselves. This night was going to be their first NYC-area show in some fifteen years, and only their fifth show since reuniting for the huge Sub Pop twentieth-anniversary weekend party in Seattle a few months earlier.

"The first Fluid show," Bischoff remembers, "there were hundreds of people there already. All kinds of people that were just dying to not have to go see that kind of hardcore cookie-cutter, polka-beat shit! Gimme a groove sometimes, sheez!" And that's what the Fluid did, taking the classic hard-charging Detroit sound (MC5, Stooges, Alice Cooper) and slapping on a shimmy via Robinson's lanky prowl and Shavlik's shifty drumming that could jitter like a lawnmower headed toward a cliff, until he jerked it back and slammed it upside down on its gas tank. The kind of seamless rock prowess of the Fluid wasn't exactly in line with the, uh, novice abilities of what would be called garage rock.

"But see, we were super isolated," Robinson makes clear. "It wasn't until we toured that we saw other bands like the Cynics kind of doing a similar thing. That wasn't happening in Denver."

The band's debut, *Punch N Judy* (1986), first came out on a small local Denver imprint, Rayon, but was soon reprinted by the German imprint, Glitterhouse. "After the second record, *Clear Black Paper*, was released in Germany," says Robinson, "Glitterhouse told us there's an American label in Seattle that's making rock records, and they have a band called Green River. I want to put that record out in Germany, so I'm gonna suggest a licensing trade: *Clear Black Paper* for Green River's *Rehab Doll*. So, sure."

The Sub Pop deal helped get them out on the road more often. "But I have to say," Robinson adds, "that I felt the Fluid was a little bit shadowed by Seattle bands, and by Sub Pop itself. We weren't in that city as the scene started happening, and it was kind of an incestuous scene." "We played with every town's grunge band," Shavlik adds, "even on the earliest tours. You would see people in the audience with their brand-new Doc Martens and flannels."

"Sub Pop was really a great experience as I look at it now," says Kulwicki, "but we were kind of the stepchild. We never had much money; we thought they had money and were just blowing us off. But little did we know, they were doing all of this with smoke and mirrors—they actually had nothing. They spent all of their money on advertising." A 1989 European tour got them loads of good press, in England especially; but a double-bill UK jaunt with Tad in 1990 was disastrous.

"That tour was terrible," Robinson laments. "Our work permits got denied, so we couldn't bring our own equipment or anything." Plus, the *Sounds* magazine writer who always raved about the Fluid lambasted their new EP, *Glue* (Sub Pop, 1990)—odd, since it's the band's best record. Due to *Glue*'s good notices in America, the Fluid finally got swept up in the bidding-war world of early-'90s alternative rock, which led to the ubiquitous major label travails, via Hollywood Records.

"There were people at the label who were really enthusiastic; they just didn't know what the hell to do with us." Are they at least happy with the Hollywood ending, *Purplemetalflakemusic* (1992)? "No," Kulwicki states, "because that was right after *Glue*, and *Glue* was the top. We recorded and mixed *Glue* in nine days and spent six grand on it. And with *Purplemetalflakemusic*, we spent four and a half weeks recording, and 125 grand before even mixing it, and it didn't sound as good. . . . That was the nail in our coffin."

IF YOU THINK it would be weird to be a high-energy glam guitar army stuck in the flannel-lined log cabin that was Sub Pop, imagine having to be the class clown in the algebra lab of Touch and Go Records. Such was the fickle fate of Champaign, Illinois's Didjits.

They started in 1985, not far from Chicago around the same time Windy City–based Touch and Go label got going. At the start, T&G was a hardcore outfit, dishing up angular howlers like the Meatmen (fronted by T&G founder Tesco Vee), Necros, and the Butthole Surfers (with whom the label ultimately had an infamous contractual flap, defining the parameters of "selling out" for the '90s alt-rock era). T&G was one of the great American punk labels, valiantly trying to find some way out of the backseat of hardcore's sputtering Escort. By the early '90s, though, the label had become the honors class of punk, a template for the math-rock most of the Chicago scene would gravitate toward during the rest of that decade.

Into this equation dropped the Didjits, who actually did fall into the art-noise camp at first. But soon enough, their surrealized love for tawdry '70s boogie came to the fore; as did lead singer Rick Sims's sense of humor—his lyrics like spun-out Marc Bolan gulping down boiling Jolt! cola; his stage persona that of a smarmy, snotty game-show host with a penchant for sharkskin suits and lightning-quick audience putdowns.

"We did feel like oddballs on Touch and Go," says Sims, "because most of the stuff like Scratch Acid, then Jesus Lizard, was like heavy '60s psychedelic acid rock—which I love, don't get me wrong. Or they had Big Black industrial kind of boys. We were just a little bit more 'rock.'" The Didjits hit the stage with mosquito ass–tight rhythms and riffs that buzzed and squealed around like the guitars were jacked right into said mosquito's sphincter, shooting sharp hooks and smug-silly vibes like the name of their best rec, 1990's *Hornet Pinata* (Touch and Go).

"Early on, we were being booked with hardcore shit," says Sims. "When we went to California, we'd be on six-band bills where everyone sounded the same and had Mohawks. People would see us and go, 'What the fuck is this?!' When we finally saw the Dwarves, it was a breath of fresh air."

It was always fresh to see how a small fellow in a shiny dinner jacket, round glasses, and shellacked coif could piss off a "modern primitive" tattoo dude who thinks he's seen it all because he worked enough late shifts at T.G.I. Friday's to afford that bad skull job on his forearm.

"Yeah, or there were the other ones who got on us for our lyrics," says Sims. "Pretty 'un-PC,' I guess; not advancing the culture. People couldn't understand you could do a song in the third person. They thought everything you wrote you were taking a stand. We took a page from Big Black a bit—bizarre stories, macabre, weird. I mean, that's no secret, every band in the world has done this, get high, drunk, do acid, whatever; then get the guitars out and, *whoa*, what the fuck?! But it was also in response to people who were tight-assed, just to fuck with those people."

Aside from Sims's rapier wit, the combo of bassist Doug Evans, who resembled a shirtless, bandana-topped human equivalent of a three-days-unfed rottweiler, and drummer (and Rick's brother) Brad Sims, with his tree-stump limbs, usually kept spats with such audience members to under one minute. Eventually, with more touring, a number of killer videos, and another excellent album, *Full Nelson Reilly* (1991), the band got some attention.

"It was kind of cool and kind of weird with Touch and Go," says Sims. "They didn't just do promo work directly proportionate to how many they sold. They were very democratic that way. Even though the Butthole Surfers outsold Didjits ten to one, they wouldn't do many more ads for them. . . . There's something to be said for sticking with Touch and Go, having some loyalty. The world wouldn't have given us shit if not for T&G."

This sort of rational pragmatism did not extend to Sims's onstage antics. But even given the muscular men behind him, Sims could handle any sticky situations that might have arisen. Circa 1992, us New Bomb Turks decide to hop in Jim's '83 Caprice Classic to ramble down about an hour to Athens, Ohio, home of Ohio University, to see the Didjits at the Union. Downstairs bar, bands upstairs via terrifyingly steep stairs,

The Didjits enjoy fan support, 1992. (Photo courtesy of Al Quint)

like twenty of them. A real bitch of a load-in, but always an excellent place to see bands. Just don't yell "fire."

So we're there watching the Didjits do their dastardly deed, which always included Sims's requisite greeting, "Hellooooo, St. Louis!" His parody of the disinterested rock-star greeting was always an asininely appropriate set-starter. Unless you're the wasted dumbass who stumbles in having misread the club poster outside and thought the local tie-dyed funksters were to perform. So as Sims continues to defame Athens as a lame-ass backwater (as if it weren't, and as if most locals didn't like it that way), aforementioned wasted dumbass keeps climbing on stage grabbing the mic and slurring, "Hey, look! If thissss guy doesssn't like our town, I say get the fuckchglch outta here!! Am I right?!! Fuck this guy!" Laughs, groans, and "No, fuck you, idiot" echoed back, and the fellow must've felt that the horde was turning on him in some revolt against local pride. He continues his on-off-onstage bogarting for like four songs in a row, yalping in between tunes too. Finally Sims, who's been quite patient so far, says, "Buddy, I am *kidding*."

No matter, the sauced sap keeps jumping onstage, only one time he grabs the mic midsong. Sims shoves him, the guy flings a beer, then Sims—in one swift move—slings off his guitar, leans it against his amp, and leaps off the stage to chase the clueless one down. Meanwhile, the band was in midriff race mode, barely blinking at the whole melee. And within two beer swigs, Sims was down the exit, then back up on the stage, straightening his tie, flinging on his git, and getting right back into the song, stuck right back into the groove. We heard later he'd caught the guy at the end of the steps, pummeled him with a quick left-right combo, and booked right back up the steps.

"That became part of the show from early on," Sims recalls. "If there wasn't a scene like that, I would usually try to start something. I don't want it to seem like it should overshadow the music, but it just became an urge for something more than just playing the songs. All of a sudden it's more than a rock show, it's a riot. I mean, we didn't want to be GG Allin . . . more like with you guys [New Bomb Turks], I always thought it was just, 'We're really pumped about our band! Our band's the best in the fucking world!' Arrogance, that can be the gasoline, which is not necessarily a bad thing. But if I'd have seen me onstage back then, I'd might've been like, 'That guy's an asshole.'"

Now, when I say the Didjits were locked in and tight as hell, a distinction should be made between where the Didjits were coming from and where mainstream pop punk was going. The Didjits inclination to snugly pummel grew from the Ramones' night school of the instinctual caveman awareness to take no chances when taking no prisoners. So hit the beats repeatedly, wow 'em with couple-chord riffs, neck-jarring bridges, and quick, not overcooked solos in order to bring on the most primal response—so Sims could then belittle same caveman tendencies in the crowd with those zippy putdowns.

"My credo, my motto onstage every night was," Sims declares, "no matter how many people are there, we can't let them down. I felt very serious about that, very concerned about our connection to the audience, the shenanigans, make sure we're still a band to be reckoned with. Every night. I still maintain that, live, we could get respect from anybody."

Seeing the Didjits was a constant stream of batty bait 'n' switch that was in stark contrast to the cardboard musicianship going down via the skate rat-ism of the Lookout/Fat Wreck Chords ilk. That brand of tightness rose out of jocky assumptions that playing with laser precision meant you were "good." First off, if technical ability were the preeminent prerequisite of music, we'd all be bopping along to the NY Philharmonic on our iPods. Second, punk rock—given its platelet-shifting thesis that "anyone can do it"—should never be about instrumental proficiency, unless it's in the service of confounding expectations or just because you can. The Didjits' rhythm section was preternaturally unable to be anything but a muscular, monolithic tempo truncheon. But again, aligned with Sims's smarm, it was hilariously new, confrontational, but never showy. The band's cockiness was instead reserved for Sims's smart-ass stance. Until around 1994.

"With my brother and I, it was sort of like patching tires at that point," says Sims. "Put out another record, do another tour, put out another record. . . . So then we had a show in Chicago with a new drummer. His wife and friends show up. By that time, we had a lot of crazy shit onstage—transvestite dancer, fire, all kinds of shit. My wife, girlfriend at the time, said, 'That show was truly disturbing.' Then at the end of the night, they were doing a bunch of coke and decide to drive two and a half hours back to where everyone else lives, and they got in a horrible car wreck. The drummer's wife got killed. So the bass player kind of went off the deep end, because he was in the car. Things kept getting weirder and weirder. He just vanished one day. After, I realized I was the only original member left—I didn't want that."

After a brief respite, Sims spent about a year and a half in Seattle's bofo buzzpunks, the Supersuckers, when their lead guitarist entered rehab. Then, not long after that, rumors ran through the punk community that Sims had cancer. "No," Sims clarifies. "They took out my thyroid. I was really freaked out. Radiation treatment. Then four weeks later, 'Your thyroid's in Philadelphia right now.' My goddamn thyroid's on a world tour! But they assured me I didn't have cancer." The yin to that yang was the Offspring had recently covered the Didjits' "Killboy Powerhead" on their 1994 *Smash*, and Sims finally got paid something for heading up one of the more original punk bands of the '90s.

After all that drama, it was somewhat of a surprise when Sims popped right back up with a new band, the Gaza Strippers. "I'm just crazy, I guess," says Sims. "I just thought, Now I have the experience, so do it right this time. Tour a lot, find a cool record label, make more accessible music, and have another guitar player so I could do more stuff. Don't make the same mistakes as the first band. Though I've since come to realize there weren't that many mistakes, other than rampant drug and alcohol abuse. Of course then I came up against the same shit as in my first band. And everything was overshadowed by my old band—'Oh, here's Rick Didjit again, just with a new wrinkle.' That was kind of insurmountable."

An amazing 10" and some great singles came before the band ran into some ubiquitous label hide-and-seek. "Yeah, we were doing almost better than Didjits," says Sims, "which is not all that good, but you know." Today, Sims has settled into his family life and creates music for various local Chicago theater productions, including "a kind of punk rock *Hamlet*."

5.
TELEPATHIC HATE

WHAT DID CHIEF Wiggum say? "Why are the pretty ones always crazy?" That's the unfair dung long flung at Peg O'Neill, drummer for Detroit dustups the Gories. "I don't know what the rumors are, so I can't say," says O'Neill.

"Well, Peg has always had kind of a volatile temper," says Dan Kroha, the trash trio's guitarist/singer. "Mick (Collins, co-singer/guitarist) and I, being young men, had our little boys' club that she was never really a part of . At the time I thought nothing of it because as Rudy Ray Moore said, I was young, dumb, and full of cum. I was just being a dude. I wasn't sensitive to her desire to be part of what we doing. Mick and I kind of knew more about music, figuring out the songs and stuff. Peg was the one with the temper."

The "crazy" that really defined the Gories was their utterly willful destruction of what was left of the carcass of garage rock at the beginning of their brief burn. Burped up in late 1985, it could be assumed that this trio was simply the next step in Detroit's fabled ugh-rock history, blueprinted by the Stooges and MC5 in the dream-dying end days of the '60s. Except the Gories were already tired of that fable before most punk fans had memorized it back then.

"All those things—the Stooges, MC5, *Creem* magazine, Motown, Fortune Records—they're just signifiers now," says Collins. "We rejected all of that—except for the soul music part. I picked up the guitar with the sole reason of killing classic rock. *Creem* magazine was the '70s, man, and the '70s bands were bands I hated. I didn't hear the MC5 until I was in late high school. I wouldn't say we rejected it *all* out of hand, but it wasn't that important to what we were doing." So they set about reaching farther down into the muck of '60s garage rock, well past the paisley. The Gories were a living, breathing, drunken, twentysomething version of the most scraggly sounds of Crypt's *Back from the Grave* compilations that were just starting to make their mark. . . .

"There were these magazines that would review these [new retro-'60s garage bands]," says Collins, "and talk about how 'wild and primitive' these bands were—but when I'd finally buy it, it'd be some jangly folk-rock thing, and that would just piss us off! So then we thought, Well okay, we're gonna be as raw and primitive as these guys are writing about. Our mission was to be a band that was so raw and primitive that it would change their definitions of those words."

Mick Collins, now in his early forties, had never moved from the house he grew up in. Which is why I was shocked to find out in early 2009 that he was living about four blocks from my pad in south Brooklyn. We met up at a local watering hole, Abilene. Collins walks in and of course knew the bartender by his first name.

Constant touring with his soul-garage band of the last twelve-plus

Gories press photo, 1988. (Photo by Steve Shaw)

years, the Dirtbombs—and meeting a girlfriend from Brooklyn—has him laying his hat in the borough—though his 7,300 records are still in a storage bin in Warren, Michigan. "I love Detroit, I want to move back," Collins says. "But it's Detroit, it's corroded out of existence. I couldn't ask her to do that with me. I like New York, but I felt tied to Detroit my whole life. If I wasn't from there, I probably would've ended up there anyway."

"Detroit," and all that implies to the fans of raw rock—who have turned the dying auto industry hilltop into a mythical musical Atlantis—has held onto Kroha's heart too, as he still lives there. "I was still living with my parents back in 1985," he says about the Gories' beginnings. "Mick, Peg, and I would hang there, in my bedroom, listen to records, and drink beer. I was really getting into *Back from the Grave* comps at that point."

Collins says, "Yeah, and the *Scum of the Earth* comp too. We thought, Man, these bands are terrible! We could be at least as good as this. We thought we'd form a band just long enough to put a few records out, make our mark in record-collector nerd history, and that would be it. If we could get a single out, we'd be happy. I'll play bass, Dan will play guitar, and our friend Fred will play drums. But he wasn't home that night. So we got Peg because she was sitting there. I couldn't play at all, Dan knew like two chords, and Peg had never touched a drum set. Then we had our first rehearsal, January 6, 1986."

"I got my first set from our friend Jerry Bartarian in '86," says O'Neill. "It wasn't a full set, though, it was a floor tom and two rack toms. The kick didn't have a head on it. No hi-hat, no cymbals. It cost fifty dollars. I used the set from the time we started until the time we broke up."

The fact that Kroha and O'Neill were an item at the time probably nudged in the drummer stool. "Dan and I would go to these mod parties every week at bars or house parties where I'd DJ," Collins recalls. "Dan's early mod band would play, and Peg would be there, and she seemed to be the only one who knew anything about the original mod scene. The first time we saw Peg, she was wearing this A-frame dress with an arrow that went right down to here, and the arrowhead tip was right there . . . and me and Dan thinking, 'Oh my God, are you seeing this?!' Then Dan was like, 'I'll be right back. . . .'"

It wasn't just short skirts and Detroit's dank that offered inspiration. The drinking age in Windsor, Ontario, about an hour north, was eighteen—if they checked IDs, that is. "Almost everyone I knew had been over to Windsor," says Collins, "and then tried to get back into the U.S. when they couldn't even drive yet. Drinking and driving was just not enforced in Detroit. My dad once got pulled over for weaving. Now he was an alcoholic, so he was probably pretty crocked when the cops pulled him over. They said, 'Well, we really wanted to pull you over for drunk driving, but we realized you were just avoiding potholes.' They let him go!"

The Gories carried on this tipsy tradition. "But the band reached a point where it was either we keep drinking or learn how to play," Collins says. "Early on, I learned if a song had more than six notes in it, the Gories couldn't play it. This realization came right before we cut the first album. We were definitely trying to sound like the bands on *Back from the Grave*. But at some point we also thought, Well, we're not that 'good.' So how do we sound like that with what we have? So we worked out some kind of formula.

"We knew going in that we were going to strip everything down because we just could not play. And even with that, after our first few rehearsals, we realized I couldn't play bass well enough, and Dan couldn't play guitar well enough, and we'd switch up instruments. Finally, we realized that I sound really good on songs with single-note runs on the guitar, and Dan sounds really good on the barre chords—so why don't we just ditch the bass altogether? And that's the only reason we didn't have a bass player. There was no conscious effort at having a bassless band—it was purely practicality. Then we took the music we listened to, which was already pretty basic rock 'n' roll, and stripped out all the frills from that until there was nothing left other than the rhythm and the lyrics."

That basic spark—to see '60s garage rock not as a rehab project but as a demolition detonation—put the Gories in the same camp as just a few post-Cramps tramps like Tav Falco and the Gibson Brothers But Collin's groovy pipes and the band's overarching preference for rust-belt R&B roots ultimately landed the Gories in the driver's seat of trash punk's plow—not that it wasn't sputtering at first.

"You have to understand," Collins reiterates, "we were terrible! The first show, I barely remember because I was hammered. It was at St. Andrews Church, a coffee house environment. They used to have an open-mic thing. Before we went on, Rob Tyner (MC5 singer) played a two-hour set of Vietnam protest songs on Autoharp. I got drunk during his set, so I don't remember when he got off and we got on. Dan was kind of sober, Peg was on mushrooms, and I drank a whole bottle of Thunderbird ESG before we went onstage."

The scene the Gories stumbled into wasn't exactly dope, guns, and fucking in the streets outside the Grande Ballroom in 1969. A straggling mod scene was about it for musical action, though Kroha mentioned a few local bands from the late '80s that inspired him, forgotten locals like Hysteric Narcotics, the Vertical Pillows, and the Zombie Surfers, who "played surf music and wore masks way before anybody did that! The Detroit neighborhood Hamtramck always had a reputation for having cheap rent, a lot of artists. . . . The two happening places at the time were Hamtramck Pub and Paychecks. Coke was going around, but as far as heroin, you didn't really start hearing about that until the mid-'90s."

"Well, I never went out much," says Collins. "Maybe there were regional bands playing, I just never heard them. But once the Gories got going, well, I recently found a day planner from 1987, and the Gories had a show literally every other weekend."

Though the band hadn't even recorded their first album yet, Collins says that Kroha and O'Neill's relationship was already strained: "All three of us hung out less after we became a band. We formed in January of '86, and they broke up in June or July of '86. So it became like a hobby for all three of us." That hobby was making O'Neill dig even deeper into old soul and R&B, more punk rock, and even introducing the band to the Velvet Underground whose influence added a drone underneath the Gories' garage rattle. "Then I remember around late 1986 or so," says Kroha, "Peggy bought Thee Mighty Caesars' *Ides of March* album. I remember going, 'God, that is the studio sound I want! These recordings sound unbelievable!' There was nothing that sounded like that at the time. It blew my mind."

The even more frequent older band that always gets name-dropped when the Gories came up was the Cramps. "I will make an admission," states Collins. "I did not hear the Cramps until 1984. I did finally hear *Smell of Female* while in college in 1984, which I still think is their best record. But back when we started, the Cramps were not that big an influence. It was cool, but we didn't really think they had much of a bearing on what we did until people started saying things like, 'The Gories did for R&B what the Cramps did for rockabilly.' So, hmm, maybe we should check these guys out." (*laughs*) . . . The thing about the Cramps, by the mid-'80s, the hardcore punks liked them. I'd see some kid with a Mohawk and a Cramps shirt, so I thought they were a hardcore band. Not to take anything away, they're an awesome band. But we had no idea when we started with two guitars and no bass that the Cramps had done that."

Kroha is even more adamant: "We were *not* trying to be like the Cramps. We were *not* influenced by the Cramps, at all. We were listening to really obscure '60s British R&B stuff and weird early '60s greaser rock. . . . I went to college in Connecticut for a year, mainly to get away from it all. My dad wanted me to go into the business, which I had no intention of doing. I always wanted to be in a band. There was a punk scene in Connecticut, and I went to a hardcore club there. I wasn't into it though. It would be a fuckin' sausage party, a bunch of dudes slam dancing and making pig piles. It was too fast and macho. I like girls, man!"

Nevertheless, there was an especially influential hardcore scene in Motown, featuring Negative Approach and the Necros. "Yeah, but those guys played an entirely different circuit of clubs than we played," says Collins. "I almost joined the Necros before the Gories, like '82, '83. I actually auditioned for Necros. They thought I was great, but too young."

"See," says Kroha, "the thing about Mick is he's the youngest in his family by ten years. He's from a family of seven brothers and sisters who grew up in the '60s. Not only that, but their dad was buddies with a record distributor. That guy would just give him boxes of singles of whatever was current at the time. So Mick grew up with this amazing collection of singles from the '50s and '60s."

All this "expertise" didn't instantly translate to the Gories' abilities. "We got a lot of crap for not knowing how to 'play,' even from our friends," says O'Neill. "We even got voted "Worst Band in Detroit" one year. We just thought, Fuck you, we're great! It was pretty fun to watch the looks on people's faces when they were watching us. There were about fifteen friends who would come to shows—although they were never all there at the same time!"

One fan had no reservations. "Lenny Puch loved the Gories because they reminded him of the Cramps," says Kroha. "He said, 'I'd really love to put out an album.' He drew up this crude contract. It was kind of funny—he wanted our publishing. Can you believe that? The oldest trick in the book. We're like, No, you're not getting our fucking publishing. I guess Mick and I were pretty smart about that stuff.

"So Lenny had a place outside the city almost in the woods, forty-five minutes away, in New Baltimore. His parents lived out there, and his brothers repaired semis or something; so they had a corrugated steel shed that you could drive a semi in. And Lenny had attached his little studio to this giant corrugated shack. Totally lined with carpet remnants. He had a stage in the studio, and a recording booth, and he would have parties out there. We went in there, set up all the amps, and just played. It sounded awesome. Three two-hour sessions. He had a Peavey mixing board, had a built-in spring reverb, somehow had a built-in slap-back echo. That's how we mixed it, it was a half-inch eight-track. And that was the Wanghead with Lips debut (*Houserockin'*, 1989)."

"Then we got drunk one night and figured we should go down and mix it ourselves," says Collins. "So we piled in our car and weaved on downriver. We banged on Lenny's door, his mom comes down in slippers and rollers, like ten-thirty on a Tuesday night. 'Where's Lenny?!' We drag him into the studio and remix the record right there, hammered, in like an hour and twenty minutes. We messed over the entire album, then split." With only seven hundred originally pressed, the record was later reissued on Crypt.

Today, recording an album and getting it out there is about as exciting an announcement as saying you finally set up a MySpace page. But you'd think in 1988, having a debut album would impress other bands at least. "August of 1989, first time we ever played in NYC, first time I was ever there in fact," says Collins. "We played three shows, none of which I remember, except the first one. I can't remember the club—it doesn't exist anymore—but it was a Friday night. We played with a band called the Neanderthals, a jangly folk-rock thing who thought they were primitive. And I'll never forget—they sneered at us. There they were, in their paisley and Beatle boots. And they looked at our gear, and they looked at us—at this point we're about half in the bag, about to go on the stage—and they sneered at us! I couldn't believe it. And that was kind of the beginning of the way I choose to I play rock music. Okay, we don't care what you think. All our shit was busted, and we just said let's take it to the hole. The kind of thing we do when we get really mad with people. And after the show, they wouldn't look at us, they couldn't look us in the eyes. They actually didn't sound that bad, it was just their attitude, that snobbish, elitist attitude. The only reason I'm harping on this is because I didn't realize it until the words were coming out of my mouth right now—I just now realized it, that's

The Gories and Alex Chilton bring their twisted noise to the Big Bad Apple . . . and New Jersey! 1989. (Courtesy of Larry Hardy/Art by Steve Shaw)

when it started! The look they gave us pissed me off *so* bad, I thought, I am never taking that from another human being, ever! I'll be damned if I'm gonna let some other band of a bunch of fuckin' rich suburban kids look down on me. So from now on, I am slaying every band that crosses my path! I swear, I didn't realize that until this moment. That was the night rock 'n' roll became a contact sport for me."

The Neanderthals might not have been impressed, but Alex Chilton was. The former leader of legendary '70s power pop innovators Big

Star had then been dabbling in production jobs that included trash-vets the Cramps and Tav Falco. "I met Alex in 1990," O'Neill recalls, "when we went to Memphis to record our second record with him, at Easley Recording. Our friend at the time—now my husband—Dan Rose, had played him our first record, and he loved it and wanted to produce our second record." Chilton hooked the band up with New Rose Records in France, rightly assuming that Euros would go for this band more quickly than Americans. When Kroha first got a call from Chilton about recording the Gories, "I didn't even know who he was," he says. "I'd never listened to Big Star. One of the first things he asked me was, 'Who's your drummer?'"

Universally great Gories singles started flowing out of all the new 7"-loving labels like Sympathy, Estrus, In the Red, and even Sub Pop, where the band did an amazing cover of Spinal Tap's "Gimme Some Money." "Danny first started sending me cassettes in 1986, '87," says Tim Warren. "Then I saw 'em at the Knitwit Factory [Knitting Factory] in October 1989 and wanted to do something with them but had drained out the coffers putting out the Headcoats' second album, never mind the insane moola hemorrhage of the first Raunch Hands tour."

"Finally," Kroha continues, "after we'd put out that second album—and we were almost ready to break up at that point—Tim Warren got back in touch with us. I was renting this Victorian house built in 1900 with a cinder-block garage in back. We recorded there in March when it was freezing cold, on Jeff Meier's four-track cassette recorder. Sent it to Tim, and he said, 'This doesn't sound like those great singles I heard; you've gotta rerecord some of this.' So we went to a real studio. Some of the four-track stuff ended up on the album, some singles, an outtake. It was kind of a hodgepodge, wasn't really what we wanted it to be."

Meeting the already infamous Tim Warren however surpassed expectations. "Oh, he was just a maniac," says Kroha. "A fuckin' toothpaste-eating nutcase. He had really sensitive teeth then, I don't know why. To relieve his sensitive teeth, he would eat it. . . . I was really pissed off at Tim for a long time because he also gave us a contract that stated that he would own 100 percent of the publishing in perpetuity. When I saw that, I was like, Fuck you! You're the guy who does *Back from the Grave*, and claims you track down these old '60s guys and pay them, but you want our publishing. Fucking hypocrite. For many years I was estranged, hated him. . . . But I'll say this—Crypt is the only label that ever gave us sheets of accounting, whether they're right or not. And we did get a regular check. Despite all the shenanigans, he's the only label that did that."

"On that only European Gories tour," Warren recalls, "I picked 'em up in the VW LT 40 at Schiphol Airport in Amsterdam, but their moods seemed not so good. I remember Peg tossing bottles of Franziskaner off the roof of the Insel club in Berlin after a major argh-fest with Margaret (Kroha's new girlfriend). It was really odd seeing them rip it up in July 2009 at Festsaal Berlin to six-hundred-plus raving fans, because the 1992 Berlin show was played to about forty people."

There was no classic practice blowup or label dispute at the Gories' end. It was a slow dissolve. . . . "What happened was after the one European tour in 1992, we'd had it with Peggy," says Kroha. According to Micha Warren, ex-wife of Crypt's Tim Warren, O'Neill had also had it with Maragret (who would play guitar in Kroha's next garage-crotch band, the Demolition Doll Rods), with her constantly getting up onstage and stripping while the Gories played. "Yeah, I brought my obnoxious girlfriend on tour," Kroha states. "Margaret and Peggy are both Leos, so it was like cat claws, you know?"

Plus, O'Neill just wasn't the type who wanted to jump in the van for months at a time. "But that was funny," Kroha says, "because we never toured that much at all. But she thought, Ah it's so fake, same thing night after night. She'd throw her drums in the middle of a set. So we just told her, You've walked out of too many shows on this tour, we've had it with you. We decided to find another drummer. But the Gories had a certain chemistry between the three of us. By that time, my heart wasn't really into it anyway. Dave Katznelson [Warner Brothers A&R] got in touch with us, I think through his friend Larry Hardy (whose In the Red Records label would soon be pressing up loads of Gories-influenced groups). Dave was like, 'Man, I really want to sign you to Warner Brothers. We'll give you seven hundred dollars to do a demo!' For us, that was a fucking fortune. We can do a demo for fifty bucks! But of course, they'd get all the rights, blah blah blah. Tell me another one. We were basically done.

"At heart, Mick and I are not at all fighters. We played this music that was totally outside of what was going on, sure. But Peggy, just by her presence, brought that badass edge."

JUST AS THE Gories were starting to unravel (if ultimately to expose more threads of their influence), the other end of early-'90s garage rock—that of the '80s dress-up retro ilk—was tightening the knot. Bands like the Fuzztones, Chesterfield Kings, and others were practically devolving into nostalgic tribute acts (though they probably thought of themselves as staunch keepers of the keys).

One band born of that '80s scene—the A-Bones—had already gone beyond the Beatle boots roots with their fun, sloppy stance on the genre. Then, in 1986, A-Bones bosses Billy Miller and his longtime lass, Miriam Linna, began one of the most active reissue imprints, Norton Records; they also began to publish their *Kicks* magazine, both of which dug even deeper into the well of lost '50s and '60s trash-rock archeology.

Billy and Miriam are fixtures to this day on the NYC area garage scene. There's a documentary waiting to be made on Miriam alone, with her globe-spanning life and drool-inducing stash of ga-ga goodies: old pics of her hanging around 1970 Cleveland (where she lived in her early teens) with a long-haired Stiv Bators; amazing unseen shots from the front row of a 1971 Iggy & the Stooges show; a lurid library of vintage pulp paperbacks, and much more . . . not to mention the mondo museum the Norton nabobs have concocted in their Park Slope, Brooklyn pad.

Comparing 12-inchers, NYC, 1984. *Left to right:* Miriam Linna (A-Bones), Billy Miller (A-Bones), Tim Warren (Crypt Records), Todd Abramson, and Vince Brnicevic (Raunch Hands). (Photo courtesy of Norton Records)

"I met Miriam in October 1977, at a record show that I was deal-
ing at, and sold her a copy of 'You Must Be a Witch' by the Lollipop
Shoppe," says Miller. "I'd seen her play in the Cramps a few times
before that [Linna was the Cramps' first drummer], and once she was
sitting behind me at the movies with [Cramps guitarist] Bryan Gregory.
The first thing I ever said to her was, 'Aren't you the girl that does the
Flamin' Groovies magazine?' She had a killer fanzine going called *The
Flamin' Groovies Monthly*. Miriam came to my loft and brought along
Todd Abramson [future NYC trash-rock promoter and head of Telstar Records, who would release records from '90s garagers the Mummies, Muffs, Swingin' Neckbreakers, and more], who looked like he
was about nine years old.

"I had started the Zantees in the summer of 1977. Miriam hooked it
up for us to play a Halloween party at the Fleshtones' house in Queens.
She was really cute at the party—she went as Dusty Springfield. Miriam and I started dating, and one of our first dates was going to the
studio to watch the Dictators record 'Stay with Me.' We started our
magazine, *Kicks*, in 1978 to write about unsung rock 'n' roll people that
we held in high regard.

"After the Zantees split in 1983, [bassist Mike] Lewis, Miriam, and
I, along with Peter Greenberg of DMZ, backed up [wild '50s r 'n' r
howler] Esquerita at a basement party. Mike Mariconda was there and
said that if we ever did anything like that again, to count him in. So a
few months later, we put the A-Bones together. But then Mariconda
was getting busier with the Raunch Hands, so we brought in Mike's
old roommate, Bruce Bennett, to replace him. Bruce's impressive cre-
dentials included stealing his parents' car to attend a Zantees show in
Maryland as an underage teen.

"Miriam and I started Norton Records in 1986 solely to issue ['50s
kookabilly one-man band] Hasil Adkins's early rock 'n' roll recordings,
but we began to uncover unreleased recordings by Link Wray, Esquerita, Jack Starr. . . . We did a record and a tour with Hasil in 1986. [Then
came a few lineup changes], lots of tours and records, and the A-Bones
back up people like Ronnie Dawson, Roy Loney, Cordell Jackson, and
more. Miriam and I continued with *Kicks* magazine until 1992, and
Norton's still wailing away."

The crazy comps that Norton put together from the mid-'80s on
started to scratch and expose the even deeper, wilder wounds under the
Nuggets scab that covered the '80s retro garage scene.

"Billy hammered out *Hipsville 29 BC* in November 1983," Tim Warren recalls, "three months after *Back from the Grave Vol. 1* came out. Billy always reminds me that *BFTG* started because I kept pestering him to put out records where people could actually *hear* the stuff they were writing about in *Kicks*. That mag's coverage and attitude really was a huge influence on Crypt. Of course, Norton's first official release, Hasil Adkins's *Out to Hunch* album from 1986 is a beast."

The *Back from the Grave*s sliced that era's excavation wide open, and soon new groups like the Gories were pouring alcohol on to let it bleed. . . .

IF THE GORIES were the soul-roots stepgrandchildren of Detroit, Pussy Galore were the Lower East Side's test-tube babies, rising as they did from the very last moment of lower Manhattan as the glorified dung heap at the end of American empire. Pussy Galore fired up screeching detonations of ripped-apart '60s garage riffs, metal garbage-can bashing, cheap amp-bleeding, and curdled cursing—and an image of crassly couture NYC heroine hoppers running a rusty Ginsu through their Rolling Stones fixation. (And if you had paid ten bucks for the Stones' *Dirty Work* right around then, you figured a rusty Ginsu through 'em is just what they needed.)

Pussy Galore palled around the late-'80s NYC post–no wave noise scene of Sonic Youth as CEO; but were themselves the most severe destruction yet of *Nuggets*. The band's soaked-in-crude-oil looks and sonic surge made for one of the loudest, most chaotic live blasts of the era, featuring guitarist Neil Hagerty slicing, syphilitic Keith Richards licks through singer/guitarist Jon Spencer's stuttering barre chords, while third git-kicker Julia Cafritz howled snotty shouts just behind Spencer's bark.

So it was always surprising when the few times I ended up bumping into Spencer over the years, he was always nothing but cordial, even understated to the point of having a guard up. Frequently absorbing half-praise/half-rich-kid-poseur accusations—in addition to all the drug use that was instantly assumed if somewhat unsubstantiated in the Pussy Galore camp—no doubt created such barriers.

Spencer grew up in Hanover, New Hampshire, setting for the tony Dartmouth College. "There was nothing there," Spencer flatly states. "Not even a record store around. Don't think I saw a live show at all. It was not a hip place." So a place like Brown University in Providence,

Rhode Island—where Spencer studied, and from which dropped out, in the mid-'80s—was a step up. While there he saw Black Flag, Gun Club, X, Link Wray, local punk bands, and numerous hardcore shows. "I think that's where I got inspired," says Spencer, "but I got frustrated soon, at shows where people were like, 'Oh you can't smoke or swear. . . .'" He also made frequent trips to NYC to see shows with new pal Julia Cafritz. They started Pussy Galore, and the two took off to Washington, DC, thinking the scene there was hopping. Of course, "hopping" isn't really the word for the politico-punk DC scene of the late '80s.

"The hardcore thing was still going on," Spencer explains. "It was pretty straitlaced. There was room for different kinds of things, but it took us a while before we could even get a show at DC Space, which at the time was *the* room to play or whatever. . . . The DIY thing was set up but still pretty new. There were people like Blag Flag who went out there and really broke the soil. You know, there are all these fucking books written about the Sex Pistols and London; and yeah, there's stuff written about NYC and L.A. But hardcore really was this country's punk in some ways. I'm not the biggest fan, but it was very inspiring and liberating. But by about 1984 or so, I was really down on it because there were a lot of knuckleheads in it, really stagnant. But maybe we weren't friendly enough, maybe I wasn't open enough for it."

Hearing Pussy Galore's early recordings, one can only imagine what they sounded like to the mosh hordes that were splitting off between regimented politics or speed metal, neither of which aspired to the willfully decadent mess Pussy Galore was aiming for. "Yeah," Spencer says, "in my head I wanted to bring together two things I was really into at the time: '60s punk and industrial noise. But what they called 'industrial' in the mid-'80s is very different than what they called industrial in the '90s or now. Bands like Throbbing Gristle, Einstürzende Neubauten, the Swans—very heavy noise stuff." Hence, off to the Lower East Side of NYC in 1986 . . .

"We thought New York would be a better place for the kind of thing we were into." Having flopped into a sublet two blocks from CBGB, the band soon released their second EP and enlisted Bob Bert, who'd played with Sonic Youth, on garbage cans. "We were playing all sorts of shows, started touring around the U.S., and were embraced by the *Village Voice* as a 'hip band,'" says Spencer. "It worked out pretty good. . . . Certainly Kim Gordon and Thurston Moore especially were nice and helpful."

And the atmosphere for the sound of gutter-garage riffs shoved into a junkyard hydraulic press was thick in the East Village. The Honeymoon Killers were already out a-scrunching. "That was Jerry Teel and his girlfriend at the time, Lisa Wells," Spencer explains. "That was their band. I had one of their records in college, and suddenly me and my wife, Cristina [Martinez], were in the band for about two years. Jerry was one of the first people we became friends with when we moved to the city."

Some music critics seemed to only fixate on the fact the Spencer bellowed blue like an AWOL sailor who was charged another twenty

Cleveland, 1989.

dollars post–nut bust; and that—heaven forbid!—they had no bass and three guitars; or, even more teeth-gnashingly silly, that the band "couldn't play" and were being brazenly offensive. It seemed some people were still catching up to punk's most basic principles, even in the late '80s. If anything, Pussy Galore to me sounded like the Electric Eels, who'd been dead since 1975.

"Well, you know, we *were* kind of miserable," Spencer concedes. "Certainly I was, I was quite angry about lots of things. So there was some genuine bad vibes and hate coming from me. But also, I was into nasty punk. Some of it was like Angry Samoans, some of it was '60s bands, the Swamp Rats, or whoever. So for me a lot of that was just the nasty music I really loved, and it inspired me to try to do that." Sometimes literally. The band gained some notoriety for a 1986 cassette-only release where they played scathingly and sloppily over the Rolling Stones classic *Exile on Main St.*, which apparently came off as sacrilege to some as making fun of the Stones—but which has presaged the destructive intentions of nearly every interesting garage punk band that followed.

As their rep for violent stage demeanor spread, Pussy Galore finally got out on tour, those expectations getting to soundcheck before they did. They played with every town's "crazy band." Spencer explains, "But to be a kid from New England in some Midwestern city or down south, whatever, they'd take you to this cool diner, thrift store, the local punk rock record store—it was all before this stuff was codified." Though Pussy Galore's image at the time was a band of intense big-city sewer rats crawling out to gnaw at your feet and steal your drugs and women, it seems Spencer looked at their tours as a chance to keep searching for that mythological "authentic" experience, and he found it in Columbus, Ohio.

"We went to Columbus and played with the Gibson Brothers, which was a real eye-opener," Spencer admits.

THE GIBSON BROTHERS were an amazingly original, Southern-fried-in-Midwest-canned-beer shrillabilly foursome who'd formed in Columbus circa 1984—the yeasty yang-wang to the Gories' yin wingding going on, unbeknownst, not three hours away. Sprung from the punk impulse, but preternaturally and geographically inclined to dig farther back for inspiration, the Gibson Brothers created some of the most de-rigged roots rock ever. No doubt there were some sauced uncles and

The Gibson Brothers visit Olan Mills Studio for a family portrait, 1989. (Photo courtesy of Ellen Hoover)

Charlie Feathers records in the wood-paneled basements of this posse. But where their other cirrhosis-sunk spooks came a-haunting from is anyone's guess. This bunch seemed to decide much earlier than the rest of us that the Cramps were too campy, and oozed a Martian's take on the gospel-stomped American dread that goes back at least to the slave trade. Onstage they stirred up a boozy, cacophonous fisticuffs like two of them were Hatfields, two McCoys, and all hoping that Saint Charlie Feathers would protect them should a real fight break out. Their influence is still being figured.

"Columbus really made an impression on me," says Spencer. "And the Gibson Brothers were such a great band! Jeff [Evans, singer/guitarist] was wearing paper sideburns; he didn't have real sideburns yet. He was being an old-fashioned entertainer or showman. And back then things were either this heavy, really angry thing, or something ironic. So I hadn't really seen anything like that. Don [Howland, singer/guitarist] was an early Pussy Galore supporter. He'd written some pieces about us. . . . I'd heard the Gun Club, the Cramps. And the Gibson Brothers were in that vein, but they were doing it really well. With Jeff and Don, that was the start of a good relationship and an education."

"Purely by coincidence," says Howland, "the Gibson Brothers were sort of at the epicenter of the nascent garage rock scene—right when the band self-detonated at Sun Studios in 1992."

PUSSY GALORE MADE it over to Europe a few times and gained a solid following in England. But soon, with the usual clashing personalities and musical differences, the band started to unravel. "When Neil quit for good [he'd already quit once before in 1987], it wasn't a very good show that night, and we made seventy bucks. He wanted to get out of the band anyway, and that was just an excuse." It's doubtful Hagerty's next band, the slinky sleaze rockers Royal Trux, topped $140 too often in their early days. "Yeah, well, I think he lunged at me in the van that night. At the time we were all still sharing an apartment, so it was weird. . . . That was a point where the band was done, certainly in my mind. Julie and I weren't really getting along anymore. After [the previous album, 1989's] *Dial M for Motherfucker*, the band did a six-week tour around the U.S. in August without her. "And that wasn't very good. Julie was really important to the band. Then Neil moved to San Francisco. . . .

"After a few months, I thought I missed that band. Neil came back, and we recorded *Historia de la Musica Rock*, just me and Bob and Neil," says Spencer. That final album exuded a very Gibson Brothers–bent version of what was to come with Spencer's next, more successful venture, the Jon Spencer Blues Explosion. Hagerty was gone before *Historia* was released in 1990.

"We did a deal with Caroline/Rough Trade. And then when it came time for them to promote that record, they wouldn't return phone calls, and that was the end of it. I was pretty upset. . . . Then when the 'classic' Gibson Brothers lineup fell apart, I volunteered," Spencer says. "It was me and Cristina plugging in a hole. We did some touring, we recorded that record [*Memphis Sol Today!*, Sympathy for the Record Industry, 1993] at Sun Studios in Memphis after Jeff Evans moved there."

"We'd met grocery store clerk Larry Hardy, early into his In the Red label, and Long Gone John on the tour that finished up with the Sun Studios recording," says Howland. "It was Long Gone who Jeff had talked into putting up the hundred dollars per hour for recording at Sun. In terms of rock 'n' roll music, there is no more hallowed ground than Sun. Elvis, Howlin' Wolf, Roy Orbison, Johnny Cash, Jerry Lee

Lewis, Frank Frost, Ike Turner—a panoramic Mt. Rushmore of legends had sat in that little room. The Gibson Brothers were devoted to that music, true, but we *sucked*! It's true, we made music by demented outliers even more demented still. But the knotted squall that issued forth when we plugged in was really just the best we could do."

"We did one whole tour of the States," says Spencer, "went to the West Coast. It was good, but it was a hard tour. Jeff and Don were butting heads."

"It had been a grueling trip," Howland states, "the only full U.S. circuit we ever did. A panel van with 180,000 miles on to start, in midsummer. When we finally made it to Memphis, we were as close to "musicianly" as we'd ever been, but fucking exhausted."

"The Sun session was at the end of that tour," Spencer adds, "so some of that tension kind of spewed out. And they do those tourist tours at the studio during the day, so if you wanted to record, you had to start late in the evening. So we went from 8 P.M. to five in the morning. It was pretty amazing. The equipment is modern, but you're in *that* room. But there was a bunch of fighting during that."

"When we arrived," Howland says, "we were still hungover from a late show at the Antenna Club the night before. We'd supped on some greasy BBQ with beans and slaw on the side, and a number of beers immediately before. I wish I could recount some other insights or ghost stories from the Sun experience, but with the Gibsons, blackout drinking was pretty much a given for important events. In my recollection, we all had our own fifths of whiskey upon entering, except of course for Rich [Lillash, drummer]. Aside from an enormous photo of Jerry Lee Lewis's face—which got more demonic as the hours slurred by—that's about it for memories. I groggily 'awoke' around 4:30 A.M. with Jeff and me facing off in an angry, stumbling fight, while Jon tried frantically to persuade the engineer to turn on the room mic to commit it to posterity.

"It was a great way to end the Gibson Brothers Until I met up with Jeff to mix it all down at Easley's studio, I might not have been sure that happened at all if not for a cassette Jon smuggled out, and some snapshots Jeff took: puffy crimson faces exploding in idiot grins, eyes utterly devoid of that which allowed us to rise up out of the savannah, middle fingers at full mast, sixth-grade style, in every one. But that tape is the shit. It has six takes of 'Knock Down My Blues.' The devolution from take to take is one of the funniest things I've ever heard in my life. And what more can you ask from rock 'n ' roll?"

Bassholes (*left:* Bim Thomas; *right:* Don Howland), Cleveland, OH, 2002. (Photo by Jay Brown)

Howland and Lillash (later replaced by Bim Thomas) soon formed the sickly punk-blues duo the Bassholes; and Jeff Evans would cobble together varying lineups of his roots-chewing crew, '68 Comeback. Both, due to their frequent killer releases, would surpass the Gibson Brothers for influence on the sullied, stripped-down, grave-robbing habits that underground garage rock was picking up as the decade wore on. . . .

THOUGH MATADOR RECORDS reissued most of Pussy Galore's catalog in 1998, those are out of print again, and the band's last album has never been reissued. In recent years, loads of fringe noise combos overtly bite from Pussy Galore, including the Hunches, the Horrors (U.S. *and* UK), Human Eye, the Blowtops, Functional Blackouts, Jay Reatard, and others. Yet Spencer seems in no rush to revisit his gory days. "It's just so long ago," Spencer says. "I can't even relate to that person, or who I was then. Now, it's like listening to somebody else's records. It's not my band. . . . But back when Pussy Galore or Blues Explosion played Seattle, it was a huge deal, all these people coming out of the woodwork. At some point it went from like a high school feel into a business and people making money."

ONE OF THE NUMEROUS subsets of the genre-name-crazy alternative rock era was the skuzzy squeal of the "pig fuck" scene from whence the Action Swingers swung, if just out of back-pat reach of pig fuck-ers Pussy Galore, the Honeymoon Killers, Black Snakes, Surgery, and Chrome Cranks. The unfortunately named subsound was a dark, heavy, urban, burning pileup of Birthday Party/Gun Club/Cramps–culled explosions centered in New York City's Lower East Side. "I don't know if I was down with those bands," says Action Swingers larynx-shredded croaker and guitarist Ned Hayden. "I was kind of friendly with a few people on the scene, the other party animals. Never had much time for all the ones who took themselves so seriously. . . . Jon Spencer pretty much hated my guts because he thought I stole half his band, which couldn't be further from the truth. . . . I like Jon, he just didn't like me. We're both a lot older with kids and stuff now, and realize how stupid all that stuff was back then. He wouldn't let me use his amp at the Pussy Galore practice space after I couldn't put out some Honeymoon Killers record he was trying to get me to put out on a label I was running for Caroline. Then he would glare at me all the time whenever we were in the same place."

Spencer's response: "Ned Hayden? Gimme a break. Any serious questions? I mean, I like some of their records, but there was no feud going on there."

Hayden had been a Bowery scene scrum-starter long before any swine had been violated. The Action Swingers' self-titled full-length de-but (Primo Scree, 1991)—featuring former Pussy Galore gal Julia Cafritz on guitar, bassist Pete Shore (Unsane), and all-around scene skin-slapper Bob Bert (Sonic Youth, Pussy Galore, Bewitched)—relied less on the clattering noise of the members' previous outfits than an aggravated ad-herence to cutting Ramones riffs in half, dragged forward by Hayden's razor-drank hate vibe possessed of an impeccable sense for herniated Hemingway-esque bone-cut verbiage. Sample lyric from "I'm Sick":

> *I'm sick, I'm sick, I'm sick, I'm sick*
> *I'm sick, I'm sick, I'm sick, I'm sick*
> *I'm sick, I'm sick, I'm sick, I'm sick*
> *Yeah!*
> *I'm sick!*

"The Action Swingers started after I met Julie Cafritz and Johan Kugelberg in 1989," says Hayden. "We decided to have a band on a Friday, I wrote "Kicked in the Head," "Bum My Trip," and "Miserable Life" in about fifteen minutes on the following Sunday, and we recorded the first single the next Friday. We basically existed for a week with that lineup." Such bruising brevity comes as no surprise when you hear that first Action Swingers single. "I don't think I was going for anything on the first single. It just came out. . . . We recorded those first two Action Swingers singles at a place called Waterworks on Fourteenth Street. Both singles were recorded in about three hours for a hundred dollars each. All I remember was Johan said he wanted his drums to sound like garbage cans."

"Ned Hayden was like the Tazmanian Devil in the Bugs Bunny cartoons," says Kugelberg, "like this whirling dervish that throws shit around. He was amazing, and that was such a fun session. He kicked me out of the band and replaced me with one of the biggest douche-bags that ever lived, J Mascis [Dinosaur Jr.]. But what an unchampioned genius Ned Hayden is."

The Action Swingers, like the rusted region that birthed them, were of course too inspiringly gritty to last. "The lineup kept changing because people always kept quitting," Hayden explains. "So I would find somebody else and make a sound that fit the new people. . . . Like I met Julie Cafritz when she was on her way out of Pussy Galore. She would come by the CBGB Record Canteen, where I worked. Then she quit Pussy Galore and asked for a job at the store. We became good friends. Then Kim Gordon [Sonic Youth] talked Julie out of being in the Action Swingers after we played with Smashing Pumpkins one night."

The thought of Hayden spewing his bile right before the Smashing Pumpkins laid their pretentions on the stage is hilarious. But finding any band back then to match the Action Swingers' surly sensibilities would've been tough. As Hayden recalls, "I didn't feel any other bands were doing anything similar to me then—maybe the Dwarves later on. In the mid- to late '90s, there were a lot of bands that sounded very similar to me who started sending me their records. They all deny it now, but it's true. . . . That was always the problem with the Action Swingers—we never fit into any scene. The more serious grunge/Sub Pop/AmRep/Touch and Go people all hated us; and the Crypt/Norton garage party purists all hated us. I was always on my own."

Hayden's loner persona has come to cloud the man's solid musical grounding. "I mostly grew up in Larchmont, New York," Hayden explains. "My father was a musician who made some doo-wop records in the late '50s for labels like Klik and Ember. In the '70s he was in a band called Laughing Back, with Michael Bolton and Kenny G. I wish I was kidding. My godfather was Bob Lewis, aka Baba Lou—one of the original WCBS-AM disc jockeys in NYC in the mid-'60s. He discovered the Shangri-Las and was the first American DJ to play the *White Album* on the radio."

Hayden's first job was in the fine tradition of many a punk (Ian MacKaye, Henry Rollins, Jello Biafra, Thurston Moore, yours truly)—he scooped ice cream. "My first job was working at Baskin-Robbins in high school. I used to get high off the nitrous oxide from the whipped cream dispensers in the back of the store. When I got kicked off the freshman baseball team in high school, I went directly into drugs and rock 'n' roll."

Like many of the bands in this book, the Swingers got more play overseas. "The last show on our first tour of England in March 1992," says Hayden, "was headlining the Camden Palace, which was supposed to be some big honor. Before the show, me and Bruce Bennett were next door at a pub having pints with some fans. We got pretty drunk. All of a sudden, two big security guards grabbed me by the arms and dragged me across the entire place and threw me up on the stage. Somebody handed me my guitar, the stage lights went on, and there were like two thousand people there. I can't really remember anything else about the show except we trashed all the equipment at the end and I stage-dived into the crowd. I woke up a short time later on the floor. We played our Peel Session the next morning and then flew back to NYC the next day. I woke up at home after a good night's sleep from three weeks of mayhem and realized I had shards of broken glass in my palms from the floor of the Camden Palace. Then a couple of days later we opened for the Ramones at Columbia University and the entire band quit the next day. The record we'd made in England during that tour, *More Fast Numbers*, ended up as our second straight record in the UK Top 20 Indie charts. Go figure.

"After I stopped doing the band and was working for eight dollars an hour at HMV, *Beverly Hills 90210* used our *Decimation Blvd.* posters on the show for a few episodes. It was when the character David was addicted to crank. But that record ruined my 'career.' Caroline sold six thousand copies and wouldn't repress it. It got a one-line review in the *NME*. We couldn't get a show in America for more than a hundred dollars. . . . But hey, have you ever heard the Toe Rag Action Swingers record? It's my best record! *Trouser Press* reviewed it as 'the sound of shit on speed.' Do you know that *Kerrang!* voted *Quit While You're Ahead* (Caroline, 1994) the most antisocial record of the year? But I didn't even know until ten years later."

It struck me that *Trouser Press*—and the import we once placed in such fleeting blurbs in print mags of that era—was long gone. But not the fire in Hayden, who says he's working on some more music again. "But I'm more into stuff like Neil Young, '70s Jamaican dub, and rare Funkadelic-related stuff. . . . I have a seven-year-old daughter, Juliana. I manage a record store and follow the Mets."

6.

LARGE MEAT SOIRÉE

By 1991, I was in the twenty-fourth gear of my collector existence, racing through LP bins and bruising kneecaps on record store floors. My commitment to finding the elusive stupidest punk record ever was at its height. At that point, I'd cobble my pennies for any 7" with a vaguely twisted band name and a less than five-dollar price tag stuck on the front. I was the kind of guy who took a long time to finally quit buying Sympathy for the Record Industry releases—not so much for their quality as their exhausting quantity.

Sympathy was, arguably, the most important indie label of the 1990s. Sub Pop was hardly independent by 1991; and Matador and Merge both built demi-empires of business and aesthetic focus well worth the envy of all the indie rock label wannabes since. But Sympathy was a massive auditory storage tank for the many strains of where underground rock and its sick siblings were going, circa early '90s. It was a diving board for a few future stars (Hole, Rocket from the Crypt, White Stripes), and many underground punk soothslayers (Supersuckers, Teengenerate, Oblivians, Claw Hammer, Humpers, Bassholes, '68 Comeback, Red Aunts, New Bomb Turks, Muffs, Nomads, and many more); side projects from fringe realms (Spacemen 3, Free Kitten, Junkyard Dogs); established bands with B sides to spare (Billy Childish, Melvins, Bad Religion, Redd Kross); occasional unreleased rarities from almost lost alt-heroes (Gun Club, Black Randy, Wreckless Eric); and at the dark corners of the endless label inventory, loads of really weird noise sludge and stuff that, frankly, no one else wanted. Via an insistence on creative packaging, the label also helped kick-start the careers of many a "lowbrow" artist (Savage Pencil, the Pizz, Coop, Frank

Arrrgh! Long Gone John, 1989. (Photo by Kirk Dominguez)

Kozik), whose work was later dubbed "pop surrealism" by the galleries that deigned to show the stuff once the decade turned. And as far as "do it yourself," you'd be hard-pressed to find one man who spread his taste farther, literally by himself, than main sympathizer Long Gone John.

Starting with the Lazy Cowgirls' *Radio Cowgirl* LP in 1989, Sympathy has released more than 750 singles, records, and CDs, every one of them conceived, executive-produced, packaged, and distribution-figured at the hands and from the living room of Long Gone John. His nasally drawl is one part pooped mogul, one part chemically grogged larynx, and one part Long Beach beach bum bummed the sun is setting. But when the topic of his fave artists comes up, his tone goes a little higher and one can imagine the teen scavenger who bounced like Br'er Rabbit through the flea markets and record stores of late-'80s Los Angeles.

After establishing himself to near statue-proposal stage in the sprawling City of Angels music scene, he actually decided in 2008 to pack up his mounds of ephemera and move to a charming hut in the woods outside of Olympia, Washington, to concentrate further on his new toy company venture, the Necessaries Toy Foundation—just about the time a fine documentary on him was released, *The Treasures of Long Gone John*.

LONG GONE JOHN: I wanted it to be called *Pictures of a Gone World*, and I didn't want my name in the title. But the director did a great job. The premiere was a big deal; all the artists came, and some musicians. For one day, I was the center of attention. I didn't like it.

ERIC DAVIDSON: Many of the label people I've interviewed for this have cited you as a template.

LG: I'll tell you it was a fucking template! The majority of them do what was my manner of business. The bottom line is whether or not you give bands money to record—which in the beginning I didn't have to. You gave them a percentage of the record, helped with equipment if you were able, a van, plane tickets, etc.

ED: For the most part you didn't sign record deals, right?

LG: The only time I ever did was at the insistence of somebody else— let's say the Muffs on Reprise, or Geraldine Fibbers on Geffen, who had started with me and wanted to continue doing little side projects—then I'd have to sign contracts. It certainly never worked to my advantage.

ED: When you started Sympathy, were you planning on having a real label or just put out some friends' stuff?

LG: Yeah, friends' stuff. About 1988. I stumbled through the process with no help, I didn't fucking know anybody. Then people I knew were like, "Do my record." Some friends in Australia got in touch, which led to a lot of Australian stuff. . . . I'd worked myself into a pattern of four singles a month and some albums. At ten years, it worked out to a record a week for every week I'd been in existence. In November, it'll be twenty years. Sub Pop just had their twentieth anniversary last week. I was just a few months behind them, without knowing they even existed. Look at what I did and you can see I had no concept at all—everything from noise to country to garage rock, whatever. But I'd say that I really went out to support and rally female artists, an enormous amount. Much rather look at a girl on a record cover than a guy . . . Keep in mind, I've had one success story in twenty years—White Stripes.

ED: I would say Rocket from the Crypt were a success too. . . .

LG: I love RFTC, but did I make a lot of money? No—better than some, though. . . . I had decent distribution. There was a time when I could sell a thousand copies of just about anything I put out. But you give a band five thousand dollars to record a single, then give them a hundred copies—there's no money there. I did sometimes get money from majors. Dude, I sold ten thousand each of three different Bad Religion singles! Brett [Gurewitz, Bad Religion guitarist, Epitaph label head] never fucking asked me for anything. He thought he was getting something from me, aligning himself with what he thought was a cool little label. That was fine with me. He was an amazing guy. He took Claw Hammer, Red Aunts, the Humpers—three of my bands all went to Epitaph. But think they did any good on Epitaph?

ED: Around that time, early '90s, there were a lot of Sympathetic garage indies popping up: Empty, Estrus, Gearhead, Junk, Rip Off, etc. Did you feel any kinship, or influence on any of those bands and labels?

LG: No, I never paid attention to what other people were doing. I was the first to use opaque colored vinyl early on. The time I put out the Supersuckers single, which was their first record, I had probably fifteen different colors of records. At this time, Sub Pop and AmRep—they were the big visible labels—were doing five hundred records with a hundred in color, and they'd charge more fucking money for the colored ones! Fuck them! All mine are color and they're all the same price.

ED: What about Crypt Records?

LG: I thought the world of Tim [Warren, Crypt honcho]. To me, he was so militant about going out and telling people how much he hated shit. Basically, if it wasn't in his narrow corridor of coolness, it was shit. He's funny, successful, and he's very important.

ED: What was it that drew you to the White Stripes?

LG: I hate to admit it, but I really loved them. Hard to admit that about someone who basically royally screwed me. I traveled with them to Japan, Australia, New Zealand, East Coast tours. There are only two bands in my entire career of Sympathy that I traveled with: Rocket from the Crypt and the White Stripes. But they got involved with a completely unscrupulous manager. He wanted to control everything, take away from me, and start all over again. They went along with it. I didn't have a contract. What are those three albums I put out worth today? Millions of dollars.

ED: Did you see any of it coming?

LG: Yeah, the minute they got that manager. We're standing outside the Troubadour, and this guy corners them, and that's the beginning of the end right there. In New York, we met with [the manager]. Promises, promises, promises. Slowly, each thing they promised was taken away until all that was left was, "We want all the records." I said, "In your motherfucking dreams." I couldn't control the records because they put a stop on my distributor. They walked away because if it went to court, there was a chance that the judge might've leaned my way. I had a moron attorney, who didn't think of anything that I hadn't already thought of first. All I've got to say is I think that Jack White is a miserable fucking person. There's a good reason he moved out of fucking Detroit—people hate him. He's very successful, he's very talented. Meg is completely useless; she just fit the bill. She couldn't do anything unless he told her what to do. I used to see him make her cry almost on a daily basis when we were on tour. He's just a mean fucker. She put up with it, I'll give her that. She was smart enough to stay with it. But she didn't write a fucking drum note. He did everything. . . .

ED: But he included her in the publishing?

LG: Yeah. Don't forget that she was his wife once.

ED: From early on, did you expect them to be some million-selling band?

Various Sympathetic mag ads, early '90s.

LG: I knew they were special. The story was something the press could grab—brother and sister; red and white; stripped down; both attractive and young. Jack was such a fucking ham. Onstage, he was like a little girl who knew when to wink. He captured people. But you and me and everyone involved in this music knows that they weren't really special. There were hundreds of other bands just like them. Not just two-piece bands, I mean—the same exact influences, people doing the same thing. So they weren't unique, the time was just right.

ED: *Well, I think in a weird way, you did at least get some acknowledgment for putting out their records first.*

LG: Maybe. And acknowledgment is something that you rarely get. You'd be surprised how many bands don't even thank you. Speaking of which, Jeff Evans [Gibson Brothers, '68 Comeback] was the one who put them on to me.

ED: *He put a lot of people on to a lot of things.*

LG: That's a guy who deserves a lot of credit and never got it. It's a shame he doesn't get the nod for helping create the Blues Explosion.

ED: *You did some Dwarves records fairly early on. . . .*

LG: I like anything the Dwarves ever did. I have the greatest admiration for Blag. We have the greatest relationship. I know that guy is a brilliant songwriter. Y'know, some bands don't say thank you, but that guy could never say thank you enough. He's a gracious guy, appreciative of what I did, never made a lot of money from me, some money, but you know, he's unique among people I worked with over the years. I could never say enough good things. He's a writer, he's articulate, well spoken, a talented producer. He borders on genius.

ED: *So how did you deal with master tapes over the years with no contracts? Would you say, "I put this out, so it's my master."*

LG: I certainly feel they were mine because, like with Hole [and this track they were trying to use for a Holland compilation], I paid for the recording. A DAT is not worth anything. It was the real reel-to-reel I want; the artifact. It's completely unfashionable to say you like Courtney Love or Hole, but I did. I thought she was a poet, the closest thing to being somebody important like Patti Smith. She got a bad rap, some probably deserved, but she was great. Obviously the real deal, because she's a nutcase. . . . That's one band I can admit to doing bootlegs of. One day I'm in L.A. at some Rock for Choice show, and here comes Courtney. "Hey John, you've been putting out bootlegs of my band. Oh, we don't care, we love you." And then she drags me back to meet Kurt Cobain. That was really early, a month or two into their relationship, before Nirvana blew up. The guy wrote a couple brilliant songs, the timing was right. But I don't rate him like people do. I've seen too many talented people come and go and never have their day in the sun.

ED: Seems weird that a band like the White Stripes would hassle you, when they already had money.

LG: If I was still in the bootleg mode, which I left behind years ago, I could've made a billion dollars on the White Stripes. A lot of the early bootleg stuff funded the label.

ED: You had some kind of work accident too, right?

LG: Yeah. I was working for a warehouse, 1976 or so, right before punk rock. Worked for ten years, hating every day, hating everyone I worked with, always in trouble. They always wanted to fire me until one time I got in an actual fight. Anyway, I was up in the air on a forklift, and I fell. Shattered my kneecap, got a concussion, knocked out teeth. People thought I was dead. Woke up for about three seconds, said, "Oh, my back," woke up in the hospital, and said to my wife, "Where's Maggie?"—my one-year-old daughter. Then woke up days later, on morphine, all fucked up. I did eventually get a settlement from that.

ED: How much?

LG: Nothing, for the time—twenty thousand dollars, because we had workman's comp. I put down the money on a house. A year in therapy, went back to work. They said they didn't want me there and didn't like me. About a year later, I pushed someone. You know what a forklift looks like—the heavy thing above the driver? I grabbed the bar, swung back, and kicked this fucker out of it, then swung back, and rammed him. Well, that was it for me. I got fired. Kind of the same situation with the White Stripes—the company was afraid I might win. They took it all the way up to the morning of court, and then settled. Made me an offer, ended up getting what I wanted, walked away with a bunch of money. . . . That was the money I started Sympathy with.

NINE POUND HAMMER, like the Gories, were first released on the tiny Indiana imprint Wanghead with Lips (*The Mud, the Blood, and the Beers*, 1989). Where numerous grunge acts in that era were *acting* the hilljack, this stompin' squad from the outskirts of Louisville, Kentucky, were a documentary. In their own shit-kicker way, Nine Pound Hammer updated the bottom-of-the-moonshine-barrel otherness, and without resorting to campy country dress-up—impossible, given their preference for the ragged realism that runs the through-line from Johnny Cash to Black Flag. No doubt, they upped the Tex Avery eyeballs of it all, which felt fresh with the encroachment of grumpy grunge and humbled indie rock. "Bands really started to take themselves way too seriously," says lumbering lead Hammer Scott Luallen. "Like it was blasphemous to crack a smile onstage."

"We had our first practice in 1985 in Owensboro, Kentucky, our hometown, population 55,000," Luallen continues. "We had our first show in Evansville, Indiana—all covers, Ramones, Clash, Eddie Cochran, Johnny Cash. . . . Then we moved to Lexington in '87 and became house band at Great Scotts Depot, a dive sandwiched between two really nasty strip clubs. So you had an interesting mix of punky kids and students running into working-class rednecks. One night, [while we were] sitting in my '75 convertible, drinkin' Boone's Farm, this stripper walks by us and proceeds to give us a 'special show,' sticking matches in her nips and swingin' them around on fire! We were speechless! Many a brawl there, lots of gunplay."

While irony was beginning its ascent to pop-culture dominance, out and out yuks were receding in America's heart of hearts, which helped to explain the reception Nine Pound Hammer got in Europe. They were tailor-made for many Euros who actually think any American raised south of Michigan runs around with a jug marked "XXX" in one hand and a BBQ-chubbied Daisy Duke in the other, shotgun sticking out the ass-crack of our dungarees. Nine Pound Hammer knew it, worked it, and ate up the praise.

"It's America's best export," Luallen says. "Sorry, but we did invent rock, punk, rockabilly, and the blues. There is a reverence for American music. People worship the originators. The fact that most clubs [and those youth centers] are subsidized by the government doesn't hurt either. We played Odense, Denmark, on a Monday night to six guys in Motörhead shirts and got paid 1,500 euro! That obviously doesn't happen here, where if you ain't somebody, you're lucky to get drink tickets! Did I mention deli trays, hotels, and all the beer you can drink? So obviously socialism is vastly superior!"

Dig, Luallen's socialism line is, characteristically, tongue-in-cheek, sort of. For decades, there were enviable squatting laws throughout Europe. These laws allowed youth groups—be they anarchist collectives, students, rehabbing junkies, or whoever—to move into long-abandoned spaces like old factories, warehouses, empty storefronts, etc. But

Nine Pound Hammer, 1994. (Photo courtesy of Ruyter Suys)

the kids had to prove that they were doing something productive in said space: repairing plumbing and electricity, putting on performances, offering after-school activities, etc. Then, after a period of time, if these fix-ups stayed consistent, and if the group proved adept at successfully doing whatever it is they were trying to do, they would—get this—*be given ownership of the building*!

Can you imagine this even being *suggested* in America? The laughs from city councils would drown out the obvious fact that this is a very good idea. If an old midcentury tenement has been sitting there rotting for decades, what's wrong with some kids getting in there and putting on punk shows and soup kitchens? Isn't that the kind of initiative we want to engender in our youth?

Of course today, the new world order of "free markets" has increasingly promoted the much more positive step of having Walmart, CVS, or criminal condo speculators snatch up these old spaces. Over the last few New Bomb Turks Euro tours, we were told a number of sad tales about these youth centers being shuttered, the groups being tossed out for all-important cell phone stores and real estate offices. That's cool, those kids can always join those fun al-Qaeda or neo-Nazi gangs that are multiplying in European slums. And since needle programs and socialized health care are also being gutted in Europe, there's bound to be solid work in the drug trade soon enough.

Now, with all that lefty spiel expunged, quick—name your favorite band from Odense. Or Cologne. Or Utrecht. As far as rock 'n' roll, it seems that America's underhanded existence of illegal drugs, unsupervised roaming of the streets, and shitty touring conditions have created some kind of hardened soul in our musicians that has resulted in the most important music of the twentieth century, from blues, jazz, and rock 'n' roll right through to hip-hop and techno—all much loved and emulated across the globe.

"I never really detected outright ridicule from anybody," Luallen says. "I think being from the South increased interest in the band. People saw us as ambassadors in some respects."

Nine Pound Hammer soon found a welcome home at Crypt Records. "It was the home of the misfit toys," says Luallen. "I think about the killer tours and bills with y'all and the Devil Dogs and Raunch Hands and just thank my lucky stars. As far as our town went, at the very beginning there was some resistance, but otherwise we were embraced. I think it was our country element, and when we went to Europe we were gods! Funny how that changed things."

THAT CHANGE MAINLY came about because of Crypt Records and its suavely incensed (hung)overlord, Tim Warren. He started Crypt in 1983, doling out some early original acts, like the Gravediggers and the Wylde Mammoths. Both great bands who disappeared fairly quickly, and whose recs Warren never got around to repressing, probably because of the enormous impact of his wild '60s garage compilations, *Back from the Grave*, that started slithering out of the Crypt crypt in late '83. "When I started planning the first *Back from the Grave* comp," says Warren, "there were all these '60s comps like, 'Hey, groovy! Remember those groovy years!' All these psychedelic covers and folky tracks that shouldn't be on a garage comp. So I just thought, Let's make a real hateful, inept '60s comp."

The *Back from the Grave*s became the *Pulp Fiction* of Crypt—sure, the label had great original bands before and since, but the *Back from the Grave* comps are the thing everyone comes back to. Following in the sauced steps of the 1971 big daddy '60s garage rarities comp, *Nuggets*—and even after so many *Nuggets* copycats like the *Pebbles*, *Boulders*, and

Highs in the Mid-Sixties series—the *Back from the Grave* comps bested them all for digging up the sheer bored, horny madness that hid inside the white slacks, paisley button-downs, and gawkish homemade bowl cuts of suburban American Stones, Sonics, and Starkweather wannabes.

Each volume got progressively crazier, louder, and more surprising. I remember when Tim first came to Columbus to visit us in 1993, a full decade after the first *Grave*. I was already impressed with his story that the only other time he'd been to Columbus was on a cross-country research trip to scour local libraries for old phone books to track down band info for upcoming *Grave* tracks.

Not only did the *Grave* comps staunchly stick to the nastiest, blasting-est, crewd 'n' lewd loser teen rants, but Tim used only the best possible sources he could scrounge up, meticulously mastered them to be the loudest they could be, and included copious liner notes and pictures. The often shoddy *Pebbles* et al comps pissed Tim off to no end. The *Graves* went way beyond another fanboy hobby trip. They gave you a strange belief that there was an infinite pool of such sounds out there, well past the usual nerd obsessive collector realm, and into a never-ending fourth dimension of possibilities that dashed past the usual boundaries of Beatles vs. Stones, Kinks vs. Sonics, Velvets vs. Stooges, past vs. present. . . .

Tim himself seemed like a band guy, and the *Graves* were his albums. He wore prescription sunglasses 24-7, seemed perpetually, uh, caffein-ated, dropped James Ellroy, Johnny Burnette, and Jim Beam into half a sentence, and was absolutely nothing like the few geeks I knew who ac-tually bought all the *Boulders*. Those guys were home poring over their "want lists," while we were out egging frat houses in Columbus. . . .

Not saying Tim didn't pore over want lists, he just did it at 6 A.M. Sleep was an option for Tim. When visiting Hamburg, we'd be out drinking till all hours, then stay up yanking violent B cheapies out of his amazing VHS collection. A few times we also aided Tim in one of his favorite pastimes. He would gently place eggs on the windowsill the morning before. Then we'd take said rotten eggs, poke a small hole in them, gingerly slide in a firecracker, turn off the lights, light the fuse, and time the egg-bomb drop so it exploded right in the faces of the johns four floors down—as Tim lived in the Reeperbahn, the red-light district of Hamburg, of course. "We're egging them on!" became a standard New Bomb Turks rallying cry.

Then there were the times where Tim would have too much, even for him. While we were hanging backstage at a show in Koln, there was a perfectly agreeable middle-aged German biker couple with leather vests and pants, beards, the whole package. But after a couple bottles of Four Roses, Tim pegged these two as representatives of all the hippies who had "fuckin' screwed up everything with your fuckin' psychedelic bullshit *Sgt. Pepper* LSD, motherfuckers! I'll fuckin' cut 'em with this bottle. . . ." Okay Tim, take it easy. After a while, even those patient krauts could take it no more and stood up bearing down on us. Tim took off. Later, we're packing up our gear, and there's Tim, wedged in and passed out up in the wobbly compartment above the backseat where we shoved our personal bags.

"Tim, c'mon man, get up, we gotta get our shit out of here."

"Ah, fuckin' hippies, fuck 'em daddy, what the . . . goddamn fuckin' Grateful De . . . I'll be grateful when they're dead . . . fuckin' . . . uhhhg . . ."

So we go back in for a nightcap, Micha gets Tim out of the van; then, later, when we come back out, there's Tim in the driver's seat, sunglasses on: "Come on, lads, I'm drivin'! Where're we going? Let's hit the goddamn au-to-bahn, daddy!!!!!"

"Uh, *no*, Tim! You're not fuckin' driving!"

But he probably could have. Tim works on a whole other clock. That was like four in the morning, and by the time we got to whatever gawdawful squat we were crashing at, Tim had apparently had enough sleep, and I could smell the coffee brewing as we dozed off, Tim no doubt on the horn, tracking down some acetate or hooting over some Lee Marvin flick on the tube. . . .

IT WASN'T ALWAYS three cheers for Crypt Records from Andy "the Fabulous Andy G" Gortler, leader of the Devil Dogs. When I moved to Brooklyn in late 2004, he was still out and about with his band of the last decade, the horn-hopped party starters, the Roller Kings. But around late 2007, he just seemed to have vanished. Nearly a year after the last e-mail I'd received from him—and on the *same exact day* that I'd set up a phone chat with Devil Dogs bassist Steve Baise (the two haven't talked in years)—I got an apologetic response from Andy, twenty scrolls long. Essentially, he needed to drop out for a while, as he felt a lot of old friends had dropped out on him. Despite his respite from the rock life, when we finally plopped down in a Brooklyn pizza joint to chat, he went right back into the mode, railing about the recent demise of the Roller Kings.

"Sax players are the biggest fucking pain in the ass in the world!"

Gortler announced. "I mean, it's not like I know cello players, so I can't compare it. But these guys are a mega pain in the ass. My theory about sax players is this: The reason you wanna play sax, it's not because you wanna be like the Fabulous Buddy Bowser on the second New York Dolls album. It's because you wanna be John Coltrane. But John Coltrane is a jazz guy. And you don't learn jazz like, 'Hey, lemme put this record on and see if I can copy it,' like you would with a Ramones record. No, you go to school and you study. So when you get out of school, you want to work on Broadway or at a jingle studio, you wanna get fucking paid, right? The same way a guy who studies medicine wants to be a doctor. You don't want to just help your friends with a headache, you wanna get a practice going and make the big bucks, right? So sax players have this thing in their head, 'I'm gonna be John Coltrane,' even though that would be impossible, for the guys I played with anyway. They wanna do something significant, or they wanna get paid. Neither one of those things are gonna happen in rock 'n' roll."

The Devil Dogs began their scooch-pooch in 1989, the end days of the ol' Bowery landscape, featuring CBGB, boarded-up tenements, and gutter junkies that have since become an American fairy tale. It was anything but, of course, for this trashy trio. They barked out a bawdy bash of Ramones rush and Johnny Thunders & the Heart-breakers stumble-slash, an amphetamine-amped uptick on the kind of shit that's been tagged as the mythologized Bowery's soundtrack. But like many of the players in this drama, their timing was terrible, except in Europe, where their perfectly pugnacious sound was embraced. In America, what consensus existed seemed to be that the Devil Dogs were "just" another Ramones-loving bunch. And they were, only there weren't many of those by the end of the '80s (aside from ultrafast hard-core bands whose sense of Ramonesy jocularity was long dispatched), or at least any that did it as freshly as the Devil Dogs did.

Since their demise, the Devil Dogs have become the Smiths of the trash punk world: The two main canines still don't talk; conjecture spreads of the members' whereabouts; rumors of rejected hefty cash reunion offers abound. Meanwhile, the wonder of how exciting they actually were welts within the band's incrementally intrigued and grow-ing fan base.

We've got the records of course, all super slabs of shake, though there's no replacing catching them in action. I saw the Devil Dogs at least twenty-five times—including a twenty-three-date Euro tour New

Bomb Turks shared with them in October 1993—and I can relay the fact that, yes indeed, the Devil Dogs were as great a rock 'n' roll band as has ever lifted its leg to let loose on any stage, anywhere, ever.

Bassist Steve Baise has spent his post-Dogs days intermittently playing in bands and developing a rep as a solid punk producer and/or tour manager between truck-driving gigs. He recently moved to L.A. from Richmond, Virginia, where he had lived, married with two kids, for the last few years. "I haven't talked to Andy in like eight years," Baise begins. "And you know, it really bums me out."

Baise grew up in Englishtown, New Jersey, but was soon making teen treks into the Big Apple with his buddy, Joe Vincent. "We would drive into Manhattan to go see the Heartbreakers at Max's, or go to CBGB or any punk place. I was like sixteen; but it really didn't matter, because when you dress all crazy or whatever, you could be fifteen or twenty-one. . . . Then, right after high school, we started a band, PT 109." But things ground down, and Baise moved to Brooklyn in 1987. Diving right into the NYC punk scene from the get-go, he soon met Gortler.

After skulking around the edges of the early '80s hardcore scene, Gortler had figured out that wasn't his bag. And in fact at eighteen, he found himself trying out for local retro-garage vets the Fuzztones. "Whatever people say about the Fuzztones and [leader] Rudi Protrudi, he was very nice to me. I was nervous, and I walk in the audition, and there's Marc Bell filling in on drums—fucking Marky Ramone! So Rudi asks, 'Well, you got a cover you wanna try?' And I said, 'How about 'Loose' by the Stooges?' The Fuzztones covered that, right? So we start it, and right where the drums are supposed to kick in, everything just stops. Now I really didn't wanna do this, I mean it's fucking Marky Ramone. But I said to him, 'Uh, you come in there, right?' And he goes, 'Eh, I don't really know this song. I never really liked the Stooges much.'"

Gortler didn't get the Fuzztones gig, but through Protrudi he met guitarist Pete Ciccone, and the two started working up obscure garage covers. "Andy was in this band the Thugs, with Pete Ciccone and Joey Psycho," says Baise. "I met them at the Strip, which was like the '60s garage rock scene club." So Baise palled around with the paisley types for a while but didn't dig the music that much, and he wasn't gravitating toward the city's hardcore cabal either. "No, I didn't really know anything about 'NYC HC.' New York City for me was the Ramones and the New York Dolls."

"But don't think the hardcore guys didn't know about Johnny Thunders," says Gortler. "Around that time, everything was about Johnny Thunders. Everyone at shows would be like, 'Hey, did you hear Johnny's gonna be here tonight?' 'Johnny's in town, Johnny's gonna be here.' Of course he was in Sweden most of the time back then, because of their easy drug laws." Which made it that much more shocking when, while tuning his guitar in a dank basement backstage before a show in 1987, Gortler looked up to see Johnny Thunders stumble in, searching for what he was always searching for. Gortler only had guitar picks on him. A quick couple of mumbles, and Thunders was gone.

So soon enough, the Thugs begat the Rat Bastards, with Baise joining the lineup in 1988. "We practiced like three days a week, five hours every night," Baise recalls. After grabbing scene stumbler Tim Warren's ear, the Rat Bastards would soon be recording with Billy Childish. "It was good recording with him," says Baise, "pretty raw, but that didn't bother me. He wrote three songs with us—'Pussywhipped,' 'Hosebag,' and 'Suck the Dog.' It was fun, but the whole time, Pete didn't like the new songs, didn't like all that nasty 'Fuck you, suck my dick,' and all that shit."

Ciccone thought that the record "wouldn't be sold in the Bible Belt," which is ludicrous to the point of hilarity, considering the name Rat Bastards—and a production gnaw that might make a nun crap her habit—would obviously preclude the record from ever getting spins at Liberty University's radio station. "It was funny," Gortler remembers, "because Pete was the one who loved all the '80s British garage stuff—the Cannibals, Stingrays, the Milkshakes [a Billy Childish band]. So when Tim said Billy was going to produce, Pete was freaking out."

That session—supposedly the same tunes and roughly the same sound that would eventually end up as the Mike Mariconda–produced, self-titled Devil Dogs 1989 debut album on Crypt—has become legendary amongst trash rockers, as no one seems to have a copy or even to have heard it.

"It really is just hard to listen to," says Tim Warren. "It was just really shrill. And it's weird, because I usually love Billy's production, and the stuff from the Gravediggers and Double Naught Spies [two other budding Crypt acts Childish produced at Coyote Studio that same week] came out sounding fine. Then the stuff with Pete was happening. . . . Mariconda tried to salvage it, and sent me a cassette, but we

NYC, 1988. (Courtesy of Cliff Mott)

just gave up. So that's when I said, Hey, why don't you just go back in and rerecord and produce it? And that's when Mariconda became the Crypt house producer for a while."

"The Rat Bastards tapes were great!" says Mariconda. "But Pete had this thing about wanting to sound like a power pop band or the Real Kids. Billy Childish had left, so Tim decided to put them up in the studio with me to rerecord the stuff. They broke up while I was recording them."

"Tim Warren said to me," says Baise, 'Look, you can go play with Pete, or you can go play with Andy. I say you go play with Andy.' I said

Okay, I'll listen to the record guy. Not that I really had any desire to go with Pete. So that's when I went with Andy." Ciccone did release some solid power pop with his next band, the Vacant Lot.

Mariconda joined the Devil Dogs, adding his seasoned roots racket on guitar. "He would go on tour in Europe with us," Baise explains, "but when we played in the States it was always as a three-piece."

Drummers floated around this milieu like pepper in a Bloody Mary. "Steve Crowley, from the Raunch Hands, was our drummer around then," says Gortler. "We were borrowing him. . . . He must've played like one gig in the States with us—every other time was in Europe. That's like saying, I'm going to dinner with you, but all I'm having is ice cream. He played with us when it suited him." Dave Turetsky then came on board. "He was in the band about 1990–'92," Gortler clarifies. "He was older than me, been playing for a long time. He was in the Headless Horsemen, a short time with Syl Sylvain. We kinda snatched him from that."

And then there was Andy G. His supreme six-string slinging somehow combined the booziest Johnny Thunders low-slung slop with his hardcore scene–sprung severity and classic '50s hooks. He always made sure to hit the stage decked out in a weathered leather, then later a cool vintage suit, or at the least with a pompadour that put all retroid greasers to rest, since Gortler did a lot more than just Elvis calf-swings on stage. He was more than willing to fling himself into the crowd, and always came out as slick as he went in. And of course, that voice— Handsome Dick Manitoba's Big Adam's Apple, Chris Bailey's kid-Iggy soul-sneer, and Gortler's own bagel-abilly Hebrewisms—all used in the service of driving the Dogs' loft bash dogmatics home and/or defaming those in the crowd who didn't yet get that punk rock was about to become really fun and funny again.

Gortler's alley-Catskills between-song banter often extended into back-and-forths with Baise that were an Abbott and Costello routine sucked up through a Lee Ving–head bong, only slightly clouding genuine visceral anger at their core. "On the first European tour with Mariconda," recalls Baise, "he had this cassette tape of Paul Stanley raps. The Kiss soundman had compiled a forty-show soundboard recording of all the stupid raps in between the songs. We listened to that and realized that, man, we can say whatever we want, they don't understand what we're saying anyway."

"But it was never me being nice and funny, then being *made* to say fuck you to some heckler," Gortler says. "It was me heckling them first.

And then people liked it, so why should I stop doing it! It was like a comedy act—the rude comic. It wasn't much deeper than that. I never insulted somebody's girlfriend, just 'Fuck you'—y'know, the classics. The show is supposed to be fun. If people get mad . . . Well, see, you're up there on the stage. If they're looking down their nose at you, that has elevated them up higher than the stage, because you're already up there. That's why people do it. These insecurity things are subconscious. People don't think they're doing anything for a reason, but they are. They don't even realize they have that reason. You wanna be the perfect person, but you're not. No one is, y'know."

"Plus, if you can back it up with the music, the crowd is not really going to cause any trouble," says Baise. "You kick ass for two minutes, then you wanna take a minute break and say some stupid shit—you've earned that right."

By the time the mini-album *Big Beef Bonanza* came bounding out in 1989, the band had really spit-shined their Bondo-caked hot rod. The record smokes from start to end, via Mariconda's sizzling production, un-ironic bawdy bravado, and sliding out of Cliff Mott's iconic sleeve with a cartoon of a devil doll and her devil dog driving a hot rod, on top of a pic of a sizzling slab of beef. Back cover: the lads hanging at Coney Island. Perfect.

"After that record came out, we couldn't record enough stuff for everybody who wanted to put out our records," Baise recalls. "I went to see the Lazy Cowgirls in New York. I sat outside and I picked Pat Todd's brain for like three hours in the rain, and he told me, 'Stick with Crypt. Fuck everybody else. Stay with this guy, he's doing you right.' And he was right."

"The first time we went to Japan," says Baise, "was during the Gulf War in '91, so we got these round-trip tickets for four hundred bucks. We flew NY to Detroit, Detroit to Anchorage, Anchorage to Seoul, Korea, and then from Seoul to Tokyo—like twenty-two hours—for two shows. But it was amazing! When we got to the airport there were about fifteen kids waiting for us—it was like we were the Bay City Rollers! Japan was always great for us, better than Europe even."

As the Euro tours commenced, Baise noticed that "we were playing with all the fucking Beatle-boot-and-haircut bands, like 75 percent garage rockers, because we were on *the* garage label. But as each tour went on, there were less and less of those people. We had more of the punk types at the end. So Crypt needed a band like New Bomb

Early Devil Dogs flyers: The Pyramid show with the Raunch Hands was the first Devil Dogs gig, 1989. (Courtesy of Cliff Mott and Andy Gortler)

Turks—younger, harder, faster. That was good for Crypt, and good for the other bands too, to get them off their ass. If you weren't kicking ass, that's when you were on the Crypt shit list."

Just as things were revving up, the Devil Dogs had to find a new drummer. "All of a sudden, Dave Turetsky said to us, 'Hey I'm going to go back to law school, I'm not doing this anymore. He is a fuckin' big lawyer now." "The way I remember it," says Gortler, "Dave was as much a drummer in the band as Joe [Vincent]; he just didn't record as much with us."

Baise's old high school buddy, Joe Vincent, henceforth known as "Mighty Joe Vincent," became the beater for the busiest era of the band. Goofy grin, big wavy hair piled high, vest over wife-beater tee, and holding the sticks jazz style, Vincent elevated the Dogs above whatever prejudice one might've harbored about "just three-chord punk." His slightly busier style helped fill out the band's sound, especially since, after recording their third album, *We Three Kings*, Mike Mariconda moved to Spain.

To complicate things further, Tim Warren had recently moved to Hamburg, Germany, and left the planning of *We Three Kings* to the band. "And I said, Tim, I don't fucking know anything about that! So we did everything—and the mastering was awful. Tim thought it was too slick, he hated the cover art, he hated *everything* about that record." Nevertheless, somebody was digging on the Dogs, as they were suddenly a hot commodity in the garage label nexus and had to come up with more tunes for promised singles.

"*We Three Kings* was mastered in this apartment in midtown, with this guy Don, who'd done some Kinks mastering in the '60s," Gortler recalls. "It was a long story, a new Dolby thing, and it wasn't really our fault—we just wanted it to sound good. It's got 'Rock City, USA.'— that's one of my favorite songs." Gortler had been digging on more '70s glam faves, even covering the Sweet's "Hellraiser" for a B side. "Yeah, Tim hated that shit," says Gortler. "I don't know, to a certain extent, what Tim really liked was not the Devil Dogs, it was the Rat Bastards, doing garage covers and stuff. Because when the Devil Dogs kind of became their own thing, it was not solely based on '60s garage music."

Live-wise, the Devil Dogs were as good as ever, as New Bomb Turks found out when we went on the road with them in Europe in 1993, about five months after we had our first Euro jaunt, and with our debut gaining steam through the growing Euro garage punk scene. "That tour was great," says Baise, "but it was weird too, because after three weeks on our own, all of a sudden that van was full."

"Well, that was kind of a bumout," Gortler admits. "Theoretically, two bands in the van at once is a good idea because it's a money saver. But it was our third tour, and we were hoping to keep movin' up. Then we start going around, and people translating zine reviews saying, 'Nine Pound Hammer—way better than the Devil Dogs!' All of a sudden we became this thing to dump on. Promoters telling you guys to headline. So it was a letdown. Plus the three of us weren't getting along well. Steve would be cranky, and I'd ask what's wrong, and he wouldn't answer me. What were we gonna do, bring it up on the tour? None of this was your fault."

Nevertheless, Gortler was always a total character. Some of my favorite memories from that trip are watching him stand up in the van and hold court like a demi–Don Rickles, juggling insults about some douchebag in the previous night's crowd with a sudden eight-year-old's excitement when a Tom Jones song came from the mixtape currently being eaten in the van's crap stereo. Even at the low moments, Gortler would drum up guffaws.

"We were in Antwerp, Belgium," Gortler remembers. "and we get to that hostel—eight guys in one room with no heat, wooden bunk beds, standing around with our coats on, and you can see your fuckin' breath in front of your face as you pass around one bottle of wine, talking gibberish, trying to kill time. And let's face it, where do you see beds like those? In jail. That's where they have those, in jail."

Tim Warren had recently repackaged *Big Beef Bonanza* as a compilation, adding the songs he liked from *We Three Kings*, and called it *Bigger Beef Bonanza*; then later still adding more cuts as *30 Sizzling Slabs*. "Yeah," Gortler laments, "anything to erase the existence of *We Three Kings*." So we were all yakking about that, when Gortler went off: "Fuck, how about another one—Fifty Hot Hamburgers! Sizable Sandwich Gala! *Large Meat Soiree!*"

"But overall, of course we had a lot of fun on that tour, and that's what it's all about!" says Gortler. "But I remember having these conversations with my dad when I was a kid, when I'd see some fucked-up musician guy on the street. My dad would say, 'Well he's a musician, and he's probably on drugs.' But why is he on drugs, just because he's a musician? 'Well, son, there's a lot of waiting around, hard times, and not a lot of money.' But I still had these romantic notions. That night

The Devil Dogs protecting Andy's '77 Oldsmobile Cutlass from douchebags, Jersey City, NJ, 1992. (Photo courtesy of Andy Gortler)

in Antwerp in particular though, it's times like that you really wish you *were* Miles Davis with a heroin problem, just to finish it off right."

We all thought the Devil Dogs were the kings of Crypt, the ones who picked up the Raunch Hands ball and bounced the Crypt manifesto around Europe, so that by the time the rest of us made it over there, the wheels were greased. And that grease had spread all the way to California into the San Francisco, post-Mummies trash-rock rabble rousing, which included a Devil Dogs show with the Trashwomen. "The woman who booked us at the Chameleon," says Gortler, "she didn't like us at all. She thought we were like lady haters, one of those. She booked the Trashwomen on the gig, though I don't think she really knew who they were. She just figured she was going to stick it to us because they were a *grrrl* band. But not only did they love the Devil Dogs, they basically performed in their underwear. So that kind of backfired on her."

Being such shit-starters means you will pack 'em in should you travel to Spain, where the Devil Dogs became personal favorites of infamous Basque punk promoter Kike Turmix (pronounced KEE-kay, short for Enrique; Turmix was taken from a popular blender in Spain). "We had *Big Beef Bonanza* out in Spain, and everybody had that record, everybody went to our shows," Baise says. "We were playing at discos with revolving stages and shit like that. . . . We played in Vigo in 1992, and I guess that night there was a robbery at a pharmacy, and somebody got pistol-whipped. Our friend George Sulley [Raunch Hands bassist] and Mariconda had gotten up early the next morning to go get codeine. These small-town cops saw them and thought they were the crooks who robbed the pharmacy because they had leather jackets on. Then the cops came to the hotel and hauled away Mariconda and George and put them in jail! So we get down to the jail, and Mariconda's got his Spanish dictionary out. Meanwhile, the cops are asking me, Andy, and Turetsky to sign autographs for their kids!"

Royal Shit Party. That was a proposed name for the Devil Dogs fourth and, as it turned out, final full-length. Instead, they chose *Saturday Night Fever*. That wasn't the only big decision involved in that album.

"When we were talking about the next record," Baise explains, "and Mariconda was the one who suggested trying another producer. And that's when that Supersnazz record came out on Sub Pop, and it sounded great. That's how we got hooked up with Kurt Bloch." Bloch was the guitarist in the swell Seattle mainstays the Fastbacks, who—through the end of the hair metal days (Guns N' Roses bassist Duff McKagan was in the Fastbacks at one point) and into the grunge era—kept crafty pop rock chewing through that town.

"When we did the *Saturday Night Fever* sessions," Baise says, "we were in Seattle for five days, in the studio every day, recorded twenty songs, and played four shows. We were ready. We already had like 70 percent of those songs written, and we toured like two weeks out to Seattle playing those songs. We worked in the studio from ten to six, go eat dinner, then go play a show, then be back at someone's house at like 3 A.M., and then back at the studio at 10 A.M. We were fucking busting our ass the whole time."

The sound was the loudest and the pace the most electric of any Devil Dogs album yet; and the theme of it all going down at a house party, with guys and dolls whooping it up between the tunes, fit like relish on a Nathan's foot-long. "It was our best record," says Baise. "Mariconda was right."

"But see, that's another thing," Gortler adds. "They talk about these famous studios—the Hit Factory, the Power Station, Olympic Studios in London. The places that I work in are like in some guy's house, in the basement, next to the recycling bin. That's what Egg Studios is, Conrad Uno's basement. But Kurt really did know his shit. It sounds great!" Tim Warren was raving about the record to anyone in earshot; Sympathy did a U.S. CD version with extra tracks. Pop-punk on the radio was fueling hopes. *The Fever* was rising.

Need I explain the rest? Trends pass fast; the Dogs were still too raw for radio; the band's American tour was fraught with the usual maladies; the Matador distribution deal got messy; the band was dissolving; and, oh well, whatever, nevermind. . . .

"I actually thought at the time, Hey, Nirvana, Green Day, that's good for us—like thumbs up!" Gortler says. "People are gonna start listening to this stuff. The mind-set made it real, but was I willing to sell everything I own to make it happen? No. Still, I didn't see any reason why we couldn't be on the radio if 'Smells like Teen Spirit' was on the radio. Why not this? Can't rock 'n' roll be on the radio too? When I was growing up, you'd hear the Ramones, Joan Jett, and stuff like that on the radio. How could it be that way back then, but not now? There's no room for *this* too? Now, I never felt like no one knows who the fuck we are. People showed up at our gigs, and the ones that liked us were frothing at the mouth. They loved this shit! So how come other people don't at least *like* it?"

WHILE A NEW RUSH of speed merchants were hitting the ignition in the early '90s, there were some older vets who'd already been revving their garbage trucks outside of any contained movement. The Cheater Slicks were, and are to this day, *the* idling Buick for all that is the noisiest, cranky trash rock.

Singer/guitarist Tom Shannon moved to Boston from Connecticut in 1985, and convinced his brother Dave (guitarist/singer) to come along from NYC in '86. Via an old college buddy of Tom's, the band hooked up with drummer Dana Hatch, a man who embodies the caveman garage rock drummer conceit, often stripped down to his skivvies midset, shocked stare, arms jabbing at imaginary invaders.

Cheater Slicks, 1995. (Photo by Galen Palmer)

Not only was the Slicks' maddening mash of Velvet Underground riff debasing, Neanderthal physicality, and crushed temperament quite rottenly fresh then, so too was their bassless lineup. "The decision to go without a bass was more out of necessity than any planned thing," says Shannon. "When we had bass players, sometimes the sound came out too 'grungy' for our tastes. We covered the low end with our guitar tones and Dana has a heavy beat, so it was never really a problem."

Covering any end would seem inevitable, as the Cheater Slicks were severely loud. And within that ear-immolating burn, their über-distorted guitar gnash flails like Ghidra the Three-Headed Monster spitting sonic sparks all over the barroom, while lesser souls scurry off like tots on a Toho set. It's all pretty confounding, sometimes catchy, and intermittently transcendent in ways that such gutter pounding usually isn't. Or they sound like crap and Tom bitches after the show. But really, what soundboard is supposed to mix *that*?!

Despite Boston's status as a legendary music town, its vibe at that point was not predicated on the occiput pummeling of the Slicks' kind. "Bands were getting signed practically every week," Shannon recalls. "Some became huge, like the Pixies, Throwing Muses, and Galaxy 500. I was friends with Stephin Merritt [of Magnetic Fields] when I first moved there. But no one was like us, and that made it difficult. . . . When we first started, we were aware of Pussy Galore, who didn't have a bass; the Gibson Brothers were doing a sort of similar thing; I had not heard of the Gories until a couple years later. But overall, it was a low point for raunchy, distorted rock 'n' roll. We were openly disliked in Boston. But the Boston radio stations supported us, which I will always be grateful for."

But way out L.A. way, Larry Hardy, who had only started his In the Red label around 1991, picked up on the Cheater Slicks right away, and would eventually release most of their albums. Another ardent supporter was burgeoning alt superstar Jon Spencer. "We opened for Boss Hog and he really liked us," says Shannon. "Then Jon started getting us on early Blues Explosion shows in New York. That really pissed off people in Boston who couldn't understand how a terrible band like ours could get good shows."

The Spencer connection, while fruitful (he produced 1995's *Don't Like You*, many fans' favorite Slicks record), became a kind of thorn in the band's side. Tom admits that "maybe it was a bit frustrating that we couldn't get people to take us seriously on our own merits at that time.

**Now that's what I call a Mideast summit! Boston, 1990.
(Courtesy of Tom Shannon)**

. . . I know we influenced Jon with our wild approach to playing, but he
had his own thing well established by that time."

In 1996, the Slicks moved to Columbus, Ohio. "We knew there was
a somewhat active scene in Columbus," says Tom, "and both David
and I had gone to school in the central Ohio area. Our family is originally from the Cincinnati area. The Bassholes [Don Howland's new
duo] were here, and we'd done shows with them. And we needed to
get our personal lives together, which were shambolic." Their timing
was good, as Columbus—with its huge student population and bargain
living—facilitated one of the most active indie scenes of the mid-'90s.

So much so that even *Entertainment Weekly* came to town in 1995 for a four-page feature.

"We felt comfortable in Columbus," says Tom, "but then our booking agent dropped us. So we decided to hunker down and write, which became *Forgive Thee*. We were still on In the Red, but it was hard to get any attention for the releases. The musical intensity was still there, and we didn't have to constantly wonder how we were going to survive each day. . . . Ultimately, I think we have influenced bands here and made a healthy contribution to this scene. There is still frustration that we can't do a little better in the music business. But then again, we've never fully tried . . . so we get what we deserve, I guess."

DEAD MOON LEADER Fred Cole's age and music industry lessons go even deeper than the Cheater Slicks'. Cole's first two bands—the Weeds (re-christened the Lollipop Shoppe by a manager) and Zipper—flirted with the big boys through the late '60s to early '70s. (The Lollipop Shoppe in fact had a minor hit, a great Love-like ripper called "You Must Be a Witch," that was on Rhino's *Nuggets* box set.) His unique warbly vocals and assumption that he's going to do things his own way doomed any chance at stardumb. Later, galvanized by the spirit of the mid-'70s new wave, he formed the Rats, which ultimately mutated into one of the most mysterious bands on the '90s indie garage scene, Dead Moon.

"Dead Moon worked from the very start," says Cole via e-mail—his use of which was surprising, considering that for Cole's taste, a push-button landline would be considered some real Buck Rogers shit. "My wife, Toody [bassist], and I were more inspired at that point just to play very simple and get off on what we did. We all got chills just getting on stage and playing together, no explaining it, it was like magic."

The sound was an anthemic midnight hooch-lurch through Roky Erickson's demo demons, grounded by the most base AC/DC riffage swung out with a junky jangle; each song clogged with desperate tales of hardy hearts doggy-paddling the toilet flush of western civilization, garbled by the members' long, rodent nests of graying hair sucked over their eyes and into their mouths as their leather-clad frames burned hotter. Unless you've seen Dead Moon, it's hard to explain their curiously catchy, oddly uplifting, timeless quality. "We were pretty lucky," says Cole. "We seemed to touch enough bases that we could get away with playing with any type of band and the crowd didn't care. We even played some death metal shows. It's all cool by me."

Cole, Toody, and their drumming pal, Andrew Loomis, took to the hills of Clackamas, Oregon, near Portland, circa 1987, and went on to self-release more than fifteen albums on their Tombstone label. Dead Moon are another example of the way end-of-the-century rock germinated in unpredictable outposts. "Portland has never been starstruck like so many other cities," says Cole. "All the bands here play for the right reason, because they love it. There is very little backstabbing that goes on here, and everyone tries to help friends get off the ground. Way cool."

Dead Moon harbors an outsider-artist aura—their previous bands' impossibly obscure back catalogs; sub-cult status in the States, a higher profile in Europe; limited releases featuring cryptic, Scotch-taped B&W cover art dripping with tombstones, spiderwebs, and that bad-ass half-moon/skull logo. Yet Fred and Toody are incredibly approachable, like Ozzie and Harriet as biker bar regulars. Their mystery mostly comes from fans' amazement at how folks who have been searing their livers and eardrums for so long (to very meager aboveground reception) have sustained a level of recording and touring quality and quantity to shame most of the acts herein. Which comes at a price. Cole suggested doing this interview over e-mail rather than phone because his ears are shot: "Like driving a V-8 on three cylinders."

For most of their existence, Dead Moon toured much more frequently in Europe. "We spent most of our time going to Europe because of the demand, and no one seemed to know us in the States, according to promoters," Cole remembers. "We made a million mistakes during some of our early tours, like getting too fucked up every night," he continues. "We learned very hard lessons that this cannot happen night after night without repercussions. Most of our tours are fifty-plus gigs long, and trying to hold a band and crew together is a bitch. Crazy shit happens every night, good and bad, but the memories are priceless."

The not-so-priceless memories most rock fans do not imagine are the banalities of touring life, like hoping to find a Laundromat open on a Monday off in Europe to give your booze- and sweat-soaked wraps a spin or three, as needed. Nasty-ass clothes are rarely a "look" but an awful reality we bear in order to be on time. Dead Moon took the second skin of tour apparel to a level that created mythical assumptions that they simply never took off their clothing, maybe even when they got back to Oregon.

"Yes, we do wash," Cole clarifies, "but only on a day off. We went

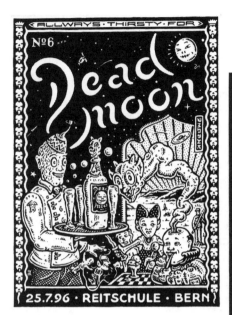

Various Dead Moon European handbills, early '90s. (Courtesy of Fred Cole)

twenty shows in a row one tour, putting on wet shit every night. Nothing ever completely dries, and the smell got so bad that we had the windows rolled down and the heater going, freezing and stinking our way across Europe. On summer tours, we'd hang our shit out of the van window, roll the windows up, then let the shit fly as we raced down the road."

This revered form of rock sanitation is little known outside of back-stage conversations. Sure, with this window practice, once the van speeds off into the night, flies, dust, and exhaust aplenty will riddle your Wranglers, but dammit, they'll be dry! Plus the looks from pass-ersby create good travel conversation and ample opportunity to hoist the middle digit to those who get to go home to their fancy fucking "washing machines."

Aside from Dead Moon's long locks and weathered couture, the other eye-grabber was the always-burning candle perched atop a Jack Daniel's bottle that was shoved into the top of the kick drum, seemingly around the time of the Iranian hostage crisis, with caked-on wax run-ning down to the drum legs.

"The whole trip with the candle was because Andrew decided to lose his ride tom, and we had the hole there," Cole explains. "Our son Weeden stuck the Jack bottle in the hole. We can't remember who came up with sticking a candle on the bottle, but it just worked. We broke so many bottles through the years it was insane, even had people steal it and get beat up by the audience trying to get away. One time at a large show in Berlin, six guys dragged in a five-hundred-pound candle thinking we would not stop playing until it burned out. It's probably still burning."

The hard-slogging work of being Dead Moon certainly didn't cease when they returned home. Cole, having digested and upchucked the bile of the music biz long ago, decided from Dead Moon's start to re-lease their own records, literally, as they even procured a record-press-ing behemoth to cut their own discs. "Mostly it's been a time and con-trol thing. Most record companies take so long to get a release out and want to do all this prepress crap. Me, I'm immediate. When it's done it should be for sale. Also, we should be able to sell to who we want to, and do production and artwork to our liking [all their releases are in mono]. CDs took me a while to come around to, and I look at them like cassette tapes—they will never be collectible."

After Sub Pop released a two-CD retrospective in 2007, the band finally eclipsed—though Cole and Toody soon decided to take up the axes again as Pierced Arrows, and are out playing and recording again. "Musicians are a funny breed," says Cole. "We're all doing something in my opinion that makes the world a better place. We give people a break from the daily monotony. We're not a detriment to society or causing wars. In this sense, we're like a brotherhood of sorts, with a code."

7.

BORN TOULOUSE-LAUTREC

"ACTION THWUP!"

That's the term Tim Warren used in Crypt ads to describe the New Bomb Turks' second LP, *Information Highway Revisited*. But really, one could use that phrase to describe the vast array of—wait, no you can't. You couldn't possibly use "action thwup" and have it make sense to anyone, ever. No doubt a devourer of numerous elongated *Rolling Stone* reviews, *Creem* mag proselytizations, and *Bomp!* beamings, by the time he got his own label going, Warren obviously decided this square globe had tainted all terms used to describe rock music. And since anything known as "rock music" then probably made Warren want to retch, it was time for some new lingo. Ergo, "Action thwup!"

I remember when I was crashing at Tim's pad for a few days after a Turks tour in 1994, and whilst tipping back some suspect Chianti, he was imploring me to help him come up with the Crypt catalog description rant for the new Blues Explosion record, *Now I Got Worry*. There were utterances that the most erudite William F. Buckley buff or half-cut Jersey lounge Elvis impersonator would've had a hard time fumbling through. But Tim tossed 'em out like he was reading *Dick & Jane*. "Savage ungaw-abilly ass-crackin'!" "F(l)unk-tastic poonk rammin!" "Steam-abilly hoot!" And on it went. I would've been dead drunk by the end, except I kept heaving out spit-takes every couple of seconds as Tim rolled out the barrel full of monkeyshine slang.

Crypt's catalogs didn't just hoist Crypt product proper, but also the mile-high mound of underbelly artifacts from all the labels they helped distribute, and other quasi-legit stuff that came from . . . *who knows where*. Perusing them felt like sneaking in the back door of a whole

Tim Warren, fully loaded at Bazooka Joe's wedding, American Legion Post 605, Dallastown, PA, 2008. (Photo by Aaron Lefkove)

hidden world where a 1955 R&B howler could cut a rug to Ramones bootlegs, cheeky '60s strip club novelty songs, Charlie Feathers, Horace McCoy novels, '60s sleaze rags, kooky calypso, B-movie posters, film noir VHS traders, Wanda Jackson comps, lost primitive punk singles, the latest buzz-punks ("poonks") and garage revivalists, '50s doo-wop, freaky fanzines, vintage soul comps, and *Back from the Grave*, of course. These sordid treasures made even the wee-est hours of freeform college radio seem more square than a yuppie's Billy Joel ticket stub.

Norton's catalog of reissue ramalama was a jam-packed fun run-through; Estrus's mostly new garage rock roster pitch looked cool; and Get Hip's seasoned list was way extensive. But nowhere in the music world—hell, in the whole world—had I found such a borderless terrain of unapologetic id. Reading the item descriptions and music industry finger-pointing was like getting a hidden history lesson told tipsy by a livid Nick Tosches, were he a younger one of those leering, hooting drunks at the opening of *Faster, Pussycat! Kill! Kill!* "Go baby, go go go!!"

Jay Hinman, publisher of early '90s trash-rock zine *Superdope*, has a good bead on the Crypt head honcho. "Tim Warren deserves to be lionized for his contribution to even the term 'garage punk.' The guy basically force-fed '60s punk to people through the 1980s, and I maintain that those *Back from the Grave* and *Garage Punk Unknowns* compilations—as well as the snotty, superior-than-thou attitude in all of his ads, artwork, and liner notes—really helped make that music snarl a lot louder than it actually does. Then when I finally met him, he was everything I'd heard: big sunglasses on at 11 P.M., hat pulled down as far as it could go, and a giant, perpetually refilled alcoholic beverage in front of him at all times."

For our purposes, the *Back from the Grave* comps are the molten core. But Crypt Records also made its name amongst the swigging set with the *Las Vegas Grind* collections that jiggled back even further and foofier to forsaken, dirty jukebox singles that once set the mood at peeler joints throughout the States in the late '50s and early '60s. Songs like "The Whip," "Little Girl," and the classic, "Hooty Sapperticker" bumped and ground out blurry visions of the seediest sides of middle-class, after-work shenanigans that went down while the wife was home figuring out the new radar range.

Soon enough, the *Grind* series encompassed all manner of cheap novelty tunesmithery (sometimes peppered with solidly sweaty R&B) that exploded alongside the analogous, cheap tawdry B flicks filling drive-ins midcentury. Other outré tipsy tunes came along with comps like *Ho Dad Hootenanny*, *Swing for a Crime*, *Wavy Gravy*, and others, often

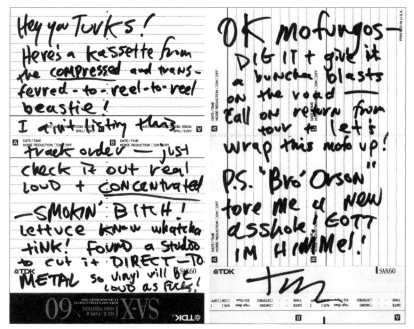

Tim Warren's track list opine for New Bomb Turks' *Information Highway Revisited* rough mix cassette, 1994.

with old greasy movie trailers or dialogue snippets tucked between the steamy songs. Of course, Tim Warren was not the first or only to compile lost novelty singles, but the consistent sleazy character of Crypt's made them into a kind of genre, as the *Grave* series had.

"I gave up drinking about six months before I'd met Tim Warren," says Norton Records' Billy Miller. Norton's core coordinators—Miller and his wife, Miriam Linna, also leaders of longtime, NYC party slop-rockers the A-Bones—were closer to the somewhat calmer collector norm, if no less googly-eyed feverish in their unearthing of all things midcentury musical insanity. "Once Norton started," says Miller, "I got straighter and straighter to where now my worst vice is an occasional french fry. But Tim is excessive in everything he does. That's what makes Crypt so great. Any notable record label should reflect the owner's personality. This one time, Tim got a video camera and he brought it to Maxwell's, where the A-Bones were backing Ronnie Dawson. He was taping us with one hand and drinking with the other. The tape ended up having three or four well-shot songs, then three or four wobbly-looking ones, then a half hour of the ceiling above the band. That's Tim!"

BEHIND EVERY GOOD man, as they say. Though Micha Warren was usually in front, utilizing her bottomless patience to cover the nuts and bolts of the running the label. Usually when stopping by Tim's pad, we'd shoot the shit about what tooth got knocked loose the night before, some crappy new "loaf-eye" band, and what have you. Then, once we settled in for a bit, we'd catch up with Micha about what was *really* happening with our records, the label, etc.

Tim was the "idea man" with the ears and excitement to rope in the talent. And actually, his supposedly lax accounting skills have since been blown out of proportion. Like any indie, Crypt wasn't exactly Lehman Bros. But when Tim said he'd cover plane tix over to Europe, he did; if he said he'd make posters, he made posters; place ads in some zines, they'd be there eventually. And nabbing Crypt freebies while in Hamburg didn't hurt either. If some of those "gifts" showed up in an accounting fax two years later, no different from most indies. Eventually Micha—whom Tim met in Hamburg while on tour with the Raunch Hands in 1989, and married soon after—started to try to tighten the screwiness a bit.

"I was dealing with distributors, stores, organizing tours, accounting, employees, promotion . . . actually, I did everything except ordering records, signing the bands, and artwork. That was Tim's job. Also, Tim dealt with the U.S. side of the label. But he struggled with Matador/ Atlantic, so I flew to New York and tried to solve the accounting mess there." In the wake of New Bomb Turks' debut selling well, and especially the Jon Spencer Blues Explosion exploding, Matador—then a subsidiary of Atlantic Records—took on Crypt for distribution. So technically, for about a year, the Country Teasers were on a major label.

"We were doing manufacturing and distribution deals for a bunch of different U.S. indies—Crypt, Teenbeat, Siltbreeze, PCP," says Gerard Cosloy of Matador. "And in general those deals didn't work out too well for anyone, including us. It was tough for the labels in question to afford our distribution fee, and the minimum number of records we were manufacturing was too many in some cases. We were set up purely to act as the sales/warehousing function for said indies; they were still supposed to be doing all of their own promo and marketing. Suffice to say, some of them were better equipped to do so than others."

As was an outgrowth of much of the energized, suddenly deeper pockets of the music biz in the go-go mid-'90s, it was all kind of a well-intentioned mess. At that point, Crypt was really shifting into mainly working their new bands—or "*groupes moderne*," as Tim called them—and that brief flirtation with Matador did at least spread the idea of Crypt as more than just a retro reissue label to the American indie landscape.

"I often functioned as a mediator between Tim and bands/labels/ people/distributors he had problems with," says Micha. "What a job that was! Oh, and then I was supposed to be the wife! This is the difficult part, especially when you run a business together." Another of Micha's tasks: serving as wingwoman for the late-night band shenanigans at their apartment.

"The bands usually behaved very well in our pad," Micha says. "But it was just a constant in-and-out party of booze and drugs. And oh, the egg/water bombs! For a while it was a ritual at our house that when you came for a visit you had to throw an egg out the window at someone. Eventually, the eggs got boring, so Tim and Billy Childish made water-balloon bombs. Billy and Tim once attacked the clothing line of the Brazilian whores in the backyard. They threw water bombs until the clothesline with the undies caved in."

Tim's dexterity in this sport was honed over many years, back to the

Micha Warren catching up on her reading at the Pink Motel, L.A., 1989.
(Photo by Tim Warren)

first European Raunch Hands jaunt. "We stopped in Paris," Warren recalls, "and crashed with Caroline [Tim's first wife], who was then living
with Stiv [Bators, Dead Boys singer]. We imbibed much in the way of
alcoholic beverages, headed up to their sixth-floor rooftop terrace with
around a hundred camouflage-colored water balloons, and set about
filling 'em. A good forty-meter chuck would land the balloons across the
street, the sixth-floor launch resulting in quite the velocity upon impact!
We keep nailing this swanky Mercedes, and each time the car alarm
erupts and the owner dashes out of this restaurant confused and frustrated, turns off the alarm, looks around enraged, then back in. . . . At
one point I give the old heave-ho without having first scouting the target
zone. And in midair journey, I suddenly spot said man's head rise to the
level of the Benz roof. The water balloon lands *smack*-fucking-*dab* on
the roof, like eighteen inches from the man's face. The resulting splosh
is mighty! This puts an end to this night of joy, as the guy calls in the
gendarmes, and we hide out with damaged ribs from much convulsive
yuk-yukking!"

Tim Warren was the first person to hear of Stiv Bators's death in
June 1990. Caroline frantically called Tim the morning she woke to
find Stiv had died in bed right next to her, after he'd stumbled home
from being hit by a car the night before. Let the world know that
besides being one of the best punk front men ever, Stiv Bators had great
aim with water balloons.

THE FUN DIDN'T stop at the Crypt walls; Hamburg being sort of "the
Las Vegas of Germany" (well, Vegas circa 1975), Tim's place was right
above a dive called the Molotov, the kind of cool, vintage movie posters and '60s R&B–blasting bar that always makes you wonder why you
have to go to Europe to find such an iconically American place. And
right at the end of the street was the Reeperbahn, a gated alley of
prostitutes who stood in the neon-lit windows that sickeningly accented
their northern European "tans," while they posed, discreetly brushed
off the crabs, and kept lil' five-year-old Hans from peeking through
the curtains. Entering the gates (which boast signs that no one under
eighteen was allowed, except Hans apparently) meant you'd best spend
some Deutsche marks or face the wrath of Adolf the pimp. One favorite yarn is when Rick Sims of the Didjits ambled in loopy one eve and
asked one of the ladies what he could get for $4.72. The answer was
a thrown shoe. But if that wasn't your bag, there were numerous bars

that reeked of chlorine, or troughs that dished out what could politely
be described as brutishly buttered bread.

For such a weird and wild town, gig crowds in Hamburg were fairly
stoic. "Yeah, crowds there were kind of lame," says Warren, "but it
was a fucking crazy town. Remember those two Russians who tried
to physically drag me off? That's what they'd do—they'd grab guys,
walk off with them, take all their credit cards and passports, and these
John Does would end up in a canal with their head and hands cut off."
So from either getting the drunken munchies or the fun's-over heebie-
jeebies from the leering late-nght locals, we'd soon find ourselves back
at the Crypt hive.

"There were all the B movies Tim had, endless old pulp paperbacks,
and cool vintage movie posters all over the walls," says Micha. "I believe the bands felt comfortable with all this American trash culture
around them. After all, it was hard touring for Crypt, hardly any off
days on these six- to eight-week tours. . . . Plus, I cooked good German
food, and when the movie ended and the bands wanted action again,
they could go to the strip club Kiez and check out the girls. Kike Turmix, singer for the Spanish punk band the Pleasure Fuckers, borrowed
money to get blow job from a hooker. Apparently he was done in two
minutes. He told us to just take the money out of the band's royalties."

Kike was, by the time we met him in 1994, an aging Spanish punk
fan (dented Johnny Thunders and Sex Pistols buttons on his worn leather jacket no doubt were had at Johnny Thunders and Sex Pistols shows),
now a few years into his reign as *the* punk rock booking agent of Spain, in
addition to fronting the Fuckers. Every time we played Spain, he fucked
up the shows in any number of ways: The club was often changed at
the last minute to another smaller bar. Then he'd take us to a great big
pasta dinner—a half hour before showtime (usually 2 A.M.), basically
imploring us to puke onstage. The show would be packed, but somehow
that wouldn't cover all expenses, etc. As though Kike were a mafia don,
it seemed like everyone just put up with his shit and went back for more,
because if you didn't, you simply wouldn't have a good show in Spain
again. And for all their foibles, Kike's shows eventually did go on, were
totally packed with insane, speeded-up Spanish kids, and were some of
the greatest gigs you could ever possibly ask the fates for.

"Sure," says Devil Dogs bassist Steve Baise, "in Spain we got radio,
newspaper, everything. Kike was getting like $2,500 a show, in 1993!
But we didn't know if we were making two thousand dollars or two

Pleasure Fuckers, Madrid, Spain, 1992. (Photo courtesy of Pleasure Fuckers)

hundred. We didn't concern ourselves with that, as long as we got fed, could drink, got our per diem, and got fucked up—that's all that mattered." Eddie Spaghetti of the Supersuckers recalls Kike's business acumen. "Oh yeah, great times! We had some run-ins with him for sure. We won some Spanish equivalent of a Grammy for one of our early records. Kike told us, 'Hey man, I collected it for you. Don't worry. I get it to you, man.' Of course we never saw it."

"Spain was so behind at that time," says Baise, "because of that cat Franco, who died in 1975—they didn't have any music, no culture, nothing until after '75. So they had to catch up, that's why there were dudes at shows wearing leather pants, you know, like they were back in the '50s. And we kind of played some '50s music, so that's why we did good there. And we had Kike."

Spain, as we experienced it, against all that is proper in the new world order, had seemingly remained devoted to such outmoded ideas as sitting back, savoring food and drink, and enjoying life. And Kike was the embodiment—with greasy, midlength hair on a head the size of a large bowling ball bag; a torso like a massive ale keg filled to bursting, even leaking a bit for the random sweat stains; oddly svelte extremities; achingly attempting the couture of a rail-thin Ramone; and, one of the last times we saw him, a hernia poking out the side of his gut. "Touch my hernia, man! Touch it! I get hernia like man!"

Listening to Kike describe a salacious act—with caked spittle cracking at the sides of his mouth, white boogers about to fly out his schnoz, and surprisingly attractive, deep black eyes—was the closest I'll ever come to listening to a Hun bitch about his day job after seven grogs. He told a story once of being on the road in America with a certain always-touring American shit-kicker crew featuring a quite randy gal bassist. One day Kike had to go out to the van after a soundcheck to get something, threw open the van doors—where there had just been some, uh, pie-slicing going on inside—and Kike said, "Oh man! Stinks like fish, man! She must have had seven different semen up in her poo-see!" To think that even Kike was disgusted galvanized the story into legend.

For all the tales of drugs and crazed rock action, Kike was a relatively laid-back cat, a bit weary from all the years of bringing loud punk to Spain, and retaining that hot-weather-sapped demeanor. And still he had the gumption to start up his Safety Pin label mid-decade, releasing a number of solid street-punk slabs. He'd made it through numerous punk revivals and still went on the road with most bands he booked. Oh yeah, he walked the walk. He was a great, visually arresting front man, and his Pleasure Fuckers stomped out killer punk. So he was going to be one of those guys who bucked the system, Keith Richards style, Iggy Pop style. . . . Nope.

"The Raunch Hands moved to Spain in 1992, largely because the Pleasure Fuckers were our friends and they lived such an amazing rock 'n' roll lifestyle," remembers Mike Edison, who joined the Pleasure Fuckers and played on their hard-rockin' ode to the lifestyle, *Ripped to the Tits*, which came out in the States on Sympathy.

"The first time I got to Madrid with the Raunch Hands I was astonished — it was like a blizzard of coke, the food was great, we couldn't buy a drink. . . . Of course later we found out, like everyone else, that we were paying for it. Kike promoted the shows and was skimming like crazy—he'd put half the money in his pocket and then pretend to be generous. But we didn't know that till later.

"When the Raunch Hands moved to Spain to live we fell apart pretty quickly—Chandler disappeared with his girlfriend and Mariconda was getting gigs producing. One of the first things he did was the Cosmic Psychos. And then I ended up playing with the Pleasure Fuckers. It was great for a while. We were like a gang. A very powerful band. We played constantly, all over Spain and Europe, and pretty much didn't sleep for three years. I guess when I finally quit I was pretty stretched out from all the booze and coke, I mean, it was fucking silly, and between Kike and me our egos were clashing. But at the end of the day he was a fucking thief and I couldn't deal anymore with a guy who was stealing from his own band, let alone all the bands on Crypt whose gigs he was promoting. He'd take records from Tim—Crypt had already put out a Pleasure Fuckers record—and promised to send him money and then never did, and finally Tim didn't want anything to do with him. He did that a lot. It was costing us gigs. We used to talk about firing him, but it is hard to replace a 350-pound Basque man. That's a helluva a gimmick. I loved living in Spain and playing in the band, but finally I had enough."

The last time New Bomb Turks saw Kike, he looked good. He'd lost some weight and wasn't too drunk. "I stop cocaine, man. But I still strong like fucking bull!" Mike Mariconda explains, "His weight was a problem, had some weird metabolism. He was getting gaunt, just not a healthy individual to begin with. But it wasn't just a drinking and drugging thing."

In 2006, Kike Turmix went to that great backstage in the sky, and the punk world lost its best ambassador from one of the last bastions of European siesta staunch, now fading into forty-hour workweeks and air-choking SUVs. We won't see the likes of Kike again. Probably still owes us fucking money though . . .

THESE KINDS OF savage stories seemed to contrast with the somewhat more reverential air of other noted retro-y labels and scenes of the time, and there seemed to be a perceived rivalry between Crypt and, well, everyone, even with old pals like Norton Records. But Billy Miller put a quick kibosh on that notion.

"Absolutely no rivalry. Quite the opposite, really," Miller flatly states. "I met Tim when I was working in downtown Manhattan, I guess around 1981. One day at lunch, I was shopping in this record store nearby and a lot of the LP dividers had cutout cartoons and stories from *Kicks* taped to them. I found out that it was Tim, who worked there, who put them on there. We became friends right away. I got him into buying original records, and he got Miriam and me into putting

out records. I remember not long after we met, he and I were eating
burgers at Junior's in Brooklyn, and I said, "Oh shit, this record auction's closing in ten minutes! I gotta call in with my bids!" He'd never
seen a record list before and he asked if he could get on the phone after
I was through. That was it—his first killer dose!

"When he got married in 1983, he went on a record-buying honeymoon. We gave him some tips where to look and said call collect if
there was anything exciting. He called every day with something wild.
One day it was the Alarm Clocks' 'No Reason to Complain,' and the
very next day it was the One Way Streets' 'Jack the Ripper.' I think I
ended up hearing all of *Back from the Grave Vol. 1* over the phone in a
week! Once we were record hunting in the Midwest, and Tim said we
should pull off the highway and check out this small town. At the time,
Tim had pretty scraggly hair that covered his eyes, and he always wore
this wrinkled overcoat like Columbo. So he has me pull up to this old
guy on a corner, and Tim rolls down the window and asks, 'Mister, do
you have a Salvation Army around here?' The guy gives Tim the once-
over and goes, 'Do you need someone to talk to, son?' He thought Tim
wanted the soup kitchen.

"But there could never be anything close to a Crypt/Norton rivalry.
We've always lent records to one another to make each other's albums
better, and we've always shared tips on stores, distributors, mastering
places, pressing plants, whatever. Tim moves around a lot, but we're
in constant touch. I told him that he needs a map of the world with
red pushpins for every Crypt headquarters over the years, then see if
he beats out the Motel 6 map. Tim has always been one of our best
friends. Even our dogs were best friends."

SOME WEDNESDAY NIGHT in Utrecht, the Netherlands, 1993, New
Bomb Turks were on tour with the Devil Dogs, playing the same night
as the A-Bones. We went over after our gig, and given the Crypt family code, and the fact that the A-Bones had a brief beef going with
Columbus's Gibson Brothers, we went in thinking maybe we'd be met
with grim glances. Instead, for the first of many times, I learned what
swell folks the A-Bones gang were as they asked us up on stage to yalp
along to "Wooly Bully," a habit they've stuck to over the years—and,
like Dolly Parton, it only *kind of* gets old.

"We went down the street to see the New Bomb Turks/Devil Dogs
show," says Miller, "and it was packed. We had to get back to our show,

which was starting at midnight, and there wasn't a soul there. It turned out that you paid one admission to catch both shows, so when the New Bomb Turks set ended, every single person came pouring through the door, all primed and in fourth gear. It was a pretty manic A-Bones set, and we also had all the Devil Dogs and New Bomb Turks onstage at once with us. The whole night was crazed. On top of that, it was Miriam's birthday. We were supposed to talk to Norton's Dutch sales rep the next day, but after all that, he called in sick with a hangover."

I was always fond of the word *go*. Hence the abundance of said word on the cover of New Bomb Turks' 1992 debut album, *!!Destroy-Oh-Boy!!*—the title taken from an amazing 1985 cartoon short called *Jac Mac & Rad Boy Go!*, which also featured that word spewed in Tourette's syndrome fashion from two pre–Beavis & Buttheads speeding around town (in more ways than one) until they smash their car into a truck towing a nuclear warhead, leaving them to contemplate their endless beer quest down in Hades for all eternity. But my mode of going was usually of the bipedal variety. I never even got my driver's license until I

Devil Dogs and New Bomb Turks bum rush the A-Bones show in Utrecht, the Netherlands, 1993. (Photo courtesy of Norton Records)

was thirty-one. Hey, Iggy Pop, Henry Rollins, Ron House—they never got their licenses either. It's a singer thing. People drive us. But this by no means means I wasn't properly gassed and ready to *GO!* by the time I moved to Columbus in 1987 to finish college at Ohio State University.

I was stuck in a freshman dorm, fifteen floors up in an eighteen-floor 1970s monstrosity, slow elevators flush with pee puddles every Friday night when you came back from the bars, and with tiny windows that were sealed shut for fear of high-strung students taking a dive after midterms. That's the petri dish in which I bumped into future boon companion and New Bomb Turks guitarist, Jim Weber. A Replacements picture on the wall was the icebreaker.

By early 1988, Jim had picked up some chords from another dorm mate, and gotten to practicing on a Cort guitar his parents gave him for Xmas. Then we begrudgingly roped in Jim's old high school chum, Ben, on bass. Begrudging, because this surly guy much preferred Rush, just as we were entering our religious slobbering over the Chocolate Watchband, New York Dolls, and the Saints. But Ben did have this hilarious habit of telling us to "suck-a my chub," which got us through the five pointless practices.

In late '89, Jim and I moved in with two other pals in some chintzy off-campus house, and with a few crappy drums down in the basement, I tried to keep a very lame beat while yelling out Buddy Holly and Ramones songs along with Jim's amazingly quick progression to killer lever on the git. The first song Jim and I ever slogged completely through in this one-and-a-half-man band setup was Billy Bragg's "Help Save the Youth of America."

We'd met the quite friendly, lovely-coifed, and music-history-headed Matt Reber at the now-defunct Ohio State student-run radio station, WOSR. He had played bass in a high school band and trudged through a few practices with a local speed-metal crew. Reber knew drummer Bill Randt, who resided in the same dorm Reber lived in. Randt had slammed with a few Cleveland hardcore bands in high school, and it showed in the first few practices, around January 1990, where his skills surpassed those of the rest of us. Randt told me he learned to play drums by cranking Black Flag through headphones as loud as possible while playing along full tilt. Girls cooed that he looked like new-wave heartthrob Paul Young. First time I met him, he was wearing a ripped Paul Young T-shirt with "I HATE" scrawled across the top. Word.

So one Monday afternoon, I'm in Used Kids Records for my thrice-

New Bomb Turks' calls for another round were going aggravatingly unanswered at Stache's, Columbus, OH, 1992. (Photo by Jay Brown)

weekly disc snacking, and Ron House tells me that his band, Thomas Jefferson Slave Apartments (who'd been around for about a year, but were already our favorite local band), were opening for the Lazy Cowgirls that Wednesday, but that the Cowgirls just canceled because of a death in the family, and would we like to play the opening slot. Since I knew saying yes might lead to Ron not charging me tax—and since my brain had just flipped upside down—I said, "Sure, yeah." Walking out I was shaking, thinking, "Fuck, we should probably have another practice." I'm not even sure we'd agreed on a band name by then.

EVERYONE IN TOWN had been beaten to the punch anyway by the name Thomas Jefferson Slave Apartments. Though according to singer House, the moniker "came from lyrics muttered offhandedly." Making your band name an indictment of the hypocrisy at the heart of America while simultaneously being too arcane for your average rock bar boozer was just the kind of weird wit we loved about Columbus's slightly older scene siblings. House had already established himself in late-'80s college rock demi-faves the Great Plains, who had committed such "serious" '80s indie rock crimes as being humorous, and allowing House's nasally vox to wobble freely upfront. He brought some of that vibe to the writing he did for local weeklies and some national and indie publications like *Your Flesh* and the *New York Times*. House also helped start up Used Kids Records—Columbus scene central—in 1986 and co-ran the store through the following decade.

From the start, the Slave Apartments were obviously going to be a U-turn from the Great Plains—louder, crankier, guitarist Bob Petric

American Recordings mag ad for Thomas Jefferson Slave Apts.' debut album, 1995. (Art by Coop)

slicing out bruised Eddie Van Halen harmonics against caveman beats. "I was sick of worrying about failing," says House. "I wanted to get back to the punk-volk: three chords, sex, and drink." House dished up intricately hilarious lyrics and his voice remained just as, uh, striking if more intermittently fierce when he (or the bartender) wanted to be. Here was another one of those hard to classify Ohio bands.

After some killer singles, they eventually released the Slave Apartments' debut album, *Bait and Switch*, on a major label, Onion/American (1995), and today they're a major influence on underground lo-fi post-garage groups like Times New Viking, Necropolis, Tyvek, Functional Blackouts, and Psychedelic Horseshit. At their best, the Slave Apartments exuded an odd exuberance, even some kind of jilted joy amidst the sweaty sound they plied that is extremely rare for any such record collector–core band to accomplish.

Bait and Switch pro-doucher Mike Rep—longtime local cult rock guru, former member of Great Plains, and leader of Columbus's addition to the canon of early-'70s rock deconstructors, the Quotas—wasn't quite as busy when New Bomb Turks came around, doing only sporadic shows and home recordings. We asked him to re-EQ the cassette of the songs we recorded in Cleveland at the Beat Farm with Robert Griffin in the winter of 1990 that would become the songs on our first release, a split-7" with our best-chum fuzz-punks Gaunt. I wrote in the liner notes that our tunes were "Lovingly Fucked with by Mike Rep," which led to Rep using that phrase as his calling card on all his many production projects since, including his scattered solo stuff and recs from the most recent Columbus noise-sters. Our lil' scene had the fortune of being offhandedly spearheaded not by a young, suddenly trendy blueprint to slovenly copy, but by collector cats who'd been around the indie litter box and knew the shit from the absorbent litter.

TUESDAY MORNING BEFORE our first gig opening for the Slave Apartments, I'm told Jerry Wick will be stopping by to get our band's name for the flyer. Ron had also asked Jerry's band, Black Ju Ju, to play. They'd been playing out for a couple months and would soon enough turn into one of the most underrated bands of the '90s, Gaunt. And Jerry would soon enough be one of our best friends. But on that day he was a gaunt, long-haired urchin in decrepit jeans, chain-smoking, wearing patchouli for some fucking indiscernible reason, and claiming he loved the Buzzcocks but appearing like a bass tech for the Meat

Puppets. The ever-subdued bassist, Eric Barth, came along with Jerry. Oddly enough, Barth lived right down the street from me until fourth grade, when his family moved; we used to walk to school together. And now he was twentysomething and asking what our band name was.

We got two more practices in, and got onstage May 23, 1990. Went on first, in front of about twenty-five folks. At that point, I had a ridiculous notion I'd play some guitar, but luckily the guitar cord I was borrowing was busted (for all I knew). I put the guitar down after one

First New Bomb Turks gig, Columbus, OH, 1990.

Gaunt go down to the basement, Columbus, OH, 1993. (Photo by Jay Brown)

verse of "Tail Crush," and we proceeded to have, y'know, the best night of our lives.

The next time Black Ju Ju played, they'd switched their name to Gaunt, ditched their Rush-fawning drummer, and roped in the far more preferable skin-smacker Jeff Regensberger. Jeff still plays with Jim Weber in the power pop combo the Patsys, and they were kind enough to gather recently with former Gaunt bassists Eric Barth and Bret Lewis in the backyard of Jim's new house in Columbus and forward me the results like some Morse code transmission from a Veterans of Foreign Wars luncheon. . . .

"There was a time when there weren't so many punk rock freaks," says Regensberger. "There weren't so many socially retarded–looking people that you could easily identify as kindred spirits, in a way that you can't now, because everybody looks uniformly freaky in their way. But I knew the second I saw Jerry working at a Sohio gas station that he was some kind of freak. After some show he comes up to me and says, 'You should come back to our place on Summit Street and smoke a bunch

of weed.' Which we did . . .
We were all skinny and sort
of like poverty-ish looking.
So it was going to be called
Gaunt."

Gaunt's sometimes sear-
ing/sometimes fumbling
fury churned Buzzcockian
hooks, Pagans pestering,
Superchunk's slacker yearn,
occasional Sonic Youth
noise-dives, very frazzled
guitar solos, and that un-
definable winter-huddled,
loner genius vibe that
Mike Rep modeled for all
of us Columbus yobs, and
sloshed it out in sonic shots
that could rival Sham 69

Columbus, OH, 1991.

fist-pumping or Beaver Cleaver slumping home with a D—usually at
the same time.

Regensberger put the "aw" in raw for Gaunt, reining in any of Jerry's festering pretensions, keeping Barth's busy bass barreling forward,
and showing the face—in resemblance and resolve—of Barney Fife
at his most heroic. "Jerry would talk about these big plans," says Regensberger, "all this stuff he was going to accomplish in the world . . .
but [he was] not particularly focused. . . . If you listen to some of the
sludgy, midtempo stuff on the early singles, you can hear that Sub Pop
was what Jerry had in mind. But I think that sort of changed quickly,
and part of that had to do with you guys [New Bomb Turks] getting
on Crypt, and thinking in a more traditional punk rock idiom. He was
always cognizant of what was going on musically around him, always
paying attention to what was popular."

Like us Turks, Jerry didn't consider himself "Columbus" per se. He
landed there after ditching his family in the western suburbs of Cleveland, and following a short stint at Kent State University. Jerry only
lived in Kent for about a year, but he hailed that burg like it was Paris
in the '30s. Kent was not Paris in the '30s. It was barely Youngstown
in the '50s. But being a transplant in Columbus means firmly believing

you're in a limbo between two phases. And we all know limbo is preferable to hell.

Soon, Jim Weber joined Gaunt too. By then, Jerry had his hair
shorn, had memorized the first few issues of Peter Bagge's *Hate* comics
(a huge influence on a sizable portion of '90s gutter rock), and slumped
around town like Buddy Bradley on a coffee and Doral cigs jag. "Cheap
cigarettes and cheap coffee were what sustained Jerry," says Weber,
"until he got to work and could get a proper meal on Used Kids' dime."

A sad reality of "growing up" is that you will have to put aside the in-
vigorating habit of telling off every schmo who tries to get in your face—
that is if you plan on doing stuff like having a relationship or keeping
a job. Thankfully, Jerry never learned that "truth." Bullet Lavolta—a
solid Boston zip-grunge band and friends of friends—were playing local punk hub Stache's one night. Jerry walks right up to them after the
show and says, with total energized sincerity, that while their records
really sucked, the show was surprisingly good. Jerry's jerky moods garnered him plenty of detractors in the scene, to the point that bandmates

**Jerry Wick and Bela Koe-Krompecher (Anyway Records), Columbus, OH,
1995. (Photo by Jay Brown)**

Regensberger and Barth designed a preemptive scene-strike Gaunt T-shirt with "Jerry's an Asshole" on the front. "But," Weber clarifies, "he was pissed off that their 'Jim Motherfucker' T-shirt sold better."

Gaunt's gumbo was messy for sure, but because of Jerry's quick sticky hooks, we all kind of figured they might be the ones to first get bigger label attention. And they did, when two respected Chicago indies, Thrill Jockey and Amphetamine Reptile, put out some Gaunt recs; then around 1996, Warner Brothers' feelers started wiggling. Jerry's response to label interest was akin to Groucho Marx's comment about not wanting to join any club that wanted him.

Lest anyone think that all his opinion-hoisting and onstage heart-hurling meant Jerry must've thought he swung a fifteen-incher, he was actually, in the classic punk manner, self-effacing to the point of depression. But in a really ha-ha way.

After a show in Austin, Texas, on the Turks/Gaunt road show in the summer of 1993, we were all congregating in the driveway of the pad where we were to crash, but word of a party floated in, so we all stuffed into the Turk van with the party directions holder to get over there before the keg ran dry. Gretchen—a great gal-pal who came along to sell tees and generally keep us from constantly deconstructing the many fascinating facets of fecal matter—told us later that drummer Jeff had hit the sack, and new second guitarist Jovan Karcic was dozing off in the van, with Jerry desperately trying to rouse him and yalping, as we drove off: "Goddamnit, goddamnit!! This is why Gaunt sucks!"

New Bomb Turks spent Wednesday and Thursday August 26–27, 1992, in Coyote Studios, on North Sixth Street in the Williamsburg section of Brooklyn, one humid floor up, recording our first album, *!!Destroy-Oh-Boy!!* Lots of fans say it's our best, and I won't argue (except to say that you really should go listen to *Nightmare Scenario* [Epitaph, 2000] again). It was a fairly traditional story: Young Ohio guys drive to the Big City . . . and right through it into a completely fucking dilapidated, rat-dodging district where apparently a lot of old Polish people still live but, from what we can tell, is mostly abandoned warehouses, garbage bags rolling in the wind, with Sergio Leone spaghetti western music somewhere in the distance. . . . The view of Manhattan was amazing, though. "Man, I can't believe more people don't live around here. It's gotta be cheap!"

We lug up five cases of beer and our equipment, nervously shake

New Bomb Turks, Stache's, Columbus, OH, 1992. (Photo by Jay Brown)

Mike Mariconda's hand, as we've only met him very briefly once or twice. We set up the gear, mics, and such in like two hours, already about halfway through the beer, and slam out twenty songs in nine hours, all live, most in under four takes. Mariconda would pop his head in once in a while as we sometimes debated a take, to tell us, "Eh, it's not botherin' me," or, conversely, "Nah, you can hit that one better." About the only delay was trying and failing at figuring out a way to keep headphones on Bill while he wailed away at the skins. Had lunch at a Polish restaurant. Crashed at our friend Janet Billig's place in Alphabet City. Went back the next day to do overdubs (mostly guitar leads and some vocals), and went out that night getting loaded in Manhattan with our great pal Paul Sommerstein, and thinking we could get used to this shit. We left, leaving the tapes in Mariconda's sure hands to mix. And when we played the rough mixes for our pals back home, each and every one commented, "Man, it's so fast." Yes, it was.

By early 1993, New Bomb Turks' debut on Crypt was out and more tours were certain, so Weber left Gaunt, and by 1994, Regensberger's allegiance was slipping. "From my perspective, it was impossible to really project a whole lot of confidence about the endeavor because of where I was musically," Regensberger admits. Barth counters, "Jerry knew how to work with what we had. He didn't need a lot. I think he liked the fact that he wasn't playing with the best musicians in town, yet we were still putting out good records."

"Jerry was either the nicest guy in the world or just an absolute bear to be with," says Lewis. "By the time I got in the band in '94, I was more interested in just having fun, and I think that upset Jerry. He had these grandiose ideas coming up where he was promising that he could get me bass lessons with Tommy Stinson!"

"Our '94 European tour was great," Regensberger recalls, "but by that time it wasn't the loveable loser show anymore. . . . [Then I guess] Jerry decided, 'Well, I don't want to try to slog through this anymore. I want to have somebody good.' It is quite a leap to go from me to Sam Brown."

Sam Brown had powered a couple of local grunge groups, becoming not only a welcome face through the saloon doors, but obviously the kind of guy who is so good at what he does that he'd never need to worry much about his next gig. Plus, he was adept at a number of other instruments and wrote as many songs as anyone else in town. He definitely did yank Gaunt up by its collar and made it even more of a live force. Needless to say, Gaunt was not the last band he'd play with.

Soon Barth moved on too, and the bass was tossed between the hands of Lewis and Athens, Georgia, scene fixture, Brett Falcon (formerly of Space Cookie and Supernova).

Around this time, Dayton, Ohio's Guided by Voices was gaining hype steam and playing Columbus every other month. While Jerry was always prolific, it seemed GBV's leader, Bob Pollard—and his band's incessant releases—also seemed to place a boot to Jerry's behind; as did the prolific ways of his Used Kids boss/pal, Ron House. Plus, it was a zeitgeist of the time, as Jerry faves like Rocket from the Crypt, Superchunk, Supersuckers, and his NBT chums were releasing records like the Brits come up with potato chip flavor combinations. Lewis once told me that the first time he heard some of the songs that wound up on the *Yeah, Me Too* (Amphetamine Reptile, 1995) and *Kryptonite* (Thrill Jockey, 1996) albums was on a demo in the van on the way to the studio to record them.

"I don't remember there being many bad times," says Lewis, "but

Columbus, OH, 1992. (Art by Arturo X)

there was always such drama on the road with Jerry." That's saying something for a band whose idea of a good time was when guitarist Karcic played his "game" to keep the band awake on long overnight drives. He would turn the headlights off and see how long they could go without someone screaming out, "Arrgghh, turn the fucking lights back on!" Also, the band assumed that a good way to save time on long drives was to slide open the van door, wrap the shoulder seat belt around your arm, lean as far as possible out the window, and pee to your heart's content. "Yeah, Jerry was into that," says Barth. "He peed all over himself, then took his deodorant and started rubbing it on his pants to get rid of the smell."

Once Gaunt's slicker but solid 1998 Warner Brothers debut, *Bricks and Blackouts*, didn't make the hoped-for dent, and the band tired of frequent touring, band practice phone calls started to be returned in weeks rather than hours. Jerry eventually found a new calling as a cook (surprising, considering that when I met Jerry, boiling ramen noodles would've been a chore for him). "One thing that gives me a great deal of peace now," says Regensberger, "is that if there was some notion that Jerry should've been 'bigger,' that was in the past, and he was ready to move on. He didn't leave as this completely frustrated rock dude."

On Saturday, January 6, 2001, New Bomb Turks played in town at a club called the High Five. Right before we went on, I saw Jerry in the crowd, and I went over and hugged him and exchanged the usual where-ya-beens. He started right off saying how he fucked up the last Gaunt record, how he was writing new stuff that rocked and was a big "fuck you." Jerry always did that sort of thing. One time I was in Used Kids while he was working. A box of a new Gaunt single came into the shop; Jerry opened it and proceeded to throw three of them at the wall, screaming, "This fuckin' thing sucks! Gaunt sucks!!" Then a few minutes later, under "much" prodding from Ron House, Jerry played the single in its entirety. Twice.

We had to go on, so we did, and zipped right into a boffo set. The crowd was especially crazed. Encore time, and of course we yell for Jerry to come up for our cover of Gaunt's "Jim Motherfucker." He utterly pile-drived through the song. Beer was flung, monitors got knocked over, friends stepped on friends, and all—and I do mean *all*—was right with the world. In the face of the dim light speeding toward us all at the end of the adolescent tunnel, Jerry was laughing, with eyes at you like a warning while singing, screaming, laughing…

I got up early the morning of Wednesday, January 10. Sat down to eat cereal, watch the news. Seems an unidentified man on a bike had been the victim of a hit-and-run death around 2 a.m. that morning, right at the end of the street I lived on. Weird, I didn't hear sirens or anything. I went out and came back home later to a frantic answering machine message, then another, then another. . . .

Jerry Wick, 1967–2001. R.I.P.

8.

STRONGER THAN DIRT

*L*IKE *A* B*IG* *Fuckin' Train*. The Supersuckers. It was just another 7"
in the Used Kids singles bin I was flipping through in early 1991.
There was a bald dude on the cover and some sliced-up font, so I figured it was another hardcore band. Once tossed on the store's stereo,
the rabid rock ricocheting out of that 7" wasn't any better than the late,
great Australian punk band, the Saints, from near fifteen years earlier.
But that's just it—it kind of sounded like the Saints. Now look, I realize
that New Bomb Turks aren't up there with Picasso on the originality
scale. But save for the Dwarves or Devil Dogs, I hadn't heard a band
so effortlessly invoke Aussie riffing, Ramones rush, and comic cursing
since, well, our last practice.

The Supersuckers started as the Black Supersuckers, out in the wild
west of Tucson, Arizona, in November 1988. "We just found that in the
back of some adult literature lying around our practice space, a living
room in an old adobe house," says singer/bassist Eddie Spaghetti, "As
you can guess, that name caused us problems at first, like people thought
we were racist or something. Nothing could be further from the truth.
We had a show and needed a name, that's it. Our lead singer at the time,
Eric Martin, would read out the back of these books for lyrics, while we
played the music. So it was either that or the Cock Hungry Studs."

The band kicked around the university bar scene in town. "We got
booked with heavy metal bands," Spaghetti recalls, "which was more
fun and made sense to me, because I grew up on the east side of Tucson,
which was where the heavy metal bands were. And in high school I was
in metal bands." But the Supersuckers' affinity for the hard stuff was
more raw. Spaghetti states, "Motörhead, the Ramones, and AC/DC—

they are the holy trinity of what our rock 'n' roll is all about, along with the Replacements. Holy quartet, I guess." Mix in Spaghetti's's asininely assured lyrics, and the 'Suckers twisted their retro-rock ramalama with the kind of knowing-wink showmanship and top-notch power that was missing in much punk-sprung music around the late '80s. "We listened to a lot of records on 45 that sounded a lot better than at 33," Spaghetti recalls. "We did that surprisingly often."

That's the kind of bored accidental art that can happen in a small town. But a move to a bigger city seemed inevitable. "We seriously chose on a coin toss between Seattle and New Orleans," Spaghetti says. "Seattle won, in 1989. A friend, Danny Bland, had moved up to Seattle from Phoenix, and he managed us for a while. [Bland had been in an early grunge band, Cat Butt, and was later in the Dwarves.] But all we knew of Seattle was they had the Space Needle, and you could wear your jacket longer than in Arizona." But Seattle had other kinds of needles too. Once there, Martin got heavily into heroin.

"I was the primary songwriter," says Spaghetti, "so I knew the words and would sing them when Eric didn't show for practice, which was happening a lot. We got a gig like that, with me having to sing; then we just decided to drop the 'Black' from the name, and my fate was sealed. We recorded a bunch of demos like that, just to see how bad I might be as a singer. I fully expected to get another singer. But those demos became our early singles and then were compiled by [Seattle-based indie] Empty Records as our first album, *The Songs All Sound the Same* [1992]. All of us dabbled in drugs to varying degrees of success, but Eric kept on. I wish he could've stuck it out, because he would've been a really great front man." Eric Martin passed away in 1994.

That was Seattle then—death or glory. The band's timing at least was good. "Yeah, very fortuitous indeed. We had no idea that there was even another good band, let alone a burgeoning rock scene; just happy to be somewhere they appreciate loud, aggressive rock music. It wasn't until I heard Nirvana's first record that I was blown away by anyone up here. Helping Danny Bland stuff some singles up at Sub Pop offices, they put in a cassette of *Bleach*, and I thought, Man, this is really good. We just thought we were going to go up there and be the best band they'd ever seen. Knock their fuckin' socks off, blow their minds. They've never seen anything as great as the mighty Black Supersuckers."

From early on, the Supersuckers often got labeled as cocky for their jaw-jutted, guitar neck–pointing, audience-baiting, cowboy hat–tipping, smart-ass image. It was still only 1991. Hair metal power ballads were still being released as singles by the majors, and anything that even remotely resembled the flashy swagger of '80s cock rock—especially in the burgeoning vortex of rainy-day grunge—was frowned upon. The irony of the Supersuckers' omnipresent devil-horn hand salute was sometimes drowned by the grunge scene's preferred solemnity. Then again, the 'Suckers were also a reliably fast and funny alternative to the slower, serious Seattle sounds flowing down like lava over the left coast in the early '90s. Hence the 'Suckers, along with the Dwarves, became a beer breath of fresh air to western rock 'n' roll fans, and their frequent touring quickly swelled their following.

Sure, the Supersuckers repeatedly called themselves "the greatest rock 'n' roll band in the world." But when they were on, they backed up the boast. Yet even in his most chest-puffed moments, Spaghetti would agree that, of course, the Dwarves were the greatest rock 'n' roll band in the world.

"Oh yeah, they changed my world! I saw them at the CoCA, in downtown Seattle. It was one of the first Sub Pop shows, late '89 or early '90. We got on the bill somehow. Nirvana played it. The Dwarves played the night before, I think. I was so blown away! The most fantastic band I'd ever seen in my entire life. And I made no bones about it, telling the guys in the band, 'I've seen the future of rock 'n' roll, and it is called the Dwarves!'

"Sub Pop had this idea we'd be this dancey, disco-y sort of band," Spaghetti says, "because we used to get out this disco ball onstage and kind of do goofy, party-band covers like 'Super Stupid' by Funkadelic, 'Burnin' Up' by Madonna." But the band wasn't just fumbling with their sound. "Earlier in the week before that big CoCA show," says Spaghetti, "we were at this party and devised this plan to steal this huge, rented disco ball from the party. So I had our drummer at the time bring his truck around front. Then I went, unhooked the disco ball, chucked it out the window to Eric, jumped out of the house after it. Running to the truck, I tossed the ball in the back, smashed it to pieces. So we took it to that big CoCA show, bring it out during the show, and there's a guy at the front of the stage—'Yo, that's mine, that's mine! You guys took it from me!' Hey, finders keepers, man."

Who'd have thought disco balls would impress Sub Pop back then? "Once we kicked Eric out, we thought we'd blown our chance," says Spaghetti. "For Sub Pop to come back around was a big thing. . . . That

Like a Big Fuckin' Train EP was when we really started to click. There
were surf and garage bands and stuff in Seattle too, but we never really
felt a part of that. Now I listen, and some of it, especially the Mono
Men stuff, sounds fresh, because music has really gone to shit again."
And one can assume the riot grrrl thing going on over in nearby Olympia wasn't exactly laying out the welcome mat for the 'Suckers. "Actually," Spaghetti recalls, "we played Olympia one time back in the day.
Riot grrrls were picketing our show out front; they thought we were
sexist, misogynistic, all those nasty words. But none of that stuff really
happened up in Seattle."

By 1992, the Supersuckers had released their classic second album,
Smoke of Hell, the record that cemented their rep as chrome-stripped,
hot-rod riff masters. And having an amazing Daniel Clowes cover
didn't hurt, with Clowes's rep as one of the best new graphic novelists
eventually exploding with his *Ghost World* stories that began in 1993.

What really laid the blacktop on garage punk's highway to hell—
running parallel to the gravel pavement of the lo-fi path—was the
legendary Dwarves/Reverend Horton Heat/Supersuckers triple-bill
Euro tour in 1993. "The minute they showed up, the guys in Reverend
Horton Heat were insane." Eddie says. "Taz [drummer] was like, 'Hey,
man, they got BP over here too!' Uh, yeah Taz, it's British Petroleum.
We're in Britain.' [Supersuckers guitarist Dan] Bolton had bought this
giant bottle of Jack Daniels from the duty-free and brought it on the bus
for everyone to share. Then we all went for a walk. The Reverend and
Jimbo [Wallace, bassist] stayed behind and drank the *entire* bottle of Jack
Daniels. When we got back to the bus—all three bands on the same
bus, which is sort of amazing—the Reverend is telling Jimbo 'Dammit,
Jimbo, get up here, we're gonna drive this bus back to America.' We
thought, Well, we could go into the logistics problem of that, but . . .

"And the Dwarves were awesome," Eddie needlessly states. "They
completely trashed the stage every night." Then there was the contest
going between the Reverend and Dwarves drummer Vadge Moore to
see who could have sex with the most people. "Yeah, everyone had
some money riding on who would win," Eddie says. "I bet on Vadge.
He took down this really disgusting fat girl on the very last night we
were there and won the contest. The grand total winning number?
Two. So the ladies weren't exactly breaking down our door.

"HeWhoCannotBeNamed was surprisingly quiet. But you know, he's
a crazy animal. I did a show with them, not too long ago, maybe half

Supersuckers sword fight, Seattle, 1992. (Photo by Charles Peterson)

a year ago. They were in Portland the night before we were supposed to be there. HeWhoCannotBeNamed went out right after the show, smoked some crack with some losers, wound up on some street corner somewhere; they couldn't find him. He finally called them around two, when they were supposed to leave, about to bail without him. 'I'm somewhere in Portland.' Yeah, no shit! I mean he's got to be fifty. And supposedly when he's off tour he's been a teacher for disabled kids!"

Another rowdy regional act the 'Suckers palled around with often was Zeke. They started out in 1993, inspired by the sudden shotgun blast of buzz-punks, but soon dove deeper into the flames of speedy metallurgy, becoming the monster truck of the mid-'90s punk scene, barreling off . . . but not before influencing loads of later speed rockers to add lots of mechanic lingo, flame-job graphics, and Satan praise of undetermined sincerity to their repertoire. "I think they're amazing, I love that band," Spaghetti exclaims. "Singer and guitar player Blind Marky Felchtone is one of the unsung heroes of rock 'n' roll. Amazing songwriter, amazing guitar player, cool voice."

As the 'Suckers solidified their reputation with arguably their best all-around record, 1994's *La Mano Cornuda* (Sub Pop), the endless touring offered more of the usual temptations, and for guitarist Ron Heathman, that meant trouble. "He was just like in a dark cloud," says Spaghetti. "So we sent him off to rehab and really didn't think he'd be back in the band. Whipping up a dream list of guitarists to ask, Rick Sims came up because of our love of the Didjits. I'd heard they'd just broken up, so we'll ask him. He said yes, and we were just blown away. I thought we made a pretty good record with him [*The Sacrilicious Sound of the Supersuckers* (Sub Pop, 1995)], but live, it wasn't really working out too well. He didn't really know what his role was. He was getting along with me but not with the others. So eventually we called Ron: He was working in a coffee shop in Phoenix. He was kind of blown away we asked him back." Asked if they thought it was going to be weird to deal with a newly sober bandmate, Spaghetti said, "Well, Rick was sober too, so we had already had our first taste of what a sober person would be like on tour. And with Ron, he's since abandoned his sobriety anyway."

Given the Supersuckers' now perfectly carved-out image/sound, and the climate for alt-rock bidding wars (especially relating to bands from Seattle), Sub Pop had spent a truckload on *Sacrilicious*. Even with the guitarist switcheroos, they kept on truckin' down the tour road and eventually signed to Interscope Records in 1997.

You know in mob flicks, there's that scene where one of the goombas tries to eat at a fancy restaurant or get into a swanky country club, gets denied, and then suddenly realizes that no matter how classy he thinks he is, no matter how much money or influence he thinks he wields, he'll never get accepted by the blue bloods? Maybe I'm thinking of Rodney Dangerfield in *Caddyshack.* . . .

The finished Interscope album was shelved, most of it later rerecorded, some new songs added, and released by the indie Koch International as the ripping *Evil Powers of Rock 'n' Roll* in 1999. The performances exhibited the kind of desperate energy of a rooster getting back for ten last pecks in a cockfight. But it was hard to expect anyone beyond the ever-loving fan base to rejoin the party, nearly five years after the 'Suckers' last proper rock album.

During the interim between *Sacrilicious*, the Interscope mess, and *The Evil Powers . . .*, the band had cobbled together a best-of collection and finally threw up the white flag to their country inclinations with *Must've Been High* (Sub Pop, 1997) which, while solid, was nonetheless met by longtime fans as a stopgap. "We had another record to do with Sub

Montreal, 1999. (Art by Dirty Donny)

Pop," says Spaghetti. "So we decided to do our country record. Everyone thought we were saying fuck you to Sub Pop, but it wasn't like that at all. When it came out, it divided our fans pretty solidly. But it's since become our best-loved record, I think." In the lag time, the band also became great pals with Willie Nelson and played Farm Aid (Rick Sims's last show with the band), where they hung with hero Steve Earle backstage. "That was his first show back as a sober artist, just out of prison," Eddie recalls. "He's had a lasting impact on the band since then."

The Supersuckers are far down the highway from that adobe house in Tucson and have become the trash-rock world's equivalent of the ol' ever-touring blues cats; while on days off, they teach their kids the devil-horn salute. "The devil-horn thing kind of started as a joke," says Spaghetti. "Only dorky heavy metal bands do that, right? Now everyone does it—even fucking emo bands do it!"

WHILE THE SUPERSUCKERS brought some scraggle-rock tendencies to a wider audience, Estrus Records was the Northwest's record label face of '90s neo-garage and surf, and the first garage label to fully embrace the soon-to-be-de-rigueur practice of wrapping recontexualized vintage-girlie-mag/hot-rod/tiki/B-horror-movie iconography around Sonics-centered sounds. Compared to the Crypt/Sympathy/In the Red axis of sleaze, though, Estrus was a bit more *Beach Blanket Bingo* than *Teenage Gang Debs*.

Dave Crider, Estrus label head and Mono Men singer/guitarist, was the only person I asked to interview for this book who graciously declined:

From: *Dave Crider*
Sent: *Thursday, November 13, 2008, 5:43 P.M.*
To: *Eric Davidson*
Subject: *Eric Davidson here, New Bomb Turks . . .*
Hey eric – ah the rumor mill – am still here have just been enjoying not releasing any new shit for the past while – book sounds cool but i think i am gonna pass – have been approached for several such projects this past year and while i am sure yours is gonna be pretty on the mark and a cut above the others i just aint all that interested in rehashing the "good ol days" for the kids – nothing personal and I do appreciate your asking regardless – best of luck with the book and if your ever in the nw we should hook up for a drink – dkc

The Mono Men were the stud horse of the Estrus stable. Like Black Flag on SST, Minor Threat on Dischord, and Halo of Flies on Amphetamine Reptile, the Mono Men were the best band on their own label at first. Their debut single, "Burning Bush"/"Rat Fink," dropped in 1989 and was ahead of the retro-garage curve. Heard then, it sounded slightly out of time, fuzzed-out, though not as "lo-fi" as might be assumed. They were surely digging up old seeds (their past-peering moniker nicked from DMZ/Lyres leader Jeff Connolly's nickname, Mono Man), but sounded like their shovels hit some heavier Rock on the way down.

Being on Estrus was a Good Housekeeping seal for a large portion of garage punkers, and the label let 'em have it. Aside from discs from the flagships (Mono Men, Mummies, Makers) were boss slabs from the Night Kings, the Fall-Outs, the Drags, Quadrajets, Thee Headcoats, the Fells, Jack O'Fire, and Supersnazz. Estrus also ballooned the collector curio pile with numerous limited-edition 10" records and 7" box sets chock full of drink coasters, key chains, comic books, and other nutty nonmusic loot.

But soon enough, you couldn't tell your Phantom Surfers from your Satan's Pilgrims. Estrus soon found itself out-fuzzed by new imprints like Empty, Bag of Hammers, Rip Off, and others whose "'60s" were just as much about late-'70s punk and the increasing taste for crackling, four-track basement recordings.

Estrus's creative packaging, consistent imaging, and great distribution meant the label was actually a fairly profitable enterprise for a good amount of time, and they were the first to introduce pillars of '90s garage punk like Teengenerate, the Mummies, and the Oblivians to freaks outside of the States. If they sometimes just missed the latest fuzz-punk trend train, they often caught the next one, with fine singles from Baseball Furies, Blowtops, and the Hellacopters. By the late '90s, Estrus seemed to finally follow its heavier hard rock instincts—if receiving an indifferent backlash from their Ventures-vaulted cult—releasing some interesting discs from careening kooks like the Fatal Flying Guillotines, Fireballs of Freedom, and DMBQ.

"I don't really know what Dave was or is, and I don't care," says singer Michael Maker, whose band, the Makers, left Estrus for mossier pastures later in their career. "He was a businessman doing business. Sure, he was a nerd wanting to be part of something. We all are. [That] whole scene was far too uptight for me in that regard anyway. I do know that Dave loved what he was doing, and that we had a blast with him. I think he was interested in the Makers because of our reputation, not our virtuosity, and I thank God for that. . . . Dave and his wife, Becky, were our friends for a good while when we were on the label. We left the label. We're not friends now."

The catty, insular nature of any music subculture is often slapped in the face by the real world. In 1997, Crider's world was torn asunder by a terrible fire at his home. He lost a large portion of his personal artifacts and Estrus back catalog. According to Crider, though, the label survives (if sparingly). Whatever the case, Estrus Records certainly put their time and money where their mouth was. Theirs was as impressive a run—as far as label identity and depth of catalog—as that of any '90s indie label. Further, Crider and Co. concocted some crazed nights of rock at the infamous Estrus Garage Shock festivals in the label's hometown of Bellingham, Washington, that acted as garage rock's EKG machine for a goodly portion of the decade.

THE MAKERS WERE mainstays at Garage Shock. Like their similarly chameleonic '80s antecedent, the Chesterfield Kings, the Makers switched their style incrementally, mimicking the evolution of the main garage rock strains, and winding up as New York Dolls-y sleaze merchants on Sub Pop and Kill Rock Stars, while touring around in a 1965

Garage Shock festival poster, 1993.

Pontiac Bonneville hearse. Since the Makers started quite young, their evolution is understandable. But I prefer my rock bands to be a few steps ahead of me, or just really great songwriters. Though the LP *Makers* (Estrus, 1996) is pretty kickin'.

"The Makers began in the very late 1980s in Spokane, Washington," says Mike Maker, who currently lives in Portland and runs a vintage boutique/art gallery. "Early on, we were just poor, angry kids messing around after school. Then, luckily, I was expelled from my high school for threatening a teacher. I remember being scared for a moment as the county sheriff escorted me off the premises. Then I soon walked straight to [guitarist] Tim's house and said to him, 'Let's make a tape.'"

This seems like just the kind of story that the Makers were expert at spreading. But it's really no use worrying about authenticity with a band that worked overtime to concoct an image, which has always been fine and dandy in rock 'n' roll—especially for the very young, finding their way. "We hated our town and we wanted everyone to know it," says Maker. "We would get kicked out of every club and just laugh about it. We were decked to the nines on- and offstage, mod suits and Chelsea boots day and night. And all this during the peak of the slacker-grunge movement. We rubbed a lot of people the wrong way!"

Everyone seemed to have heard of a fight at a Makers show. "It's true, fights did happen at our shows," Maker concedes, "but it wasn't always us starting them, or even being involved in them. And most of the fights happened in shitty little Spokane, Washington, so it's no surprise. We had to fight our way through school, so why would it be different when we took to the stage? We always had the element of surprise on our side. No one expected a bunch of suited-up dandies to be so vicious. . . . We'd get called 'faggots' all the time; and me and Donny are not all white, so we also had to deal with a lot of racist remarks when we'd perform."

The one time I saw the Makers, they just struck me as a solid, well-dressed garage group. We played with them, the Cheater Slicks, and Thee Headcoats in Columbus, Ohio, in 1997, at the Alrosa Villa. It was your standard dilapidated, out-off-the-highway, leftover '70s place where long-in-the-capped-tooth metal also-rans played. I saw Cinderella there—in 1999. It's the club where Pantera's Dimebag Darrell was shot and killed in 2004. The kind of place that wasn't used to the, uh, relaxed attitude toward sound engineering us trashy types favored.

"I think [Thee Headcoats] got a kick out of watching us do our

The Makers, 1997. (Photo by Vic Mostly)

thing [on that tour]," says Maker. "We were so crazy and aggressive while they were so mature and sedate. . . . We loved old bands like the Sonics and the Pretty Things, but we also loved '70s punk bands like the Damned and the Stranglers. Billy Childish and the Mummies were a great influence early on. But we mostly hated everything, very contrary, always finding weaknesses and flaws in the things we once swore by, quickly condemning them. *Everybody Rise* [Kill Rock Stars, 2005] is probably our best record, but it's probably our least heard album, being that it came out on a label comprised of people that seem to despise rock 'n' roll completely."

So whatever happened to that 1965 hearse? "That hearse was beautiful but never comfortable." Maker laments. "Maybe it was a blessing when that giant moose went through the windshield. I still have that giant rack as a trophy on my wall."

SOMEWHERE BETWEEN THE Mono Men's retro reverence and the Makers' mincing melees lay Estrus's most legendary loons, the Mummies. The Mummies rose up about the same time, all wrapped in nominal gunk-stained white gauze and possessed of scraped-up vintage gear that seemed to have been buried with them in whatever mausoleum they just ambled up out of. Their zany look and analog adherence was a party to the West Coast surf revival groups they originally palled around with; but the Mummies added *Back from the Grave* ardor and blasted it all out with an abandon that just bordered on "update."

Lasting less than four years, the Mummies nonetheless became the rickety axle of one of the two wheels of the '90s garage punk motorcycle. Where the Dwarves, Didjits, Devil Dogs, Supersuckers, and New Bomb Turks lead-footed the gas pedal on their gutter-buzz toward some unforeseen hyper horizon, the Mummies and their batty "budget rock" brood—along with more misanthropic middle-America agitators like the Gories and Oblivians—turned onto bumpy back roads of monomaniacal knocking and pinging.

Despite a predominant focus on their concept, the Mummies' cutting clatter produced some screws-loose sides that win converts to this day—witness their instantly sold-out reunion gigs in the summer of 2009. I finally saw them in Brooklyn that June, and the claims people made to me over the years that they were best heard live were completely true. The show was a blast—keyboard and bodies flying, beer-soaked rags still stinking, Russell Quan decimating the drums. Reaching singer/organ-smasher Trent Ruane at home on the eve of those reunions, I was unsurprised to find we were both calling from landlines.

————————

TRENT RUANE: This is a landline. Does it sound craptaculous?

ERIC DAVIDSON No, its sounds great. I don't have a cell phone.

TR: I have a work-issued one. Outside of that, I've never owned one. I work for a high-tech company for thirteen years, and for the first, oh, six or seven years I still had a dial phone.

ED: So the Mummies formed in the late '80s. Everyone always kind of bags on the '80s as one of the worst eras for rock music.

TR: At the time, I think what was so horrible about the '80s is what made us better. It's kind of what fueled us, y'know? I feel like when there are things going pretty well, and the established scene has been figured out, then the formulas have been set. There is not a whole lot that forces you to be original. I don't know what it was like for you guys, but before there was a scene for that kind of stuff around here, we played a lot of horrible shows with lots of bands that were all over the map.

The punks dig Mummies, New Year's Eve, Gilman Street, San Francisco, 1990. Green Day opened, Angry Samoans closed—and still no alcohol permitted. (Photo by Michaela Warren)

ED: There was a lot of pop punk crap going around there right? Like NOFX, Gilman Street, and all that. . . .

TR: Yeah, we played Gilman a few times, but that really wasn't our scene. In fact, I think the audiences at Gilman were generally bummed by us. And that was an all-ages thing. All ages, to us that was like a kiss of death. The younger the kids were, the less interested they were in what we were dong. The people who were into us from the get-go were like these drunken guys. Losers, bike messengers, record collectors, people like that.

ED: Were you into any of those sort of '80s '60s revival bands, the pointy Beatle boots and the paisley shirts stuff?

TR: Russell was probably most into that and still is. He actually lived through the '60s, so he was there. I kind of stumbled upon the Back from the Grave stuff. At the time, I had not heard anything like that before. And the thing that really stood out the most to me was the way things were recorded. . . . . Anyway, then I told those guys, "Hey, I know a guy who is playing drums named Russell, and he'd be great for this!" So we had Maz [Kattuah] take over on bass. . . . I've known Russell for a long time now—he is one of my best friends, but he can't keep time to save his life. If you ever asked him to slow something down a little bit, boy, wrong thing to ask!

ED: So how did the mummy motif come up?

TR: Maz and I used go thrift shopping all the time. And this was before you had to have a set job. Rent was cheap or we were living at home. . . .

ED: And thrift stores still had good cheap shit too, before they were picked over by vintage stores.

TR: Exactly! And we lived in a hotbed of thrift store activity. The peninsula, like south of San Francisco, had the most amazing thrift stores. My theory is that in the '60s the peninsula had a lot of well-off areas, and there was a lot of, "Hey Mom, I wanna be in a band!" So, "Okay Junior, let me buy this organ for you, this guitar," etc. And all that shit just sat in closets or garages, then in the '80s they just dumped it all. We would literally find equipment at thrift stores. Maz and I would drive around almost every fucking day, hit all the thrift stores. Then you'd have to kill time while you were doing all that sitting in traffic. So we talked about band stuff, and we were trying to come up with the dumbest idea. So that was one of the ideas—we should just dress up like mummies.

ED: So what year are we talking about?

TR: Like the tail end of 1988. So we got a show together for February of '89 and now, fuck, we have a show, we have to figure out how we're going to do this! Now we have to come up with costumes [for this new band]. In the '80s in the Bay Area there was this '60s thing going on, but it was mainly a mod thing. So our first show was kind of a mod show—and it really bummed them out. Back then we couldn't get a show to save our lives. We just weren't playing the right kind of music. We started to play a lot in South Bay and Santa Bay. There was a club down there, Marsugi's, that was actually pretty nice to us. The guy who booked the club wanted to be our "manager" at the time, and booked a Northwest tour for us. On the road as we are going up [to Seattle], we [find out] all the clubs canceled all the shows. So we went up there and played anyway. We just happened to be there at the right time and the right place; and that was one of the best shows. . . . The "right" people were there. After that, things kind of fell into place.

ED: It's true, there were some lame bands in that Northwest grunge scene, but there were some goods ones, nice people, and the fans definitely came out to whatever the

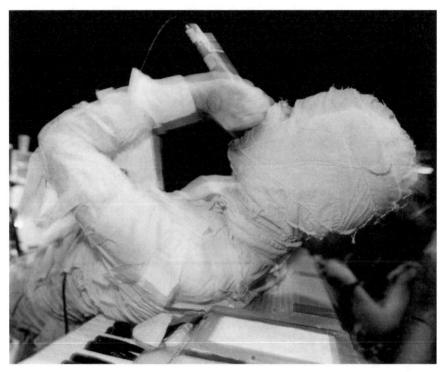

**Trent Ruane (Mummies) sucks it up, Seattle, 1992.
(Photo by Charles Peterson)**

hell was playing. Did you ever get thrown on a bill with a grunge band?

TR: Well, we really didn't get shows back then. Y'know it was the DIY thing. I was in a record store and I found Untamed Youth's first album. I bought it, thought it was great, and I wrote a letter to (singer/ guitarist) Derek Dickerson. He wrote back and said actually they were going to be in Cali this date, they would like to play a show in San Francisco. . . . So I ended up renting out the place where we played our first show. It was a place on Broadway in San Francisco called the Chi Chi Club. I think I put like two hundred dollars out to rent the place. . . . Then we met the Phantom Surfers early on. It's funny because one of the guys in the Phantom Surfers I had gone to high school with, but I didn't really know anything about the Phantom Surfers until we met them as a band. There was a band playing surf music the way it needed to be played, pretty straight.

BOTH THE PHANTOM Surfers and the Untamed Youth played a pivotal role in the late '80s by adding dollops of plain goofy fun back into indie

San Francisco, 1990. (Courtesy of Trent Ruane)

rock via their instrumental surf rock jump start. But their early records are extremely tame compared to what was crawling out of the garage punk underbelly. As a side show to the general rearview vibe of the early '90s (the space-age bachelor pad/tiki trends; movies like *Swingers* and *Pulp Fiction*), the surf scene itself grew large by the early '90s, but its overly kitschy facade and static sounds—released on Estrus, Norton, Get Hip, Lookout, and others—were soon set aside by the new trashier garage punks.

————

TR: It was one of those things where, because there was no scene, you kind of wanted there to be one—then it actually happens, and it's like, This really sucks! All the bands playing the same kind of shit, same fucking songs. . . . I guess it wasn't always this way, but San Francisco has kind of a reputation of being a really retro city, in terms of music.

ED: *I think California in general has that rep, at least as an Ohio guy looking at it. I always attribute it to weather—how the Bettie Pages and their '50s boyfriends' hot rods and suede creepers don't deteriorate because you don't have winter with salt dumped on the roads—and it kind of stems from there.*

TR: I loved those original '60s garage records, largely because of the way they were recorded. Then I bought a few of those ['80s paisley-type] records and they sounded like shit, really clean like any other '80s band.

ED: *Yeah, the level of trashiness in the recordings usually didn't get anywhere near as noisy as you guys or Teengenerate, or just over-the-top spazzy fast like the Devil Dogs, Dwarves, whatever. . . .*

TR: I think it's harder for bands to do something like that and put it out and not be embarrassed. If you listen to anything we did, it's like you're listening to something that came through an AM radio.

ED: *For most of the bands I knew in Ohio who did the whole lo-fi thing, it wasn't because they were trying to go for a certain style at first—I mean, it was fun and quick, but a lot of it was just economics. We were broke, we didn't have the money to go into some pro studio.*

TR: I can't say this without sounding totally like cheesy or hippie, but it really was like magic. Back then, no one really used old shit; it wasn't like the White Stripes had made [vintage guitars] highly sought after. We got Silvertones and organs for thirty-five dollars! That's fucking magic. . . . I was really into this mystery thing. Are you familiar with the *Garage Punk Unknowns* comps? I liked the *Back from the* Grave stuff, but the *Garage Punk Unknowns* were my favorites because they had a bunch of blurry pictures with no information on the sleeves, and I thought that was the coolest thing. That's why we never put any of our names on our records.

ED: Well how about some info on how you recorded?

TR: We recorded our first couple of singles, believe it or not, on an eight-track reel-to-reel, half-inch tape. A pretty big one, the size of a refrigerator. We'd lug it around before we had a place where we could make noise. My mom had a van and we would set up drums inside the van, go out to a community college parking lot at night, record drums in the van, and just bang away, and no one would call the cops on you. . . . . Michael Lucas, the bassist for the Phantom Surfers, worked in a furniture warehouse, and we went and record-ed the first couple of singles there in a stairwell. For a while we were renting a practice space in a warehouse; and then we recorded and practiced in a wood shop. We had this really strong DIY thing going on. I think largely it came from Maz. He was also really into put-ting out fanzines too. . . . What we really wanted to do was put out a record. And back then no one did that sort of thing. Maz found an ad for a thousand records. We all pitched in and sent the thing off, but we were really cheap and had the record sleeves printed in town at a print shop. And we ended up cutting those things by hand and folding them and gluing them, every single one by hand.

ED: Oh yeah, we had a number of those marathon sleeve-folding parties, where we'd buy a bunch of six-packs and have friends come over and help stuff little stickers into sleeves, spray-paint covers in the backyard. . . .

TR: Yeah. We had marathon sessions with the rubber cement and the rulers and the paper cutters. It was back when you were still pretty excited to do the whole thing—whereas now you're like, Fuck this! Everything was so different back then. I remember when printing something in full color was mind-boggling! It was so expensive. Now you just whip them up on the computer. . . . That whole "budget rock" thing—Maz actually coined that phrase because we were all cheap. That's kind of the guide in our lives. See, you have to take anything we did with a grain of salt. It was kind of a big joke. Plus we got set in our ways, we really enjoyed doing stuff on our own. We only ever recorded in an actual studio once—when we did a Peel Session at the BBC.

ED: You sent a demo to Crypt, and they were maybe going to do a Mummies record, but then came the ensuing drama. . . .

TR: The thing with Crypt is that I had been pen-palling with Tim Warren for a while, and he really liked the first couple records we put out. And I think at this point I was already in contact with Billy [Childish] too. I loved Thee Mighty Caesars, they were a huge influence on me. So I was writing to all these guys at that point. And Tim said, "I really love this stuff; we're going to record an album, and I am going to fly Billy out there to record you guys." Fucking great! But last minute he was like, No we can't do it, so I'm sending my good friend Mike Mariconda out there. And I kind of knew who he was by virtue of the Raunch Hands.

ED: Did you like the Raunch Hands?

TR: Not really. I don't like a whole lot of stuff. I was bummed at that point, not because he was a dick or anything, I just didn't know the guy. At this point we were practicing in a wood shop. It was wintertime, unheated, and we set up to record, and you could tell Mariconda was really kind of bummed being there. I think he was expecting us to be little more professional. So he recorded the stuff, and we were kind of unsure about it. He had to go back, so we said we would finish up the last couple of tracks and send it to him. So we sent it but felt really uneasy about it because it didn't sound like us. The originals kind of sucked, the covers were lame. . . . But at that point I guess we were thinking Tim had sent out Mariconda, and we have already wasted all this time, so . . .

ED: Mariconda didn't end up doing a mix?

TR: No, we mixed it and sent it. But Tim didn't like it and then suggested for the planned Crypt album that we put half our singles and the other half would be some of that Mariconda stuff. But we didn't want to do that because we knew it was horseshit. And I think that kind of validated that for us—Tim Warren didn't like it either. But then bootlegs of it starting showing up. Then that whole Mariconda song thing really pissed them off. [The Mummies released a dis tune called "Mariconda Is a Friend of Mine."] We were a little surprised at how personal they took it. We did that as a joke, but boy did it piss them off! I guess it was kind of petty.

ED: Had you heard the Gories by then?

TR: I think I know what you are getting at. I didn't like any of the new bands on Crypt or on Estrus. I didn't really like any new music at that point.

ED: The first time we played the Vera club in the Netherlands was right around that time, and we wrapped ourselves up in toilet paper, got up onstage and called ourselves "the Mariconds," and tried to fumble through a song, "The Mummies Are a Friend of Ours." Not sure if anybody got the joke.

TR: After we played Hamburg, Crypt gave us a bunch of shit, like they slashed our tires on the van. And Tim's wife poured a pint of piss on me, right after we got off stage and were going upstairs. I thought it was beer at first. But it was warm, and why does this stuff stink? . . .

———

HERE'S HOW CRYPT Records unwraps its version of the Mummies: "Ha! Bullshit," says Michaela Warren. "That didn't happen. Tim and I didn't even go to the Hamburg gig. I remember there was the talk about it, and God knows what Rich and Patty did, as they did go to the show. [Those two fellows were short-term Crypt tour managers.] I never threw a pint of piss at anybody.

"Only thing I remember is we saw the Mummies in San Francisco on New Year's Eve, 1990. They played with Green Day and Angry Samoans. It was great show. We wanted to put out the record. The Mummies wanted to have Billy Childish as their producer, and when that fell apart, and that Mariconda will fly out instead, they got pissed off and acted up like babies at the recording session with Mariconda. Some of them didn't even show, and one decided to go skiing instead. They'd been really anti about the whole recording, and Tim didn't want to put out the record with them having such an attitude. So we dropped them because we stood behind Mariconda, as an old friend."

Tim Warren adds, "We were on vacation, and I went to the Pasadena swap meet. I was broke, and I brought along twenty really rare-ass surf singles and sold them to Lux Interior for, like, a grand. Cool, road trip. So we went to Berkeley. I'd been digging the Mummies' singles, though I did think they were like—this song's gonna be a Pebbles song, and this one's gonna be a Childish song, etc. But they really ripped it up live! I fuckin' loved it. I thought if they could translate that into a whole record . . . So I sent Mariconda. How did I know they already had a grudge against him? The tape was okay, but I'm a discerning guy—I've been dis-earning all my life! And after the mess of recording them, I didn't want to step into a world of shit, with like one of the members skipping out of a tour to go snowboarding or something. So then Sympathy bootlegged it on CD; Get Hip did the bootleg vinyl. The band busted Get Hip on that and collected some bread. Everyone made money on those 'aborted' tapes except me! I lost $1,600. I was the loss leader!"

––––––––––

ED: So how'd you hook up with Estrus Records?

TR: Well, the first show we played in Seattle, a club called Squid Row. [Dave] Crider was there . . . probably the tail end of '89. I don't know if it was like this for you guys, but you always end up touring around in the fucking wintertime. And I was always sick back then. Y'know, no sleep and you eat crap food. And this sounds really nasty, but we would play a show and we kept the costumes in a plastic milk crate. So we would play a show, then be tired, and you didn't want to lug your equipment offstage let alone deal with wet costumes. So we would just throw them in this milk crate. So here we are in the dead of winter, we just played a show the night before. We were getting dressed, but there weren't any dressing rooms. So we're in the alley behind the club, fucking freezing, getting into these wet, stinky, cold-as-fuck costumes.

ED: *Yeesh. Were they usually wrapped around a pair of pants or something, or was it literally wrapping your whole body in these things?*

TR: When we started, we actually wrapped Ace bandages, and then we realized that took too long. So we sewed stuff onto pants and shirts. So here we are getting dressed in the alley from the milk crates, and we carried a can of Lysol with us. We suit up, spread-eagle, and one of the guys would spray you down.

ED: *Wow, that's fuckin' dedication!*

TR: No, it's laziness! It's not like the next morning you want to go to a Laundromat. You want to go to a record store. . . . One time in Seattle we stopped at a Laundromat. And because we were sort of pressed for time, and cheap, we decide that instead of washing the wraps we would just shove them in the dryer. So we put all these costumes in one dryer and the window of the dryer starts turning gray. And of course after the first cycle, we didn't want to put any more money in. They were still wet, but they were warm. It was a real nice feeling.

ED: *Billy Childish told me that the Mummies were hilarious, and the only band that I mentioned for this book that he cares a half a shit about.*

TR: I believe I sent him a copy of our first record with a letter, and I taped a dollar bill to the record that said, "Here is a dollar for you to play our record." He wrote back, and I probably still have the

letter. . . . We toured with them in August 1991. Live, I think Thee
Headcoats were really great. At that point, Billy was still drinking
and they were pretty fucked up. The tour was great and horrible all
at the same time, because Thee Headcoats were getting pretty big,
and there were a lot of promoter politics about what order bands
were playing. It was a lot of bullshit. I was getting tired of playing
music. It was just getting to be a drag here in San Fran too, it was
becoming a fashion show circus.

ED: You also toured with Supercharger, in Europe right?

TR: Yeah, but that was sort of at the end, where I was pretty close to being done with everything. We played a show at Maxwell's with Mudhoney and the Lyres for New Year's Eve 1991. On the plane ride
back I turned to Larry and said, "That's it. I can't do it anymore."
Then, see, we used to put inserts in some records, to order T-shirts
and stuff: "The Mummies will play your birthday party or tractor
pull . . . blah blah blah." So I got this letter from a guy in Germany
saying, "I want you to play my tractor pull. . . ." I thought it was just
a joke. But I said, Fine, get us the flight tickets! So he said, "Yeah,
I am buying the tickets, you are coming to Germany." I said okay,
but told him to put Supercharger on the bill. At this point, end of
1992, the Mummies were dead, so I didn't care. Before everything
fell apart, a number of us lived in the same house, which is where we
recorded our last few things, like the "Planet of the Apes" single. So
it was like the Phantom Surfers, the Mummies, and Supercharger all
living at the house . . . and we could all record down there.

ED: Were there a lot of parties there?

TR: We had a few, but people would come over and steal shit, so it
wasn't a good idea. We recorded a bunch of stuff, and I put out a
single by this band called the Fingers, and a Supercharger single
was recorded there. But we were all kind of getting on each other's
nerves. So we went over to Europe with Supercharger, and it was
actually a lot of fun. It was a three-week span, but we only played
like ten shows. It was awesome. . . . I don't know if you had the same
experience, but when you were touring the States in the late '80s/
early '90s, at the level of band we were, it was like dog shit.

ED: Yeah, then you go to Europe and they have food trays backstage.

TR: Yeah! We could not believe it, a food tray!

*ED: Yeah, you'd get there, gobble down the catering—because you'd been driving all
day and had no money to buy the crap at the gas stations on the way—and then*

an hour later, "Okay, now vee take din-ah." But wait, I just gorged on the food plate! Amazing. In America, you're lucky if they toss you a mini-bag of Doritos from the bar.

TR: We really looked at that whole thing as like free travel; it wasn't so much about playing. Like late 1993, that German guy asked us to come over again, but he said this time you need something to promote, which is the *Party at Steve's House* [Pin Up, 1994] record. So we did that tour, and it sucked ass. A month, and played every fucking night. Slave labor tour. It was literally play, pack up, and vroom— drive on to the next country. Of course I got sick again, and on top of it all, the crowd hated us. They were pissed we had just been there the year before. "You vaz betta last ye-ah." Asshole! Germany sucks!

ED: Germany was the country you had to go to because they had money. It wasn't quite the nirvana the rest of Europe was, more like touring America, bad truck-stop food and loads of traffic jams. But German shows were usually crazy fun. Except everyone smokes in Europe, and they shutter all the windows to avoid sound violations.

TR: Yeah, and it gets really hot in those bandages, like having your head in a pillowcase. I would get a pint or a pitcher and just pour it on my head, 'cause you feel like you're dying. The problem with that was the bandages are over your ears while they are wet, so it was like a membrane. Then everything sounds so loud and tinny. And it really did stink.

THE NOVELTY OF the Mummies' style and sound hit the West Coast garage scene like a sloppy spitball, the splash spreading quickly. Greg Lowery—who would later codify the "budget rock" sound with the Rip Offs—was bowled over by the Mummies. He soon scrounged up Supercharger, who became the "Chester" to the Mummies' "Spike," bouncing around Trent Ruane for advice.

"The Supercharger story is pretty weird," says Lowery. "I was into punk, the Ramones, all that at an early age, but it wasn't until I was a little older that I started Supercharger. I was twenty-eight. It all started with Darin Raffaelli getting a Christmas bonus from his job, and saying, 'Hey I'm buying a drum kit.' And I said, 'But I can't play anything.' And he said, 'So what!' This is around early 1991."

Supercharger had a dirty little secret. "Yes, we had a friend who was a full-blown hippie," Lowery admits. "He could *play* anything, but he didn't *know* anything. So we started practicing, and that guy started writing songs. After about five months of that, we were getting tired of it, and Darin decided to buy a guitar, figured we've got to start writing our own songs." Then destiny stepped in. "The hippie guitar player actually got sick and had to have surgery. It was horrible, but it knocked him out of the band. That was a sign from God that we've got to go forward. Darin wanted to buy a guitar, but he wouldn't even go into the shop. We were intimidated. We hated those people."

It may go without saying that the majority of the musicians in this book hate "musicians." Hence walking into a music store of any kind besides a record shop is tantamount to visiting the dentist. (Reference the classic Oblivians song "Guitar Shop Asshole" for a succinct enunciation of this conundrum.) "So I went it and bought it," says Lowery. "And it turned out that the guitar I chose, this Fender Jaguar, well Jon Von, who was in Mr. T Experience and would later be in the Rip Offs, it was his guitar that he had just sold to this place. A weird, vicious circle."

Then we just tried to see everything," says Lowery. "Sonic Youth. Buzzcocks, Ramones, the Didjits, the Dwarves . . . Mostly, we were trying to emulate the great Devil Dogs, of course. They were a huge influence, and the Angry Samoans. But we were not even close to that. We couldn't play at all, so we just started writing songs. We needed a drummer, so I asked my girlfriend at the time, Karen[Singletary]. She was like, 'What? Are you crazy?!' But she came down and banged around. We recorded the first album, but we were terrible, and we'd never played live. We just did it out of arrogance and ignorance at the same time."

Which is an appropriate summation of the fumbling, '50s-leaning trash that Supercharger clunked out on that self-titled debut on Raffaelli's Radio X imprint. And how was that half-ass harangue recorded? "A Tascam four-track," says Lowery. "We basically did some at Darin's parents' garage, and some at Karen's job in an office at an air freight company. If we could finish a song, we kept it. A sloppy mess. We just decided to do it as a lark, just for fun. We pressed up five hundred of that first album. Darin ran over with one copy of our album, and I thought, Wow! But then we went over to his house and saw a stack of five hundred records, and he goes, 'What the fuck are we gonna do with these?!'"

The kind of slop Supercharger were slinging was gaining a following down the road apiece among the Mummies' circle of sillies. The scene itself wasn't exactly a thunderous tidal wave, as Jay Hinman of

Superdope zine recalls: "I've had people tell me that I was lucky to see the Mummies, Supercharger, the Phantom Surfers, and whatnot multiple times while they were active, and no doubt those were some very fun shows. But outside of a few record freaks and people from the other bands, that scene was totally off the radar in San Francisco. While I think that made it even more special for the people who did get it, it mostly consisted of the same ten people screaming and hooting at each other; a real sleazoid, drunken sort of vibe, but only a tiny handful of really great, lasting tunes."

"We'd heard about the Mummies about the same time we started recording that first album," Lowery recalls. "They were an inspiration, definitely. We thought, Wow, look at these guys—we can do that!

A writer at *Maximumrocknroll* nabbed a copy of *Supercharger* and gave it a glowing review, which greased the wheels a wee more. "But what really started it all," Lowery claims, "was when we dropped those records off at the Epicenter record store. Russell Quan, the Mummies' drummer, bought one and flipped out. He wrote us a little note saying, 'This is great, stay amateur, don't go pro!'

"About a week later we got another letter, this one from Tom Guido, who would later run the Purple Onion (aged Beatnik hangout that became the budget-rock nexus of the SF scene). He asked us to play a free show at the Chameleon. So we took two weeks to practice and played a free show on a Sunday afternoon. Only about twenty people, but the 'who's who' of the SF garage scene: Mike Lucas of Phantom Surfers, Russell Quan, Tina of the Trashwomen, Peepin' John, lead singer of the Flakes. We just rambled through a twenty-minute set . . . very nervous. Then the Mummies were playing two days later on Halloween. We'd never seen the Mummies up to that point. So we go to the same club we just played—super tiny, holds like a hundred people max—and we can't get in because it's almost sold out." There were sporadic area gigs, but nothing resembling a tour, until a call from the Mummies for the 1992 European tour.

Tales of the mythical gonzo behavior of that SF garage scene, mainly framed by the Mummies' onstage shenanigans, have inflated the actual intake of party favors. "To be honest," says Lowery, "we were very much outsiders to the drug scene and all that. We were suburban kids. Trent and I had similar clean kid upbringings, but we just liked really trashy music."

Estrus, via prodding from the Mummies, had distributed the re-

Promo poster for *Goes Way Out!* LP, 1993. (Courtesy of Greg Lowery)

maining copies of *Supercharger* throughout Europe, and were planning a follow-up (Estrus also reissued the debut in 1997). "I suspected the only reason Crider wanted to put out Supercharger was because of the name," Lowery says, "and his whole hot-rod rock shtick. I don't trust anybody. But, okay fine, we'll do the second album, *Goes Way Out!* [1993]—which I thought was the better record—with Estrus. We didn't really hear from him for a month or so because he was waiting for us to make the record. So he finally called and said, 'Well, I wanted to talk to you about the artwork. I have an idea. How about we take a picture of a '60s Dodge Charger, and on the back we'll have a hot girl with the car specs, and your song titles will be the specs of the Charger. What do ya think?!' And I was being nice: Uh, well, let me talk to the other members." Already by 1992, the Rat Fink hot-rod-a-mania thing was getting stale.

"I didn't even bother telling the rest of the members because they would've laughed. I'm a total control freak, I do my own covers always. So we just ended up doing our budget cutout bullshit art. Crider kind of flipped out and said, 'If I don't like the artwork or the music, this thing is not coming out.' But a few days later he called back apologizing. 'I'm sorry, I love it.'"

Further adding to Supercharger's loopy lore was their gig at the Vera club.

Ah, the Vera. The name itself elicits long, wistful sighs from any rocker who has passed through Groningen, the Netherlands. Playing anywhere in the Netherlands is usually a treat—swanky clubs; learned, drunk, but rarely violent fans and promoters; preserved architecture; fresh food and good beer. See what you get when your mostly neutral country doesn't have to be the police of the world? Money can go into improving *your* cities instead of the estate of every third-world nation's "democratic" despot. Anyway, save for the often gloomy weather, it's a real paradise (except maybe for people of any sort of color, who I will have to conveniently, hopefully assume have been directed toward an equally comfortable locale). And the Vera is paradise's best rock club.

A few annoying steps up the front entrance and a walk back to the main hall made for a slightly tough load-in. But from there, one can hear the angelic voices of every dead musician who ever played a dank dive guide you as you stride through the place. After getting the equipment in, you head upstairs for java in the relaxed hangout room, walls covered in show flyers dating from the opening of the club in about

SUPERCHARGER — VERA-ZG. 21/3/93 ©SNORKEL

'Nuff said. (Photo courtesy of Greg Lowery)

1980, and big windows that look out on a fairly busy street in one of the hippest growing cities in the Netherlands.

A floor up from there is a screen-print room where the staff produces a monthly zine and all the amazingly bizarre gig posters that have become legendary. There's an office where the staff send out e-mail updates up until dinnertime, featuring stories of recent wild Vera shows over good Thai food, which ain't exactly abundant in Europe. There's never even a question of all-night free hooch for the performers. An easy soundcheck, then kill time down the street at the great Elpee record store. Then the show, which was invariably sold out. Crazed crowds, good sound, and a clean backstage room right behind the stage to retreat to, as the Vera crowds were notorious for demanding week-long encores. And don't get me started on the new little backstage band bedrooms they erected in the early '00s. The Vera, perhaps the best rock club in the world.

SUPERCHARGER, THOUGH, ARE one of the very few bands for whom the Vera holds sour memories, if not for anything the club caused. "That was the end of Supercharger," Lowery states. "The Vera was the blow-up show. Darin was trying to impress the Mummies. He was trying to piss me off so I wouldn't want to play with him anymore. So he was talking smack to me onstage. It got really ugly. Later, in the Rip Offs and my later bands, that was part of the shtick. But in Supercharger, because we were good friends, it just wasn't part of our act. Darin was starting to be a real asshole on stage.

"So the Vera show was packed, our shining moment, and they loved us! But Darin said some dumb shit on stage, and I was dishing it back. So the show ends, and we were on the side of the stage, and I grabbed him and said, I'm gonna fuckin' pop you right here! And my girlfriend is crying. At the same time, the crowd is screaming for an encore. But we're right there, so everyone can see what's happening. I said, I'll fuckin' walk on this tour, I don't need you. Let's do the encore, but after this, don't fuckin' talk to me in the van, don't say a word to me, I swear to God I'll beat your ass! We did the encore, they loved it, and that was it."

But tempers were rising before the plane for Europe even took flight. "Darin had gotten crazier since he moved into Trent's house. They lived in Pacifica, a huge place. It overlooked the beach, teetering right on a sheer cliff edge. When we recorded the first Supercharger single, there was a huge crack right under my feet. One foot was on one side, the other foot on the other. Nice house, but not long for this earth."

9.

ÎT GETS A LÎTTLE RED

"I REMEMBER MEETING Dave Crider from Estrus Records early on, and he was one of the coolest guys," says Larry Hardy, founder of legendary vicious sounds vanguard In the Red Records. "The first time I met him, I'd gone up to a Garage Shock, 1992. We were comparing notes, and his label was definitely taking off faster. But I remember him telling me his favorite '80s garage bands were the Pandoras and the Lyres. Mine were the Scientists and Pussy Galore. So there ya go."

The intriguing thing about Larry Hardy has been, besides his consistent taste, the fact that he's sidestepped most of the usual sinking feelings of the aging vintage-sounds scrounger and stayed positive in the face of whatever is happening to music-consumption assumptions. A mojo made more interesting when considering the volatile sounds In the Red has bred with incredible consistency since 1991, sounds that most instantaneously evoke angst and frustration.

"Pussy Galore and the Gories. They were pretty much the reason I started the label," says Hardy. "I heard of the Gories before they even had a record out. I had a friend in Texas who was doing Alex Chilton's accounting. Chilton kept telling my friend, 'You've gotta hear this band. They sound like the Cramps, if the Cramps were black!' I'd thought about putting out records for a while—it seemed like the right thing to do since I was a total record nerd. I was about twenty-four. I was friends with Long Gone John [Sympathy for the Record Industry], and I watched him start his label. . . .

"I found out about the Gories, the Gibson Brothers, and the Cheater Slicks all around the same time, around 1990," Hardy remembers. "Wow, there are these bands that are playing garage or roots rock what-

ever, but it's fucked up. It didn't sound like Estrus or that sort of stuff."
But one band that always bridged the map—offering gurgling sounds
for winter-hunkered Midwesterners and flashy garb for the Left Coast
retro lifestylers—was, of course, the Cramps. "The Cramps totally
changed me. And there was a bunch of friends I had around my age in
the early '80s, former punk rockers, that suddenly got way into weird
'50s and '60s music, all by way of being Cramps fans."

Hardy has always been quick to correct me on my Pacific pooh-
pooh presumptions. I want to point out that most of the most crucially
corrosive Cali acts of the original punk era—Crime, Weirdos, Screamers, Consumers, and others—never released proper whole albums and
didn't last long. To which Hardy reminds me that, no matter, they *did
indeed exist*, and their various limited releases and latter-day bootlegs
have created a flip side to the perceived UK-influenced punk history
of Hollywoodland. "I grew up with that first wave," Hardy explains.
"Like, the Screamers are a punk band. Devo is a punk band. They're
just as crazy and weird as any punk band, and seem just as aggressive
in an odd way. Punk was a broader term then."

"To me, Pussy Galore were a punk band," say Hardy. "I met Jon
Spencer by chance through the Gibson Brothers, right around the time

In the Red Records ad, 1992.

Spencer joined them. Don Howland [Gibson Brothers singer/guitar-ist] was keeping me abreast of the band, and I remember totally freak-ing out when he told me Spencer was joining the Gibson Brothers I never told him I liked Pussy Galore; I thought it was weird they even knew one another. But then the Gibson Brothers were all really into the Cheater Slicks and the Gories, and I thought, Shit, these guys all like the same new bands I do. There's definitely something going on here."

By the tail end of the '80s, the '60s dress-up garage groups who had plagued the East Coast were still standing around the streets of L.A. "As far as those garage bands doing that retro thing then," says Hardy, "I really hated them. Even though I ended up marrying a girl who was in the Pandoras, I fucking couldn't stand that band. The only ones I liked was that first Dwarves record [when they were still called Suburban Nightmare]. And I liked the Nomads [from Sweden]. I remember the Fuzztones moved out here from NYC in the '80s, and sometimes the Pandoras would play with them. And I remember thinking, This is the worst shit ever. Even though they're covering songs that I like the origi-nal of. I just don't see why you'd want to relive a bygone era so exactly, why you didn't want to do something to it to make it a bit more your own or more contemporary."

The pinging lightbulb above Hardy's head that the miscegenation of Pussy Galore, Gibson Brothers, Gories, and Cheater Slicks set off all happened in the span of less than two years. Which seems quick, unless you've noticed how trends and band life spans now rocket across the Internet in a matter of weeks. The time a band has to germinate has shrunken incrementally. Hardy concurs, "Yeah, friends tell me about bands now, I check them out on MySpace, and the next person I talk to has already heard about them. But I think that's a good thing overall, that it's so much easier for young people to get new music today."

But if he heard about the Gories today, and a week later a hundred people were e-mailing him about them, would it perhaps dissuade him from putting out their records? Is it possible that maybe part of the appeal of these bands is their outsider status? "Well, as long as they're good, as long as I like them, yeah, I would put out a record," says Har-dy. "If anything, [the Internet] might've made the Gories more popu-lar. They seem like a band that should've been bigger than they were. They didn't tour much, and obviously it was raw and not for everybody. But it was accessible enough. Most people I know who heard them liked them a lot."

*

AND MANY FIRST heard of the Gories and the rest of Hardy's world of bluesy-woozy through the pages of Jay Hinman's fanzine, *Superdope*. A classic B&W job, it was the first zine I saw (very early '90s) that mashed the aesthetic of old Cramps B-movie-festooned flyers and the amphetamine arts of the Crypt catalog and totally championed the lot of loons Crypt and In the Red were following.

"*Superdope* was not a garage punk magazine per se," says Hinman, "but it was being published when all those amazing garage punk 45s were coming out, and consequently I was writing about that stuff a ton. It was revelatory for me, and in retrospect I'm still surprised that there were very few fanzines focused on this stuff at the time."

Hinman, like Larry Hardy, felt something was afoot. "In the early 1990s," says Hinman, "it seemed like all of the best and most raw bands were getting their material put out by In The Red or Crypt. If those labels passed on you, then you got to put your stuff out on Sympathy. If even he passed on you—and he didn't pass on much—then you had to settle for putting your record out on Dionysus or by yourself. . . . Larry Hardy was and remains the most humble, approachable record label mogul I've ever met. I think when he was putting out those early In the Red 45s, there was not much thought toward making anything approaching a living from it. Back then, Hardy was a married grocery clerk at Safeway, a total Orange County lifer. He also happened to have the most amazing collection of vinyl, weird films, and collectibles I've ever seen. And he was very free and cool about making compilation tapes for people who might be interested in his oddball records."

Many of the bands *Superdope* slobbered over are still active today. Though the classic bands that these bands got critically compared to— New York Dolls, Electric Eels, Dead Boys, Saints, Pagans, Crime—only released one or two records and were done under four years. The assumption was always that these kind of high-energy bands were too fucked up to stick around. Maybe people want their crazy bands to burn out quickly, either to perpetuate familiar rock myths, or as a way to assuage their own unexciting existences. Like, how can anyone have that much fun for that long?

WELL, THE CHEATER Slicks don't always look like they're having fun per se, but they keep plugging along. "Yeah, that's a weird one," Hardy says. "And they still sound exactly the same. I think they'll go until a couple

Superdope zine, issue No. 8, 1998.

of them die. I can't think of another band that's like that, besides the Stones!" Making the longevity of the Slicks even more interesting is that they've always polarized the garage crowd. Retro royalty Estrus Records had no doubts when they released a Cheater Slicks single in 1992. "I went to Garage Shock that year, as the Cheater Slicks were playing it on their first West Coast trip. All that crowd was there, some guys from Satan's Pilgrims, A-Bones, etc. Then the Slicks get up and play all the shit on *Don't Like You* really loud. Sonically, they sounded closer to the first Jesus & Mary Chain record than a garage band. It was great! But, and I'm not exaggerating, *everyone* left the room, even the guy working the bar! It went over like a fart in church. And after that, no one talked to them. I remember thinking, Everyone tells me I have a garage label, but garage rock fans don't like the shit I put out, that's for sure!"

Nonetheless, Hardy stuck with the Cheater Slicks through thin and thin. "At one time I would definitely say they were the flagship artist of what I'm doing. I fucking love them, but they're not always the easiest people to deal with—though I guess that could be said about any of the best bands."

"We had such a connection to In the Red," says Tom Shannon [Cheater Slicks singer/guitarist]. "We were one and the same. Let's just say it was a failure of communication on both sides over a fairly long period of time that led to the disintegration. We have had a very rough time of it after leaving In the Red. We're still a working band but have no support from the music establishment—no label, no booking agent, no representation of any kind. In a sense we don't exist. But still, being on small labels has allowed us to do things we would not have done had we stayed on ITR. It pushed us in a different direction, and it hardened us. Our next record will be through Columbus Discount Records. Good people, close to home, and they're doing good stuff."

WEIRD VIBES WERE also raised sometimes between old pals Hardy and Tim Warren of Crypt Records when the two labels started taking off in the mid-'90s. Especially when Crypt reissued the first two Gories albums, released their third one, and then put out the debut from the Fireworks, a crankabilly crew from Texas whose leader, Darin Lin Wood (formerly of NYC band Black Snakes) then formed the garage punk supergroup Blacktop, with Mick Collins of the Gories. It seemed to most that Crypt was the natural home for Blacktop's debut album, although In the Red had released Gories and Fireworks singles too, and Hardy originally suggested the Blacktop hookup. But the arms dealing going on between the small cabal of noisy garage labels who rarely dealt with legally binding contracts meant any new crew was fair game. Bruised egos healed quickly. In fact, for a short while in the mid-'90s, Crypt even shared office space with In the Red in L.A. That setup went south, as the louse who was "working" for Crypt there ended up swiping cash from the label in various ways, resulting in Warren posting said louse's full name and social security number on the front cover of a Crypt catalog.

Ultimately, Blacktop's one and only album, *I've Got a Baaad Feeling About This* (1995), came out on In the Red and remains one of the best albums of this saucy strata—a groovy barrage of hazardous hooks, Gories-styled fritzy garage pound, echo-abilly, and noir-y nighttime

In the Red ad, 1995.

Route 66 ruminating, via Collins at perhaps his dirty vocal height. He told me that after Blacktop, he changed his singing technique to save his voice for what would become the long journey of his next band, the Dirtbombs.

"Blacktop lasted almost exactly fourteen months," says Collins, "from the day we formed the band to the final fuck-you." And from Collins's telling, that was more than enough time to deal with Darin Lin Wood. When I informed Collins that I came across a MySpace page of some new project from Lin Wood, he said, "Really? He's still alive? I couldn't care less where Darin Lin Wood is right now. I was told that at some point he found Jesus, but I have trouble believing that."

BY 1992, LED by In the Red, Crypt, Sympathy, and Estrus's action, there was suddenly a bubbling garage bounty to be pillaged. Then down Memphis way, the Oblivians—the trio of Greg Cartwright, Jack Yarber, and Eric Friedl (they all used the Ramones' band-name-as-last-name tack then)—detonated onto the crap-fi scene like a gas-filled balloon lobbed into a smoke-flavored Southern saloon haunted by the hell-held, hooch-addled ghosts of bluesmen past, but currently occupied by some grunge-sickened punks hankering for their next fix. While the Oblivians might've seemed like triplets squeezed out of some meth mom, there was, of course, some gestation to be done.

"My mother's side of the family were total rednecks," Cartwright says, "bizarre backwoods people. I don't say that disparagingly, that's just what they are. Most of them are in jail now. But they were into country music, Elvis, etc. I also inherited my dad's family's old records, a lot of weird Memphis label 45s that were never on the radio anymore. That stuff was totally mysterious to me."

Digging on new wave by the early '80s, Cartwright soon met up with slightly older bar bander Yarber, to form the Compulsive Gamblers. "Jack was coming from Mississippi, and a few years older," Cartwright says. "So in his puberty it was all mid-'70s rock, but Velvets and Stooges too. He had a great band in 1980, Johnny Vomit & the Dry Heaves, so he totally got the whole punk thing. We started the Painkillers around 1989. It was kinda punky, but the 'punk' scene in Memphis was a straight-edge hardcore-only thing. There was no audience for what the Painkillers were doing. Then when we morphed into the Compulsive Gamblers, got more country around the edges, a weird bar band, horns, kind of loungey thing—there was even less of an audience!"

Like a prodigal uncle, former Gibson Brothers front man Jeff Evans stumbled into Memphis from Columbus around 1989, attempting to track down mythological Americana ghosts, but finding only a severely depressed locale, albeit one with a simmering music scene. He soon formed '68 Comeback, a loose collective whose lineup (an all-star cast of early-'90s rural-garage boozers) frequently shifted. But its sound— the Gibson Brothers' scruffy hick-amble turned tougher via a Stones at their most opiated, with radiating distortion, and Evans's lover laments that went from unintentionally funny to unmitigatedly irate—subtly but surely spray-painted the garage scene. Once again, the Velvet Underground axiom applies here.

"I loved them!" says Friedl. "Jeff Evans is kind of a local hero. That first '68 Comeback lineup, with Peg O'Neill [Gories] on drums, was just amazing!" But come time for their first U.S. tour in 1992, O'Neill wasn't down for the idea, and Cartwright agreed to try his hand at the skins.

"I went out with '68 Comeback for two months—even though I'd never played drums before in my life" says Cartwright. "It was awesome, but a total nightmare too. Two junkie disasters; Dan Brown (bass), one of the most talented guys I ever played with; and then Jeff. The Gibson Brothers had garnered some attention, so this was Jeff's new band—but nobody was showing up at the gigs. It really demoralized him for a while."

The most fruitful outcome of that tour for Cartwright was the drumming. "I was spending every waking moment trying to play like Peggy," he says, "because that's the way I knew those songs. I played standing up, pretty much broke it down raw like her. So when I got home from that tour, I'd mastered those beats, and that's when we were starting the Oblivians. We were all fans of the Gories already, but I think that '68 Comeback experience is what made the Oblivians sound like the Oblivians."

And making the rounds with Jeff Evans meant Cartwright was crashing on the floors of the nascent trash-punk underworld—meeting Dave Crider (Estrus) in Seattle, and Larry Hardy (In the Red) and Long Gone John (Sympathy) in L.A. "It was cool finding out that there was a place out there somewhere for what we were doing," says Cartwright. "And Eric turned me on to the Mummies and all that stuff, as he was doing *Wipeout* zine and writing for other zines. He knew about all these new bands."

"Jack and Greg had started hanging out at Shangri-La Records, where I worked at the time," says Friedl, "and they'd let me get onstage and sing a Sonics or Billy Childish cover occasionally. [While Greg was on the road with '68 Comeback], Jack and I wrote a bunch of songs. When Greg came back to town, he got behind the drums for some of those songs, and we were off. Once we played "Vietnam War Blues," everything just kinda went BOOM!"

"We'd rehearse at Shangri-La Records after closing," Cartwright recalls. "Eric was just learning how to play these crude riffs, single-string stuff, with a lot of fuzz. Of course Jack's always been a great drummer. So then we started switching around instruments. It's the way most bands work out demos—but for us it became the style of our band."

Explosive Oblivians singles came fast and furious, (sometimes too fast to notice how catchy the songs were, and how achingly doo-woppy Cartwright's songwriting was getting).

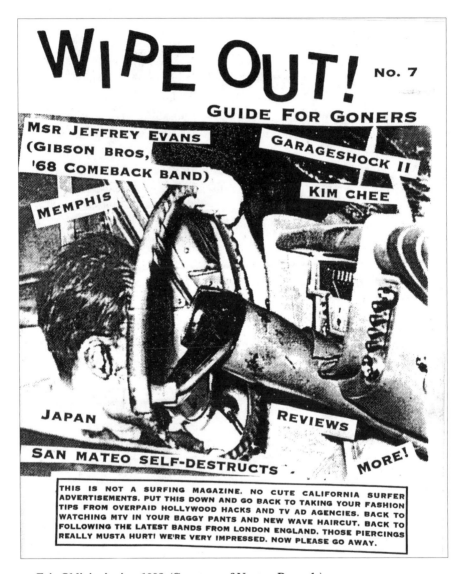

Eric Oblivian's zine, 1993. (Courtesy of Norton Records)

"It was a new age of the single," says Cartwright. "It had become a viable commercial tool again, after it had died in the '60s. All of the sudden here was this little subculture!" But now, unlike 7" bands of yore, these new groups were not restrained by "proper" studio time limits or costs. "There was always some hip guy in every town who had some kind of tape machine in his basement or whatever. For us, it was Doug Easley who was recording people in his backyard. But what really changed everything in the late '80s was the four-track recorder. It really revolutionized music for people like me. You could now tape tunes at home in a casual way you couldn't do before. And you wouldn't even want to record them in some proper studio, because they sound so perfect to you."

Additionally, since bands would now craft their stuff at home on the cheap, little indie labels wouldn't have to pony up for studio costs. So any guy who could afford to press up five hundred singles and buy a few fanzine ads was now a record label mogul. "It was just simpler for everyone to get involved," Cartwright says.

The name "Oblivians" was on the slobbering lips of every fan of fuzz guitar the summer of 1994, and indie trash-punk labels got a crash course in the concept of a "bidding war." Of course, in this universe, a bidding war promises not million-dollar deals and opening slots for U2, but instead a loose goal of colored vinyl pressings and a shmancy screen-printed poster for that Louisville gig next month. That was fine with Cartwright, who had already crapped out a moldy major label lunch when he'd lived in NYC for a couple years in the late '80s.

"I moved up there to play guitar in this band, Casey Scott and the Creeps. The Gamblers' bassist was college roommates with Scott. She was part of that 'antifolk' thing going on then. We did an album for Capitol. No contract for me, I just got paid union wage. The record's not very good, but it was a fun experience. But I saw her record get made, not pushed, and immediately become a cutout. And I thought, Man, what a drag!"

By the time the Oblivians finally started playing out, "a drag" was not the term that came to mind. Onstage, you could see whatever dysfunctional family shit there must've been inside Cartwright scrunching out of his face as he strangled his guitar neck and bellowed with a deeper reservoir of regret than you usually get from this ilk. Yarber, though as nice as can be to chat with, even shy, came over like an "energy pack"-packed trucker on his twenty-seventh straight hour of driving through God's country. And Friedl held a look in his eyes and the occasional smart-aleck insult out of his sneer like he was the little brother who always got interrupted.

After their first NYC-area gigs with the Jon Spencer Blues Explosion in early 1993, Spencer, lid duly flipped, sent some Oblivians demos to Tim Warren, which led to the first of the band's three Crypt albums, *Soul Food* (1995)—meaning the trio was soon receiving legend-

OBLIVIANS

JACK OBLIVIAN - Guitar, Vocal, Drums
GREG OBLIVIAN - Guitar, Vocal, Drums
ERIC OBLIVIAN - Guitar, Vocal, Drums

LP/CD "SOUL FOOD" (CRYPT-054) out FEB. 1 1995

ON TOUR IN EUROPE MAY-JUNE 1995
BOOKING COORDINATION:
BOOMBASTIC TEL (49)040-310089   FAX (49)040-310406

CRYPT RECORDS:
Europe: P.O. BOX 304292, 20325 HAMBURG, GERMANY. TEL (49)040-3174503 FAX 313522

USA: P.O. BOX 140528, STATEN ISLAND, New York 10314-0528

Manufactured & Distributed in North America by MATADOR RECORDS, 676 Broadway, N.Y. N.Y. 10012 tel (212)995-5882 fax 5883

Photo : Jim Cole

Crypt Records press photo, 1995.

arily wacko faxes from Warren. "Eric showed up at a rehearsal with this fax," Cartwright recalls, "and I think it started off with, 'Fuck that Stray Cat–abilly faggot!!' It was an insane six-page rant about how Darin Lin Wood ripped him off, that whole mess with Blacktop. . . . I'd worked with Darin in '68 Comeback, and I've got to say, he was not a pleasure to be around. But he did make some pretty good Fireworks records. So that fax was funny, but then we all kind of looked at each other and said, 'Wow, did we just make a bad decision signing with this crazy guy?" I liked Tim, his manic 'maybe he's on coke, maybe he's not' take on life, which is exciting to be around. And if you're going to be on someone's label, you want them to be excited."

Of course, Tim's accounting "skills" were as infamous as his faxes. "Yeah, I'd say he was on the shady side," says Cartwright. "You never knew exactly what was going on, especially with the tours Tim would book. One of our records was reprinted like three times without us knowing. Almost ten years passed and we got nothing, nothing. But I've buried my hatchet with Tim. Now he sends us like a check a year for a couple hundred bucks, and statements sometimes. I have no idea if they're accurate, but he's making an attempt."

Us mugs must make do with all the killer memories. Like when the Oblivians went over for their first European tour, on a double bill with the latest Crypt signing, the mind-melting Scottish psychos the Country Teasers.

"We'd never heard or met them," Cartwright remembers. "And as soon as we started playing with them, we thought, 'Oh my God, I can't believe Tim is into this!' They were like John Wayne's Texas Funeral meets Joy Division. It's true, Tim is a music Nazi—but he's not narrow-minded. The Country Teasers were amazing. Every day was hilarity. They were some wild, drinkin', crazy people, with a really dark sense of humor, and who loved to pick fights that they could not win. The show in Amsterdam was both of us opening for the Chesterfield Kings. So the Teasers just insulted the Chesterfield Kings the entire set, right at the front of the stage. 'Fuck you, you idiots!' They'd even made these quick homemade signs with 'You Suck!' 'Fuck You!'

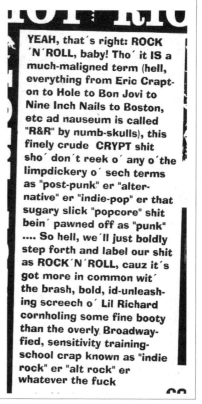

YEAH, that´s right: ROCK 'N'ROLL, baby! Tho' it IS a much-maligned term (hell, everything from Eric Crapton to Hole to Bon Jovi to Nine Inch Nails to Boston, etc ad nauseum is called "R&R" by numb-skulls), this finely crude CRYPT shit sho´ don´t reek o´ any o´the limpdickery o´ sech terms as "post-punk" er "alternative" er "indie-pop" er that sugary slick "popcore" shit bein´ pawned off as "punk" .... So hell, we´ll just boldly step forth and label our shit as ROCK´N´ROLL, cauz it´s got more in common wit´ the brash, bold, id-unleashing screech o´ Lil Richard cornholing some fine booty than the overly Broadway-fied, sensitivity training-school crap known as "indie rock" er "alt rock" er whatever the fuck

Portion of a jam-packed Crypt mag ad, 1995.

Flyer from France, 1995. (Courtesy of Yvan Serrano Fontova)

Now the Kings were not wimpy guys, a couple of them were real bruis-
ers, and they were really mad. 'As soon as this set's over we're gonna
kick all of yer asses!' And the Teasers are just laughin' and laughin'. . . .

"So the set's over, the Kings rush out to the parking lot to get to the
Teasers, who are now totally shit-faced and still talking shit—these little
tiny Scottish guys. And one of the Kings grabs the Teasers guitarist and
starts threatening him bad, about to really tear into him. And the Teasers guitarist goes, 'Oh, yer a big man, picking on the wee li-ill faggot,
like me. Ho, you're a big man!' He's out of his mind drunk, but using
this amazing psychology on the guy. So after five minutes of this, the
Kings guy pushed him away and says, 'All right, I'm not even gonna
fuck with you, you faggot!' And it defuses the whole situation. It was
amazing to behold."

On the plane home from their second Japanese tour, the Oblivians decided to call it a day. Cartwright soon turned some solo work—an outgrowth from the Oblivians final, gospel-tinged album, *Play 9 Songs with Mr. Quintron* (1997), predominantly written by Cartwright—into his current band, the Reigning Sound, whose crunchy croon tunes have developed a wider following. But all along, somewhere inside the three-headed dog that was the Oblivians, lurked the kind of true songwriters that squares will never have the pleasure of experiencing because the band didn't smile nice, wear clean shirts, and remix that shit. The gunk-punk underground, however, found another tipsy template, laying out where lo-fi garage punk could jump off of from here on out. . . .

BUT LOOKING BACK was still au courant. By the late 1980s, Andre Williams was a forgotten Detroit-based R&B howler who had a few stunningly sleazy regional hits for Fortune in the early '60s, even did a stint on Motown in the mid-'60s, then spent time Chess Records, went into the ubiquitous, drug-addled, ripped-off-African-American-musician decline, and by the early '80s was living on the streets. But a resuscitation began later that decade.

"Credit really needs to go to George Paulus of St. George Records in Chicago," says Billy Miller. "George organized a session, and we agreed that Norton would do the vinyl, so that's how *Greasy* came about. I remember Andre canceled one vocal session because he'd left his teeth at a party. That was 1995.

"I took Andre into the studio here in New York a while later. He was asking me about Larry at In the Red. I told him they had a real good rep. He said, 'They want me to make a *garage* record. What do you suppose he means?' I told him that they want it raw and not too slick. I believe I even said, for the one and only time in my life, 'Let it all hang out.' Andre said, 'I can handle that!'

"So Tim Warren wanted to license the first Andre Williams album I did on In the Red, *Silky* [1998], for Europe," Hardy says, "and when we didn't do it, he got upset about that too." Then again, maybe not getting wrapped up in Williams's world was fortuitous for Crypt. Andre Williams's comeback was a great story but often caused as many painful headaches as pulled heartstrings. Once hooked up with former Gories Mick Collins (who by now had his Dirtbombs rolling) and Dan Kroha (who was staining stages with his wild trio, Demolition Doll Rods), Williams was back-slapped into making *Silky*, which was not only a fine come-back of sweaty-sack, juke-joint foot-stomp and gut-busting innuendo (if a song called "Let Me Put It In" qualifies as innuendo), but simultaneously yanked many a garage purist's ear back further into the R&B base of the genre. *Silky* was a steamy musical muff dive as history lesson.

The few gigs with Collins and Kroha backing Williams are legendary for their meld of two messy eras of garage gunk fun; and for the first couple years of the comeback, Williams was able to secure other solid backup bands, like the Countdowns and the Sadies. All of which led to one of the most welcome, if bizarre, comeback stories in music history. This was no old boomer playing the House of Blues to graybeards griping about two-drink minimums 'tween Motown covers. Williams was packing the dive bar circuit with the trash rock crowd and a growing college contingent that got giggles from hearing senior citizens yalp naughty words.

Williams stood over six foot two, always decked out in a spectacularly peepers-popping pimp suit, wide hat, and even wider sly grin, rambling around the stage just ready to keel over, but then letting out subterranean growls and pinpoint leers right at the cuties down front. And though near thirty years removed from his first tour life, Williams was not cutting back on his vices, be they femme or pharmaceutical.

"That was the weirdest experience of my career," Hardy admits. "Dealing with Andre could be very difficult. No matter how much money is handed to him, he's going to blow through it in one glorious party. Then, when he sobers up, he cries foul. And of course it's the white guy with the record label who fucked him over. I often wondered if it was a bad thing we did, to get him involved in all that again. At first it was like, Cool, a new lease on life. His records are selling, he's making money, getting all these offers for big shows. And apparently he'd been homeless for years, really on the skids, but he'd cleaned himself up. But it was like, Jesus, this guy can't be around this stuff, drinking all day, being around drugs again. . . . You'd see these horrible shows later on where he's too drunk to be onstage, and he can only remember one line from every song, and there're all these white kids cheering him on and laughing, 'I can't wait to hear him say "pussy" again!' But when he comes through town, it's all friendly, he's nice to me, and he acknowledges that I'd done him a good thing. He was constantly asking to borrow money. He's so charming, you love him, and he's this old guy you really respect. And you're like, Okay, I'll loan you three hundred bucks. 'Thanks. I just gotta get my suit out of the dry cleaners.'"

Williams has since sobered up and recently released his first novel.

*

BUT EVEN THE historically gone tendencies of Andre Williams paled in the face of the gargantuan ingestions of the Necessary Evils, a stupor group concocted of pieces from the demise of the great late-'80s/early-'90s psych-garage monsters the Beguiled, a guitarist from the Fireworks, and even a fine British bloke, Jimmy Hole (who had worked publicity at Epitaph Records). They seemed like a sure-ish thing.

"They were a band I thought were going to make a real stand because there was an interest in them right away," Hardy recalls. "But they were so untogether. All the reasons they were amazing were all the reasons that they were never going to last. Way out of control guys. Driving to Las Vegas from L.A. for a show, and the very first gas station we stop at, Steve Pallow (singer, guitarist; aka Steve Sherman, aka Haunted George), has an eighteen-pack of Pabst, and he's pounding them by himself. Halfway there, they're empty, and he's going to get another one. By the time you get to Vegas, he can't walk or talk. Then finding out that after I went to bed some of them went off to smoke crack. That was the tour when the drummer had fallen out a window, landed flat, and broke both of his feet."

Needless to say, the Necessary Evils never got around to much touring, despite two albums and a couple singles of psychotic, fiery, fractured fuzz bombs hurled as if from the grips of jalapeño-fed gorillas.

"This one Vegas show," Hardy recalls, "they decided to do mushrooms before they played. They got onstage and suddenly felt like gods. Slam pits, amazing. But [unbeknownst] to them, there were fights breaking out in the crowd, jocks beating up on people including [guitarist] James Arthur's wife. Jimmy Hole wasn't aware of the fact that there were these fights going on, even if the show was shut down because of all the fights. Then Jimmy went outside afterwards, and there were these big guys beating up on Tommy Times [teen leader of the wild, Devil Dogs–bitten punk band the L.A. Times]. Jimmy stepped in and wound up getting a baseball bat right across the mouth, his front teeth shattered out. Then at five in the morning, they've been on coke all night, go to a stripper club, and there's Jimmy Hole—front row at the club, still in his bloodstained shirt, giving dollar bills to strippers and rubbing coke on his bloody mouth to kill the pain! They were *that* kind of band."

WHILE THE BEGUILED-cum-Necessary-Evils flung noisy dung through West Coast dives, the Humpers helped save slash 'n' burn gutter-glam from the hit it took on the Sunset Strip during the '80s hair metal era.

"There are a lot of angry people in Southern California that are living a life that isn't shown on the TV," says singer Scott Drake. "The Humpers were from the working-class areas of North Orange County and Long Beach. We were all working manual labor–type jobs: construction, house painting, truck driving. We couldn't have been further removed from that Sunset Strip attitude. We detested that whole scene."

Asking someone like Drake to toss out a few crazy stories is kind of like asking chef Lidia Bastianich how many of her recipes call for garlic. So instead, Drake just rattled off a scrappy short list: "Okay, we got kicked off a tour by the Meteors after two shows . . . got into a scuffle with wrestlers in San Francisco . . . crossed the U.S. in winter in an old van with no heat (it finally broke down right outside CBGB) . . . Billy fell down the stairs in Germany onto a pile of broken glass. . . . Jimi and I got into a fight in Denver and broke a giant plateglass window, so the band left me there, passed out on a bus bench. . . . The ceiling collapsed on us while doing a garage gig in Austin, Texas . . . . We went to the nude beach in Marbella, Spain, and by the end of the night, Jimi was high as hell and running naked through the streets, howling like a wolf. . . . In Lisbon there was a large contingent of gay kids who were convinced we were representing queer America. . . . We played at the Lesbian Film Collective in Berlin, but it turned into a brawl when some people from the venue noticed our bus driver watching pornos in the bus. They said he was exploiting women. Meanwhile, there was a giant adult bookstore right across the street that no one seemed offended by. . . . In the Netherlands, Gas Huffer presented us with a giant bottle of Czech white lightning, which Jimi took one slug from and then dropped in a giant crash all over the dressing room floor. Bastard!"

WHEN YOU'RE A touring band, there occur a vast array of such ordeals. Like the times where you have to haggle with a bar owner for an hour just to get the extra ten dollars of "percentage" on top of the sixty-five-dollar guarantee. You drive seven hours to a gig in Albuquerque, only to find out the promoter gave you the wrong date. You get home from a long tour, ready to plop in front of the TV, and the electricity has been shut off. And on and on . . . Then there are moments when a thousand kids at a Netherlands festival are simultaneously jumping up and down to a beat the four of you drunkenly jammed up on a Tuesday afternoon a year earlier because you didn't have any riffs ready for practice. Or a sixteen-year-old shyly says hello after a show, then later writes you a letter to say that your songs encouraged him to stand up to the fucking bullies and come out of the closet already. Or a Croatian guy e-mails to say he wrote "Destroy-Oh-Boy" on his helmet and blasted that album through his Walkman as he shot at his former neighbors during the Bosnian conflict. Well, that was just kind of weird. Sometimes the highs and lows are the same.

10.

BUMPED BY KARAOKE

L"O-FI" IS A descriptor that has long ago moved beyond a default rock critic adjective and settled into a wide-reaching designation that encompasses so many sounds as to have attained the useless ubiquity of the word *rock* itself. Today, most would attach "lo-fi" to scruffy, melodic pop bands that prefer a purposely fuzzy recording style—except that most current bands who employ that tactic tend to do everything on Pro Tools, utilizing umpteen tracks and samples to evoke that hundred-times-rerecorded-over analog cassette skizz.

Now dig, I'm not saying that some cat in a Minneapolis weekly didn't use "lo-fi" in a Michael Yonkers review in 1969 or something. But honestly, I never really heard the term lo-fi consistently tossed around as a singular musical adjective until hearing it fired out the gush of Craig Regala.

Regala was the mad scientist behind Datapanik Records, the Columbus, Ohio, independent label he began in 1989. When first spotted knocking elbows around Columbus shows back then, he stuck out like a soaring thumb—or middle finger, as it were. The Columbus scene tended to be populated by either slacker collegiates, tie-dyed types, frat/sorority schmucks, or new country music–weaned townies, all counting down the days until they "get out of this fuckin' town" (knowing full well they probably won't because Columbus is a pretty nice place). Despite obvious social differences, most twentysomethings tended toward lethargic, couch-on-the-front-porch time killing—or "pot," to be succinct.

Into this muted milieu came Regala—muscular, tattooed, and clean-cut, shooting off loud and bracingly intelligent denigrations of hippies of any stripe, informing you straightaway how potentially bad your favorite band was, then bouncing away to instigate mosh pits with a silly crouched-down, arms-waving motion that was, oddly, not unlike a bad hippie dance. (Found out later he liked Amon Düül II as much as Agnostic Front.)

Regala, like a number of other slightly more seasoned rock types in town, came to Columbus figuring it'd be a good place to dry out. Well, if switching up expensive heroin for cheap rent, cheaper weed, and the cheapest beer was your idea of drying out, Columbus was Mt. Olympus.

High Street was the main drag in Columbus. It ran right up from the old southern suburbs, through the dead downtown, the gingerly gentrifying Short North art gallery/sex-shop haven, right past the main OSU campus on the left and all the bars and fast food joints on the right, through the graduate student–matriculated north end of campus, where unemployed English majors would marvel that Phil Ochs used to hang out at Larry's Bar, and finally back into more postwar suburbs, eventually leading to I-71, which would take you up to Cleveland.

Dick's Den was a friendly old haunt that stood right at the end of the north campus bar crawl. The walls were blotched with fading Polaroids of '70s softball league teams, broken neon signs, and yet more photos of Woody Hayes; a pool table and pinball machine occupied the back, and a big front window looked right out on all the cars zipping by. Every Wednesday at Dick's Den, a glass of Blatz was twenty-five cents; a pitcher of same was $1.50.

Right across the street shoved into a dilapidated '60s strip center was the great and grimy Stache's. Formerly a Polish restaurant, it was the main rock hub for local and national acts in the 1990s. Local welfare poets to Nirvana graced the warped wood of the stage. Of course, every band coveted Wednesday night slots at Stache's because of the happy hopscotch between the two clubs. And two doors down from Dick's was the late-night diner, the Blue Danube, a cool old haunt (supposedly the popular kids' hangout in the 1940s) that offered gravy fries and other crap that soaked up beer like a sponge, and featured an amazingly private, enclosed working phone booth that made you feel like a film noir mob informant dropping a tip.

The cover at Stache's on Wednesdays was often zilch-o, assuring you'd have every penny ready for Dick's Den's boozy bounty, and a primed stomach of steam heading into the Stache's show. . . . When Dick's Den eventually became a madhouse on Wednesday nights, the bar doubled the price to fifty cents a glass and $2.50 a pitcher. The next week, the place was near empty in protest.

For about four years, there was a nice little ladder Columbus music fans and bands could climb up High Street. Right at the end of the Short North was Apollo's, set up in the second tier of another decaying '60s strip mall. Those kind of postwar cheapies made up the bulk of High Street's "architecture," hanging askew along the street like torn two-dollar prints across the back wall of a thrift store.

Stumble up a few blocks and you find Bernie's Bagels and its attached bar, the Distillery, which felt like a step up (or down—it was in the basement of a bank). Bernie's had been booking local acts since the '70s, though the roster leaned heavily toward the patchouli-and-patchy-jeans jive. It didn't exactly scream "punk rock ruckus," but that's what started to blast out of the place around 1991 when bands like ours, Gaunt, Greenhorn, Pica Huss, and others started asking if they could fill the room with something other than CSNY covers. There was usually no cover charge, and you'd (maybe) get 15 percent of the bar take, which in Columbus is always a winning deal. More punk spew started to sprout from Bernie's stinky soil, like the pogo-galumph of Moody Jackson; Clay, who made like the Minutemen as loopy Saturday morning kids' TV show hosts; and My White Bread Mom, a kind of Dead Kennedys carved with a potato peeler into central-Ohio whippet huffers.

At its busiest (1991–'96), Bernie's was the axis point of the Columbus scene—well, unless you considered the stench of human waste wafting through the pipes two feet above your head to be a detriment. Today, most of my Columbus cohorts can't remember the last time they went there. Still, it stands, directly across the street from the middle of the largest university in the United States, giving gigs to hopeful youngins, and defying the city fathers to come up with a better idea. If it weren't there, an Old Navy would be. 'Nuff said.

AFTER WE'D ONLY hung with Craig Regala a couple times at some of our early shows, he'd released some fine local-band singles already and asked us all to meet at Larry's to discuss releasing our first record, which he envisioned as a split single with our pals Gaunt. That record came out spring 1991, the sixth Datapanik release. We released a four-song EP on Datapanik in early 1992. Gaunt released the classic "Jim Motherfucker" 7" soon after that (co-released with new local indie, Anyway

Records), and Regala had his Datapanik Records idea going strong, if not for long.

One of my favorite Regala summations of the Datapanik aim was "Three chords and a cloud of dust," a pun on the phrase made famous by Columbus's defrocked high priest, OSU football coach Woody Hayes, describing his offensive philosophy "Three yards and a cloud of dust." Datapanik's anti-fi aesthetic arose because how the hell else were we going to record if not in a basement with Jerry Wick's three-and-a-half-track Tascam ("Cornhole Studio"). Then, if you wallow in it long enough, your ear gets used to it, and one man's abrasive din is another man's excuse to turn it up. The first Datapanik CD compilation from 1992, *Bumped by Karaoke*, was, by title and tinnitus, the perfect Regala statement of such. The insanely muddy moxie of it—featuring nearly every band of note in the region from the early '90s—is the label's crowning crud-fi achievement.

"I enjoyed the activity and a bit of the music," says Regala, "but overall it eventually pointed in a direction that meant little to me. I focused Datapanik on the stuff in my backyard. I used to say culture comes from the Midwest, you only think it comes from the coasts because, like heroin or fresh fish, that's where its ass gets peddled. But I got out, and in essence 'went metal,' following my natural instincts. Anyway Records continued the job I wasn't interested in."

JOHAN KUGELBERG SEEMED a continent away from Craig Regala, which he was. Kugelberg was an eight-foot-tall suave Swedish cat, brief de facto manager of Union Carbide Productions, and legendary collector scum. He was working for Matador Records in the early '90s, and booked New Bomb Turks for our first Big Apple–area gig, at a warehouse space in the pre-gentrifying Bushwick hood of Brooklyn, in the summer of 1992.

'Twas a doozy, the kind of rickety boho warehouse loft gig a Cleveland kid dreams of when reading his first *Creem* magazine Warhol Factory reminiscence in ninth grade. Four floors up to a rust-crusted, twenty-foot-ceiling stink tank that had, in its "glory" days probably offered endless hours of back-breaking steel forging and eventual lung cancer for the union ghosts whose moans of "Faggots!" were luckily not traveling well in the dense, stale humidity that night. A no-doubt delusional artist had covered the crumbling walls with tons of shredded cotton-ball material. And broken-padlock side doors led to pitch-black, junk-strewn rooms perfect for what pitch-black rooms are perfect for at rock shows. About seventy-five-plus people showed up in a part of town they wouldn't have paid their crooked landlords to go streaking through in 1992.

That night we shared the, uh, plywood wobble box with Philly noise-folkers the Strapping Fieldhands, and fellow Columbusites, V-3. During their early-'80s to early-'90s wellspring, V-3 and leader Jim Shepard created piles of some of the most pavement-crawling, heavens-decrying art punk Pere Ubu never got around to. They're a legend in Ohio amongst people who are sure that music is their salvation, while knowing that's a dying subject, especially once Shepard sadly shook this coil, hanging himself in 1999.

KUGELBERG CONCOCTED THE first four volumes of *Killed by Death* in the very early '90s. Named after a Motörhead song, for no apparent reason, the *Killed by Death* compilations (or "*KBD*" as they've become eBay abbreviated) were basically the *Back from the Graves* for the original punk rock era—quasi-legit collections of forgotten vinyl singles or cassette demos that straight history assumed had slumped off to a dark corner somewhere to decompose.

The original four *KBD*s contained songs from unimaginably obscure bands with names like the Lewd, the Hillside Stranglers, the Child Molesters, Mad Virgins, the Mad, S'nots, Huns, Mentally Ill, the Violators, and the Queers; and featuring lyrics of only the most depraved sentiments. Had these combos been bashing away in the mid-'60s, they would've tried to rewrite Stones and Sonics songs in their garages. Instead, they were teens when the Hughes Corporation, Bad Company, Debbie Boone, and Bread gooped out from their radios; Ramones records rumbled in the background at their local head shops; stepparents were popping Valium; and the economy offered little hope for anything beyond a job at the mall.

So spewed forth, around 1976–'81, while nobody was looking, a vast, oily pool of sub-fi, hate-filled, hilarious, and peculiarly powerful bile that, were it printed into vinyl batches at all, usually numbered around 317. The 150 that went unsold or unstolen warped away in basements until ten years later, looters like Kugelberg knocked on the front door of some born-again, post-AA ex-punk, hopefully catching them at just the right rent-overdue moment. "You'll give me fifty bucks for that crap?! Here ya go."

Cover of first *Killed by Death* compilation, 1989.

And like their post-*Nuggets* attitudinal antecedents, the *Killed by Death* comps—their template soon copied and bootlegged by punk collectors all over the world—led to many follow-up series like *Bloodstains Across*, which would focus on certain regions (*Bloodstains Across the Midwest*, *Bloodstains Across Texas*, and *Bloodstains Across Northern Ireland* being my personal faves). Famed rock critic Byron Coley drummed up the first three excellent volumes. And like the cheap treats these comps reintroduced, not only did their collector price bump up, but, since these latter-day comps themselves were made in limited runs on the cheap, they too became instantly collectible.

"The idea of contextualizing the sound of a certain scene was more interesting to me," says Coley. "The real concept had been to get rare sounds into people's hands for cheap. I'd do a thousand copies and usually sell them in one lump, or do a trade. I sold those albums for five dollars."

Back to Front was another fine lost punk comp series out of somewhere in the Black Forest of Germany, on a label called Incognito. And then there's *Hyped to Death*, a mind-bogglingly completist series of CD-only comps from an Indiana collector that spreads its tentacles all over the subgenres of the original "new wave." This only smudges the surface of this snowcapped stack.

*

SINCE CHEERILY UNCHAINING all that inspiring detritus, Johan Kugelberg has gone from low-browbeater to high-art gallery curator and Christie's punk auction catalog writer. Not that his office resembles a Manhattan art patron's mahogany-paneled den. The heap hovering around was half from Kugelberg's scatterbrained collector-itus, the other half from the fact he was in the process of packing up and shipping out a ton of stuff to some Euro museum for a Velvet Underground exhibit he was organizing.

Though Kugelberg's accent, vocabulary, and lanky posture may exude "upper crust," The Man will never completely surrender the keys of the high-pop-culture halls to someone who thinks the best musical venture Thurston Moore was ever involved with was a bootleg Venom 7" comprised only of the singer's in-between-song banter. Or who has, in a recent *Ugly Things* magazine, declared the entire musical output of 1985 to 1995 "The Suck Years."

––––––––––

JOHAN KUGELBERG: I was moving boxes in the basement of my house in Westchester, and there were like four boxes of 45s down there. It was basically like a '90s Matador promo avalanche, untouched since back then. Now we know that there were some really good records that came out back then. But the not-good-to-good ratio is frightening if you compare it to any other time in rock music history.

ERIC DAVIDSON: *I think the 2000s are going to catch up pretty quickly.*

JK: Well, I wave my old-guy flag high. And the very few times a year when I have one of my young, edgy friends hook me up with some new sounds, I end up being baffled. But you know what Asger Jorn said? Every avant-garde is incapable of recognizing its successor, because succession occurs through contradiction. That holds true for any underground music too. And in the words of the great poet Chris Rock, "There is nothing worse than being the oldest guy in the club." So whenever I see like fortysomething, fiftysomething hep cats who are still collecting the new limited-edition 7"s, or going backstage and high-fiving and stuff like that, I feel that certain kind of cold intestinal anxiety of "There but for the grace of God go I."

The idea, which is a baby boomer and post–baby boomer idea, that you can stay in touch, you can be a cool fifty- or sixty-year-old— it's a blatant, artificial lie and an aspect of the kid-cult identity of

Johan Kugelberg wonders how I snuck into his high-falutin' Velvet Underground gallery show in Manhattan, April 2007. (Photo by Lesley Kunikis)

the last four decades. . . . But the one aspect of retro-consumption culture that has a core nobility in it is the archival "dig where you stand." Digging in like "I dig it, man," but also digging deep. Pop culture has been fragmenting with increasing speed since the Age of Aquarius. And since we're talking about really marginal stuff here—marginal artists, marginal records, marginal fan scenes—it means that the time span it takes to separate the wheat from the chaff is two or three decades, easily. That's how long time it takes to get an overview of an aesthetic, without getting it too tainted by nostalgia.

ED: *Well, from the* Nuggets *rule of law, then the* Pebbles, *the* Back from the Grave, *and the* Killed by Death *comps, that span seems to have shrunk to about thirteen years.*

JK: But it's never cut-and-dried, and it's never a history of quantum leaps. It's a history of commerce, of necessity, and of distribution logistics as much as it's a history of passions, epiphanies, and spontaneity.

ED: *Like one of the things I've noticed about most of the bands I'm talking with is that their whole lo-fi aesthetic was most often just an economic necessity.*

JK: Yes, of course. Also, one of the things about *Nuggets* is that Lenny Kaye [guitarist for Patti Smith Group], who created *Nuggets*, just thinking about his deep roots in rock fandom and science-fiction fandom. And you know rock fandom is science-fiction fandom, right? Everybody who got involved in the rock fandom scene starting with *Mojo Navigator* and *Crawdaddy* in 1966 had a passion for science-fiction fandom. The idea of mimeographing those fanzines, distributing through the mail, the idea of the APA [Amateur Press Association]—where different people would send their fanzines to a central location to then get distributed—that's the history of the American rock fanzine prior to punk. Greg Shaw [*Bomp!* magazine/record label founder]had a long past in science-fiction fandom. Lenny Kaye did his first fanzine in 1959. It was called *Obilisk.* So the idea of fandom culture, of really navigating and searching in the realms of marginal, underdocumented fields of popular culture, that's where that idea actually came from. So in 1970–'71, when Lenny Kaye started talking to Jac Holzman at Elektra about the idea of doing *Nuggets,* this compilation of marginal 45s that were only released maybe five, six years ago, it was an almost absurdly great epiphany. Even though the term *punk rock* was widely used by the late '60s to describe American teenage bands aping the Stones, the Pretty Things, and the Dave Clark 5. So you also have to remember, before *American Graffiti*, there really wasn't the idea of retro consumption culture. This is something that certainly has been evolving, like in the early '70s, with the teddy boys in England and Sha Na Na in the U.S. looking back to the '50s. And another really interesting strand of rock fandom that already started in the very early '60s was there were people who compiled lists and discographies of rockabilly, R&B, and '50s rock 'n' roll records and circulated those in a fandom network to find out more about this music that they like. Which is of course how Alan Betrock's legendary magazine *Rock Marketplace* came about. Those zines didn't really have serious rock journalism or rock criticism in them, but there were certainly a part of that milieu. And the discussion of these records becomes like this holy quest because it was not a given that you could go to a record shop and find a 45 that was more than six months old. Or even an album that was older than six months. Things were cut out and deleted so quickly. So then Lenny Kaye comes from this angle of sifting for nuggets.

*ED: Couldn't it be that Kaye was already just sick of hearing about the Beatles, and wanted to expose more of the bands from that era? Many of the post-*Nuggets *'60s garage rarities comps certainly had that attitude: "Forget the Beatles, fuck the hippies—this is the real garage stuff the kids were dancing to."*

JK: The term *garage* is a later term, it's an '80s term because before the '80s it was known as "'60s punk," which is the term I still much prefer to use than "garage." The first *Pebbles* came out a couple of years after Seymour Stein reissued *Nuggets* in 1976. Then more of these rock fandom–generated '60s punk compilations came through the late '70s and early '80s. But they were few and far between.

ED: And then Pebbles, Boulders, Highs in the Mid-Sixties . . .

JK: Yeah, that was a little later. And then you have Tim Warren, who changed the game completely forever in 1984, with the first *Back from the Grave* compilation. Those comps, you can't fuck with them. They're like Picasso's *Guernica* or Caravaggio paintings or the Maine coastline or a perfect sausage-and-peppers hero. They are art that is so primeval and so perfect that you remain baffled by them decade after decade. Because Tim Warren doesn't have one atom of watered-down nostalgia in his bloodstream. He lives in an omnipresent now, and those *Back from the Grave*s are not about twenty years ago, or forty years ago, or "hard to find," or any of that. It's like Jackson Pollock—it's the pour. If you or I poured paint it would look like some asshole poured some paint. But when Jackson Pollock poured paint, it became beautiful. . . . I met in Tim Warren in 1984 in Sweden. Actually, the *Killed by Death*s was Tim's idea. He was like, "Oh, you should do a punk *Back from the Grave*." The first *Killed by Death* came out in May of 1988. I made a master tape and a record cover, but I just had no idea how to put a record out. So there was this guy here in NYC who did all kinds of clandestine record releases, and he was like, "I'll put it out for you." I think I made about four hundred dollars and twenty-five copies from each. . . . It's obviously very flattering that so many young ones have been so inspired by the series, but the mistake is to see me as the grandfather of *Killed by Death*. I certainly compiled the first four volumes, but I was following the lead of the two real fellows. In 1984, Tesco Vee of the Meatmen wrote an article in *Maximumrocknroll* about rare American '70s punk collecting, which blew all our minds. We had like Misfits, Minor Threat, and Black Flag records because we were skateboarders. But when we then found out about the Mad or the Nubs or the Pagans,

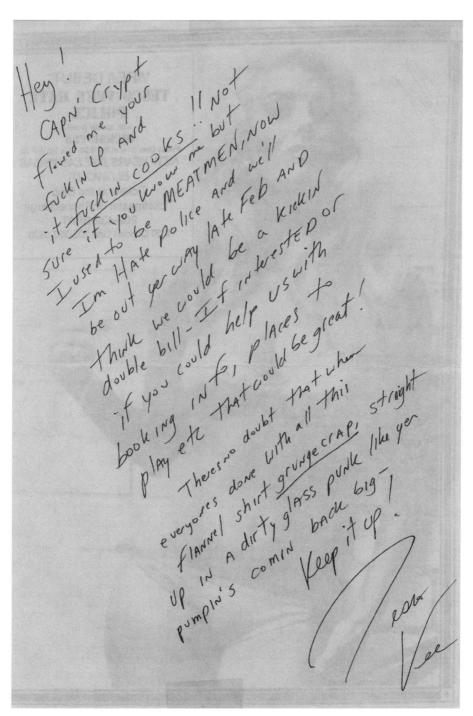

Letter to New Bomb Turks from Tesco Vee, 1993.

we couldn't believe it! And of course you had Chuck Warner's legendary record mail-order list; and those interesting Midnight Records and Venus Records store lists [two Manhattan-based stores, now closed]. Different people, record distributors, and mail-order operations had been buying all these records as they came out, but they'd been sitting in a warehouse for years, so you could still buy them. And obviously with no Internet, without those forms of mass communication, the intensity of and the thirst for knowledge was festering so severely that you spent easily fifteen to twenty hours of your week not sitting there searching for stuff on eBay, but actually writing people actual letters, making overseas phone calls, looking for extra copies of stuff at record stores that you would swap with people on the other side of the earth through trust only. It was a really superb fanboy network.

ED: So you think the way most people do it nowadays—sitting at a computer and easily chalking up rarities via PayPal—dilutes the experience?

JK: It's apples and oranges, but it is alienated consumption culture. See, we're alone and we're anonymous in a way that we've never been before. And if you look at all those '70s punk websites, and you see how nasty and competitive the verbal tone is in the blogs, it's ultimately an alienated consumption, and a consumption that doesn't fulfill any kind of collective context. You're not a part of a group, you're all—what is it that Philip K. Dick called them?—you're all monads, isolated souls, without the ability to reach other people.

ED: It does throw it all down to just a simple commercial transaction. There's no more character in it than buying toilet paper from Overstock.com. And the listings don't look much different from the Continental Airlines home page or whatever.

JK: Yeah, there's no community aspect to it. That's a side effect of alienated consumption, in the same way that the actual art of a record is cheapened. When you download, you just see a huge list of band names, and you're going to click and listen to them for the first twenty seconds of the song to see if you like them or not. And you can rapidly go through a hundred songs, which means that the context of each individual band and each individual track is completely nonexistent. You're not provided with the cultural context of that culture you're consuming.

ED: Yeah, I remember coming across a 1980 Poodle Boys 7" for fifty cents in a Cleveland record store a few years ago. I had no idea who the band was, but their picture on the back cover was funny and the song titles were good. And it certainly

felt a lot more exciting than if I just saw "Poodle Boys" zip by as I scrolled down
an Internet post of 150 rare records. Plus it'd probably be fifty dollars on there,
because that's another effect of the Internet trading thing—inflated worth.

JK: Of course. So then there was a Swedish schoolteacher who was a
real visionary collector. His name was Lars Wallin, and he was pursuing hyperobscure American '70s punk already in 1981. He was a
really generous guy who'd make you cassettes. One thing you need
to remember about the Swedes is that they are absolutely incapable of original thought. There's no originality in the Swedish soul.
But they are so quick following other people's leads. The frenzy of
Swedish rock 'n' roll fandom is based on that lack of originality. The
hunger for acquiring that sense of belonging is so frenetic that the
import record shops in Sweden in the early to mid-'80s were absolutely world class. But they would only order in one or two copies of
stuff, so you'd literally have to go to these shops every week.

ED: *So you don't think there was anything original about Union Carbide Produc-*
tions?

JK: I think Union Carbide are superb, and they are probably still the
best live band I've ever seen, with the possible of exception of Mag-
ma or the first Stooges reunion show. Union Carbide were always
amazing—for about two years. Then that other perennial Swedish
music trap kicked in, when it's not a concern of just making music
and playing gigs, but making "great" music and playing "great" gigs.
And that sort of pretense strangled that once unbelievable band.
But that's also armchair quarterback stuff. I wasn't in the band, I
didn't lug the amps up and down stairs, then sit around at 10 P.M.
waiting to go on, with nothing to eat but frozen french fries. There
are not that many bands in that era where you can say they were the
best band in the world, without being a douchebag. But you can say
it about Union Carbide, and about the Gories, maybe the Mummies. . . . Once the Mummies, in a quite superb way, started really
ridiculing Mariconda, Tim's super loyalty kicked into gear. . . . That
happens—people fall out, there's very little money, and it's a bunch
of people who are so passionate about every aspect of the craft. So
of course they're going to lock horns.

ED: *The Mummies, Union Carbide, the Lazy Cowgirls, the Gories . . . These*
bands all coming out around the very end of the '80s. They don't sound exactly
alike, but they also didn't fit into the usual frames. . . .

JK: Oh, the Lazy Cowgirls were supremely superb. They were out of time. Who knew then that they were the saviors, the true leaders, the bearers of something precious? But that's the benefit of 20/20 hindsight, it's really easy for us to sit and remember those bands, but then forget all the Vipers and Fuzztones and Unclaimed, bands that didn't really stand the test of time. So you're obviously recontextualizing a musical past in the moment when you're selecting what held up and what didn't.

ED: *True. But even at the time when I got the first Cowgirls record, I remember thinking this just seemed to come out of nowhere. . . .*

JK: Well, they were actually really hyped by the whole *Forced Exposure* scene. Though in hindsight, it's stunning how absolutely awful *Forced Exposure* was, and how absolutely marinated it was in this high-pitched whine of the spoiled, elitist man-child. I think now, as a grown-up, that *Forced Exposure* was the worst of all those magazines, just because of that crypto-fascist elitist stance toward art. And the bullying was so severe. It reminds me of *Vice* magazine, where it's obvious that people who were probably bullied in high school then spend their twenties and thirties trying to emulate the people who bullied them. *

---

*"Gee, where to start?" says *Forced Exposure* publisher Byron Coley. "*Forced Exposure*, elitist? Yeah, I guess. Pretentious, not hardly. Mean-spirited? Well, if we didn't like somebody or thought their motives sucked, sure, but we were quite generous otherwise. We gave a lot of positive ink to bands who didn't get much otherwise. It was a full-time job, and we took it seriously. But we were not scene guys, not partiers; we were record collectors and information junkies. A lot of people misinterpreted this, but Johan is reinventing history a little here. Johan is a guy I was trading with for a while. I finally met him when Tim Warren brought him to my place in Somerville in the late '80s. He burned me on a trade at that time—took a buncha good singles he wanted, failed to send exactly what he'd said he would, etc. But that was not uncommon, so I let it slide. Soon after he started bugging us to let him write for *Forced Exposure*. We let him do a piece on Swedish punk singles, then paired it was a list of great "cocktail punk" records, written by my old friend Tom Givan. He griped that we were dissing his Swedish ass. And we were, but not too bad. A while later he moved to NYC, seemingly with the goal of hanging out with Sonic Youth. He was always bussing by Thurston's place on Eldridge Street, carrying some record he

wanted to trade. He became kind of omnipresent in the WFMU record
scum circle. He was a high roller after that, and I only saw him at record fairs. Never got invited on one of his catered limo tours of record
stores. Like I fucking care."

————————

ED: You landed in that scene when you moved to NYC in 1988. . . .

JK: Thanks to Tim Warren. He fucking hooked me up, let met stay at
his house, introduced me to everybody. I'm really grateful for what
he did for me. Then quite rapidly I got a gig at Matador, I started
doing radio at WFMU, and I started writing for *Spin* magazine. It all
happened really quickly; this was all shit that I'd already been doing
for five or six years as a hobby. For a living in Sweden, I'd worked
as a janitor in an ER room of a big hospital, and as a nurse's aide. I
also got a degree in philosophy in 1988. And then the record store I
had in Gothenburg, Swine Records, went belly-up. I broke up with
my girlfriend. She actually broke into my apartment once and set
fire to my room. I came home to a smoldering pile.

ED: Shit. Did you lose a bunch of records?

JK: Hell yeah! I was kind of baffled by life after that. I didn't know what
the fuck to do. And then Tim invited me to come to New York.

*ED: Was there a notion going to work at Matador that you're actually going to help
get some cool bands signed?*

JK: You know Chris [Lombardi] and Gerard [Cosloy] were so awesome, and such wild guys. Chris was ultra-debonair, falling down
the stairs drunk on Avenue B, and he had an unbelievable '70s punk
collection. And Gerard was the funniest, most vitriolic writer. But
here's the big difference between his mag, *Conflict*, and *Forced Exposure*: *Conflict* stood up for the underdog. Yeah they were a couple of
great men, and they brought me in because they recognized that I
was a motormouth who could get anybody on the phone and sort
of sell them anything, recordwise. Working at Matador was great
and an unbelievable opportunity. But over the course of four-plus
years I worked there I got increasingly frustrated that I couldn't sign
bands. . . . Some of the things I brought in they did sign, like Guided
by Voices. But also, my first child was born in the spring of '92, and
then, you know, you take no prisoners after that. It only becomes a
matter of providing for your family. I left Matador in '94 because I
desperately needed to make more money. Of course it was an ugly
ending. It took years for us to become friends again.

ED: Then you took that A&R position at Rick Rubin's label, American Recordings, out in L.A., and helped form two subsidiary labels while there: Onion, for new signings; and Infinite Zero, for reissues (which included Devo, Alan Vega, and the first official U.S. release of the legendary '60s banjo-led, bizarro-beat band, the Monks).

JK: The main gal at Infinite Zero was Lynn Nakama, who was a true visionary. But Rick was amazing, he let me do the wildest shit, whether I was doing marketing for Slayer or the Black Crowes, or being a runner on an AC/DC session, or putting out weird-ass underground records through a major-label system. I even signed V-3 and the Thomas Jefferson Slave Apartments to Onion! I still think [TJSA's debut full-length, *Bait and Switch* (Onion/American, 1995)] is one of the best records ever made. Plus I was extremely excited about Mike Rep's superb skills as a producer. I didn't want that scene to get lost. You have to remember, in the American music business in the mid-'90s, it was sort of like the late '60s—no one knew what weird shit the proverbial "kids" were going to like next, and everybody was afraid of not being on top of it. So the company freak—and I was the company freak at American—was really empowered.

———

By 1992, inspired by the resurgence of 7" vinyl singles, the creeping acceptance of un-fi production within the indie punk set, and the snot-gob gospel of the *Killed by Death* comps, garage bands and labels started amping up their output. It was clear Crypt, In the Red, Estrus, and even Sympathy had neither the manpower nor the desire to release slabs from every Tom's Harry Dick. So like a plague, small gunky garage labels started escalating.

Empty Records, based in Seattle, was a bratty brother off to the side of the pot-smoke-filled garage of northwest grunge. But owner Blake Wright was no kid. "My love of music started when I saw the Sex Pistols at the Winterland show in San Francisco in 1978," says Wright. "In 1984, in San Francisco, an old high school friend, Volker Stewart, suggested that we start a label that he would finance. It started off as cassettes-only. I ended up in Germany in the army, and eventually moved to Seattle because that was where Volker was living. It was a desolate, small town, but did have its own scene going that was really great. Sub Pop had a lot of good stuff, but they were so image oriented, they would pass on a lot of cool bands. Good for me!"

Empty really shifted into gear at the very end of the '80s, and soon its roster burst with great buzz-punk like Gas Huffer, the Fumes, Zip-gun, Sinister Six, Scared of Chaka, Steel Wool, and the X-Rays. "Dead Moon I was really proud of," Wright says, "since I was the first U.S. label to do anything for them, since they'd done it all themselves up to that point. But there were other labels: Pop Llama, CZ; Estrus was doing the more traditional garage thing; and Jimmy Stapleton [Bag of Hammers] liked the real lo-fi bands. Jimmy was and old roommate of mine, and he was working on a completely different level."

Indeed. Bag of Hammers was an influential label in the early '90s, not just for their good taste in bad taste (Guitar Wolf, Fingers, Dummies, Supercharger, and more), but also for the staunch preference for total crap-fi sound quality—before most garage labels dove deep into that direction. Hanging with Hammers' head Jimmy Stapleton at a Turks show in Seattle in 1993, he seemed like a genuinely nice cat, despite warnings of how monstrously drunk he could get. Which he did by the end of the night, thrown out of the bar, etc. Haven't seen him since. I know he has kids and a good job now, but his rock life (besides being a frequent eBay rare-punk scout) seems to be as distant in the rearview mirror as that moment when the previously yummy 2 A.M. Taco Bell gobble-down starts to get its revenge. . . .

SINCE EUROPE WAS where most of these bands got the most attention, it was obvious labels would be springing up over there too, ready to dump this gunk around the defeated territories. Munster Records was a sprawling Spanish label who delved into numerous alt-rock strains, hence had the cash it seemed to release glossy, full color, even glued(!) sleeves for garage bands used to home-folded Kinko's numbers. Italy had Helter Skelter. Germany birthed Incognito Records. Started as the valve for the boss *Back to Front* compilations, one of the best retorts to *Killed by Death*, the label soon started finding new leather-clad kooks to unleash.

Those are just a minute smattering of the avalanche of garage punk labels that rumbled onto mom 'n' pop shelves in the ''90s. A notable imprint of the era was Demolition Derby, based in the tiny town of Kortrijk, Belgium. Chris Veruth was your average sweaty twentysomething getting as juiced as anyone about all this fun new stuff floating around; plus he was in the perfect position to see it all.

Kortrijk was home to the Pits, a wee corner pub not big enough to hold the cast of *Waiting for Godot,* but which would, about twice a

The Mummies hanging out at The Pits; cover for split single with Supercharger, 1993.

month, pack in a hundred drunken nutjobs of rural Belgium to see the best of this new breed of sleaze. We did our very first European show there, not long after the Mummies and Supercharger got the Pits spitting. Many acts mentioned in this book and loads of regional bands elbowed their way through the place. There was a decent backstage room upstairs (where I first learned how much higher the alcohol percentage is in Belgian beer). But from there, the club got smaller and smaller, until you practically had to walk sideways through the space from the "kitchen" (a sink) to the bar. Then crawl over the bar to get to the six-by-six stage.

But, as usual, none of that matters once the first chord is struck, and the Pits—with its infamously inebriated denizens—was as fun a setting as you'd want to play. And play and play. With no direct line off the stage, short of climbing back over that bar, there was no other way to get off the stage besides shoving through the crowd. After about an hour and a half, we just threw down the instruments, threw up our hands, and went belly-flopping into the folks who had us surfing to the back of the club and out the door to get some air. On his way out, Jim's foot smacked a bell hanging from the ceiling. Once outside, the bartender informed him that local tradition held that ringing the bell meant buying a round for everyone in the bar. They laughed it off, but Jim did anyway. They deserved it.

CONSIDERABLY LESS FRIENDLY and more destructive riots usually followed Richmond, Virginia's psychopathic prodigal punk sons, the Candy Snatchers. Witness the last show New Bomb Turks played at Stache's, in Columbus, early 1997, with the Candy Snatchers and Southern batter-fried boogie-punks, Nashville Pussy. By the third Candy Snatchers song, the crowd had slung more beer than they'd swallowed, and singer Larry May had already busted the metal grating on one of the floor monitors and was hanging on an electrical chord of unknown origin drooping from the ceiling. Nashville Pussy were never particularly violent, but their crowds sure absorbed combative mojo from them, and bodies continued to fly during their sizzling set. By the time we got on, the crowd was, well, what's the human equivalent of feral dogs? There were some cheap drop-ceiling tiles May graciously left for me to trash, and after about twenty-five minutes, club owner Dan Dougan—who'd seen us orchestrate such galas many times before—had finally had enough. He grabbed the mic, stopped the show, and for some reason picked our always-kind bassist Matt to bitch at while we packed up our gear. Probably just tired of chewing my ear off. "You fuckers will never play here again!" (Duh. Stache's closed a few months later.)

The Candy Snatchers were unquestionably one of the most sonically searing, physically vicious, and attitudinally hilarious bands of the era, or ever. And the motor of their smash-up derby sedan was guitarist Matthew Odietus. He was the kind of kid who picked up on the sounds of his heroes (Johnny Thunders, the Dwarves, Larry Flynt) before he picked up on their stupidly glorified drug habits and went with them, hard. So much energy and eye-darting desire to find the next better kick around the corner, he was a wicked wonder to behold.

I'd seen, numerous times, Odietus grab a beer bottle, down it all in a few gulps, and just zing it in a random direction, maybe even to-

**Matthew Odietus (Candy Snatchers), what a cutup! 1993.
(Photo courtesy of Andrea Rizzo)**

ward his own band, not even glancing ahead, without a millisecond of thought—and usually within the first three songs, well aware he'd be up there for at least another fifteen minutes, more than enough time for a bruised crowd member to forge a counterattack which, understandably, they rarely did. Medium height, maybe 130 pounds, scraggly long black hair, but with eyes under it that bored holes through all the unspoken bullshit that sat like a dung heap in his stomach, Odietus was rarely challenged to do anything but play a few more songs—which he did 40 oz.-fold. He was as shit-hot a punk guitar player as there has ever been.

The inevitable accusations that the Candy Snatchers were leaning on their bloody shtick as the years passed usually came from people who hadn't seen them in a while. Yes, they retained a Daffy Duck demeanor in even the most dire moments. But the Candy Snatchers were never just kidding around. They lasted for more than ten years, featuring tons of troubled tours, five albums, and countless singles and compilation tracks. Andy Slob—bassist for the Cincinnati band the Slobs and producer to the slop-rock stars—claims, "Oddly, the Candy Snatchers were one of the most professional and focused bands I've ever recorded. They always knew what they were trying to do musically, and could do it extremely energetically in the studio. I'll never forget recording them in my basement, Larry with a cast on his broken leg, and the two guys from Nielsen Ratings who were hooking all kinds of stuff up to my TVs and sneaking cheap canned beer from the fridge."

The seething core of Odietus and May could rarely convince a revolving rhythm section to stick around. Original bassist Willy Johns fit perfectly until he landed in jail for some genuinely awful, dastardly deeds. And May unblinkingly admitted that he tried to break beer bottles and cut the same place on his forehead every other show, "so that I'd just have that one scar." Hell, even if that is a shtick, it's a dedicated one! Plus he usually missed the sweet spot anyway.

Amidst all the gossipy battle-scar stories, the music was often astoundingly good, with May's lyrics being wittier than his constant concussions should've allowed. The band could capture a seedy smash of Stones swagger, New York Dolls swish, Misfits marauding, Saints surge, Didjits bofo-boogie and turn-of-the-millennium fear/fury in two-minute H-100s you could sing along to, with pathologically self-denigrating titles like "Deadbeat," "Moronic Pleasures," "Ugly on the Inside," "Fuck My Family," and "We Never Learn."

But even the band members themselves would usually rather chat

Larry May (Candy Snatchers) greets the crowd at the Maxi Pad, Cincinnati, 1998. (Photo by Vicki Graham)

about their latest dustup than go on about music and shit. "One time," May recalls, "Willy beat Matt to a bloody pulp at a packed Continental show, then Suke duct-taped Matt's ear back on right. Willy also cut my phone lines after pawning Goose's amp that he was letting Willy use, while we were waitin' on a call back for the amp's serial number. . . . "

"I saw Matt drink antifreeze," says Steve Baise of the Devil Dogs. "He wanted to get a buzz. He was like, 'I'm gonna mix some with water.' He drank like half a glass. He was kind of bad off at the end. He got in a big fight with his mom, she threw him in jail; then he left town and didn't go to his court date. He was a fugitive for awhile. He patched it up with his mom but was still a fugitive. He was just a mess. Nice guy though, and I thought he was a really good guitar player. He didn't really work that much, he just spent all his time playing guitar. But he also had a lot of time on his hands as a thinker. He thinked his way to death."

Matthew Odietus died June 28, 2008.

DEAN RISPLER, NYC PUNK PRODUCER AND PROMOTER

One of my personal favorite Candy Snatchers stories is when I was in a band called the Hot Corn Girls. We were invited by the Candy Snatchers to play a New Year's Eve house party in Richmond, VA, back in 1993. The house was a real punk rock mess. There were puddles on the floor of what I hoped was just water from leaky pipes, and the electricity was shoddy at best. We went on right before the Candy Snatchers. Despite their relative insanity, those guys, especially Larry and Matthew, were extremely supportive of new bands. After our set, the Candy Snatchers started to play, and it was complete mayhem as per usual: bottles, cans, and busted glass flying everywhere; blood spewing from Larry's head and Matthew's chest; and Willy's bass was set on fire while he played. Amazing.

About fifteen minutes into this set, Larry gets on top of the bass drum and grabs a hold of what he probably thought was a plumbing pipe. After hanging for a few seconds, I saw what it really was—an electrical conduit pipe. At that point I said to myself that we were all going to die here on this wet floor. The pipe did give way and thousands of sparks emitted from it—a real, beautiful punk rock dream. Nobody died, but the power went out. The last thing I remember was the drummer, Barry, just chuckling and packing away his drums—as if this was all obviously expected.

LADY MONSTER, BURLESQUE QUEEN OF THE FIRE TASSELS

In early 1996, when the Candy Snatchers were on tour with the Trick Babies, they played a show with the New Bomb Turks at Stache's, in Columbus, Ohio. I think this was right after Larry made the cover of Maximumrocknroll. The Candy Snatchers were chucking everything they could get their hands on. Larry was cutting himself, rolling around on the floor, shaking his blood into the audience like a wet dog. Then Matt just went ballistic! He threw a cinder block, then his guitar. He even beaned the singer for the Trick Babies with a highball glass, cutting her forehead. I stayed on the side of the stage where Willy was, and somehow remained unmarred.

After the show (after making out with Willy in the ladies' room), I went up to Matt and he thanked me for being so brave, rocking out up front all night. I commented that I didn't get hurt or any get blood on me, so he grabs my head, starts kissing me, and then bites my bottom lip so hard that blood starts pouring out! I scream. He laughs. And no, I didn't get hepatitis from kissing the Candy Snatchers.

ANDREA RIZZO, *THE* FAN

Those guys were badass, the real deal—nothing stood in the way of a good time. My personal stories are sometimes endearing, sometime hilarious, and sometimes horrible: waking up to find Matthew had become blood brothers with a long-forgotten friend using my disposable razor; letting the dog out only to find Serge [drummer] sleeping on my doorstep; Willy's famous toothless grin and penchant for sticking stolen cigarettes within the cracks; when Barry discovered he had cancer and he gave up on life, only to live it recklessly; and when Larry mopped my kitchen floor with a broken leg.

My favorite story is seeing the Candy Snatchers that first time at Friar Tuck's in Norfolk, 1994, when they were young, cocky, and seemingly invincible—before their talent gave way to substances of choice and they grew apart. Before their smoking jackets became tattered and the constant rotation of drummers gave way to the constant rotation of bass players. Before two of them died. Before I knew them.

Footnote: I dated Matthew Odietus for almost six years. A statement that's hard to state unflinchingly.

CHET WEISE, QUADRAJETS, IMMORTAL LEE COUNTY KILLERS

The Quadrajets had the pleasure of touring with the Candy Snatchers several times. The last time I saw them play, I was in the duo Immortal Lee County Killers. We were on our last legs as a band. My head couldn't take any more drama. We pulled into Minneapolis for a weeknight show, I walked through the door, and there stands Larry, grinning wide. Honestly, I sadly thought, "Oh shit, it's gonna be a Snatchers kind of night."

When they hit the stage, they blew the place up. One of the best shows I have ever seen. I am not being nostalgic or elegiac here either in light of Matthew's death. I'm telling you, that night the Snatchers could have played next to any band in history and blown them off the face of this blue planet. I got teary-eyed watching it. They didn't need broken bottles anymore to push people back on their heels—only needed their Marshalls. After their set, Larry walked up, grinning of course.

"We've been sober lately," he said.

11.
GET ACTION!

ALREADY WELL KNOWN as the place where rock genres go to get jumper cables attached to their nipples, the Land of the Rising Sun was burning hot in the mid-'90s with some of the most crazed bands of this sound—Jet Boys, Supersnazz, and the 5.6.7.8's, to name a few. But perhaps the most beloved and influential band on the Japanese side of the sound was Teengenerate.

The fucked-up musical knowledge of the fiery foursome—who took their name from a Dictators song—didn't stop there. In fact, about half their discography—one proper album on Crypt, a number of EPs, compilations, and more 7" singles than there are Cheap Trick fans in Tokyo—was covers of long-lost subterranean punk of the *Killed by Death* ilk. Their originals were just as nuts, and all played with an electrified energy like they swallowed Pop Rocks and battery acid and were trying to sweat it back out onto their amps, the crowd, or whatever was in the way of them surviving for another day spent searching for much stronger battery acid. They equally loved the skinny-tie stuff of the 1978–'80 post-Knack power-pop geyser, so—despite damaged fidelity, an utter disdain for tuning, and busted English—every song was still catchy as hell.

"When young, I was into general major pop and rock music from U.S. and UK," says singer/guitarist Fink. "But getting especially into the '60s music from UK (Stones, Who, Them), punk rock (Flamin' Groovies, Heartbreakers, Clash, Buzzcocks), and the Stooges, under an influence of my older brother, Fifi" (the other gums-snarling, guitar-slashing half of the Teengenerate brother front).

Smack-dab in the middle of the Green Day/Offspring spring days, had you played a Teengenerate song to your freshly orange-haired teen sister, she'd have recoiled in ear-covering fright. But New Bomb Turks toured with Teengenerate—once in Europe for about a month in spring 1994, ten days in Japan in summer 1995, and another two-plus weeks in the U.S. that fall—and I can say with assurance that they were the nicest guys we ever toured with, polite to the core. But once they hit that stage, I still would've shoved your sis to the back wall and told her to watch the fuck out!

Teengenerate were amazing every minute of every single show. Fifi and Fink jerked their arms, legs, and heads about like they were constantly dodging and exchanging switchblade stabs from imaginary enemies. Bassist Sammy stomped a bit, but mostly rocked back and forth with a knowing grin on his face like there was a girlie-mag model waiting for him back home (and there was). And drummer Shoe, cherub face but hands that slammed fast and hard like Lennie from *Of Mice and Men* making an urgent point, was the youngest, and really gave the band a solid bottom end that is sometimes forgotten by many lo-fi punks who came in Teengenerate's wake.

Fifi and Fink were already in their very late twenties when their Crypt album dropped in 1995. They'd knocked around the Tokyo punk scene for a while, having played in American Soul Spiders, an influential local band from the late '80s who revived names like the MC5, Radio Birdman, and the Lazy Cowgirls for a new generation of Japanese garage bands.

"That band sounded more Detroit hard rock–oriented," Fink explains, "but people regarded us as a trendy grunge band, I guess, and a record label unexpectedly asked us to release a 45. Thus we could have chances to release records on 1+2 and Mangrove, and cut in overseas too like on Sympathy, Estrus, Get Hip, and In Your Face [UK] and went to tour shortly over in U.S. in '91. After a New York City show, the singer suddenly decided to stay there, so the band broke up! In spring of '92, I had an idea to form a new band, without a stand-alone singer, as I got a big influence from the Devil Dogs—since American Soul Spiders played with them in NYC. But compared to the Devil Dogs, American Soul Spiders tunes were a little bit longer and more complicated. And we had long hairs."

"We played with American Soul Spiders in Japan too," says Devil Dogs bassist Steve Baise. "They were really good, but after they saw us they realized, Hey, this metal-ish stuff is not what we should be doing.

Teengenerate, 1993. (Photo by Eri Sekiguchi)

And that's when they started doing Teengenerate."

"My decision was writing less-than-three-minutes songs and playing simpler like Real Kids, DMZ, and Saints," says Fink. "But people in Tokyo at that time in '92 didn't want to know that kind of music. All music clubs were occupied with grunge, skateboard thrash, and techno. One day, I got phone call from Sammy, and said, 'Let's get action with Fifi!' I must say that we loved the Devil Dogs first, and New Bomb Turks, Young Fresh Fellows, Replacements, the Mummies, the Rip Offs, and Prisonshake. I remember in early days, the name was often misspelled on posters, like Teenage Generates or Teen Generation Nation—because no one knew us."

"When Teengenerate started," Fifi recalls, "there were no real punk bands in Tokyo. The surf or garage bands, like the 5.6.7.8's or Jackie and the Cedrics, were much more real thing to us. We used to play with them because the garage scene was hotter than punk scene in Tokyo."

Teengenerate's ingestion of arcane punk was deep and abiding, and eventually helped spread those rare sounds throughout the under-

NYC, 1993. (Courtesy of Cliff Mott)

ground punk scene nearly as much as the *Killed by Death* comps. Not that they were the first to unearth those kinds of songs, but once Teengenerate and their uncontrolled upchuck of that stuff made the rounds, KBD as a genre was really solidified.

"But," Fifi adds, "please don't forget the *Feel Lucky Punk?* comp from Crypt. It was the most important compilation album to us then."

When asked how they felt when seemingly every garage punk label asked them to do a single, Fink makes with the history: "I remember that Teengenerate's first show was at smallest club in Shinjuku, with boring reggae bands booked by the club! But the second show was Garage Shock in Bellingham, Washington, which was a big festival given by Estrus's Dave Crider. And we got tons of recording offers there from several labels. We think we were the luckiest band at that moment. Thank you, Dave, to give us a chance to play there! As for Crypt, we are honor to be on the greatest label in the world. Thanks, Tim and Micha!"

Fifi simply adds, "And I guess those labels all knew our recordings wouldn't cost much!"

One would think that getting records to sound like they'd been recorded with a burning boom box tied to the back of a 1956 Vincent Black Shadow racing straight through the front window of an emergency room would be easy. Not so. Few fuzz-fi fuckers since have nailed Teengenerate's incendiary sizzle. "We've done all our recording for ourselves," says Fifi. "So the sound was so crazy and loud because we had no real engineers or producers. Real studios in Japan were too expensive for us."

Augsburg, Germany, 1994.

"Most of our 45s and the *Get Action* LP were recorded live with four-track cassette," Fink explains. "Though we added some hand-claps and voices later. I got an idea with four-track recorder while Teengenerate's first stay in Seattle. Scott McCaughey and Jim Sangster (of Young Fresh Fellows) took us to a very old studio to record live all the songs we had then. Studio was owned by Kearney Barton (legendary engineer for the Kingsmen and the Wailers), and he was there as an engineer! Everything was as it was 1961. I think Kearney was over eighty years old, but still made an incredible big sound with big two-track recorder! Other recordings were done back home with TEAC eight-track open-reel recorder that Wallabies Records owned."

New Bomb Turks did five shows in ten days in Japan, three at one club alone, the Shelter, in Tokyo. Teengenerate were like the house band who helped bring all these cool bands over, with help from some local indie labels like Wallabies.

The Shelter was a simple square room in the basement of some office building. An American fire chief would tag it at about 150 capacity, but they packed about three hundred kids in there! The little bar was

Teengenerate slay the Shelter Club, Tokyo, 1993. (Photo by Eri Sekiguchi)

only stocked with beer that ran out by about eight-thirty. That seemed to be the way, since the whole beer ritual didn't seem as integral an ingredient in the rock scene there. So we made our way down a block to a Lawson's. That was weird, since Lawson's was the big convenience-store chain in northern Ohio when I was a tot, which I had assumed had gone out of business years ago. The troublemakers told us that we could get vodka there; and in the cooler, these little plastic cups that came with Sprite-like flavored ice cubes inside. Some little kiddie frozen treat that, with vodka tips, became quite adult indeed.

"In Japan," says Fifi, "when you play live you don't have to bring amplifiers or drum kit. Venues have it. Bad thing in Japan is tickets for shows are usually so expensive. You have to pay more than two thousand yen (almost twenty dollars) to see a couple of local bands. And if we don't have enough audience, we have to pay to venues later." Our shows were, with the exchange rate at the time during a major Japanese recession, almost thirty-five dollars a ticket. They said that was the lowest they could go.

Plus, it was hot as hell that time of year, and the packed Shelter was only hotter. Very strange that as we hung in the tiny backstage for the first show, you'd have thought the place was empty from the lack of anything like a chattering crowd coming from outside. Supersnazz and Teengenerate riled the gang up good, we hit the stage to very sweaty but somewhat sedate people. You could almost hear a pin drop across the room. But once the songs started . . . BLAMMO!

The crowd exploded, just bouncing around like Mexican jumping bean–fed chickens with their heads cut off, some of which I think went flying past us during the set, it was hard to tell. The other bands were smiling and popping up and down at the sides of the stage. Sweat literally started to drip down from the ceiling about two feet above us, and even some cold beer was flung from some folks who planned well. But the second the song ended, the crowd would simmer down like taking boiling milk off the burner. Then the explosion, then quiet, and on and on; though for the last two songs, the explosion kept going, and I've never experienced anything like it since. It was pretty much like that at the Nagoya and Osaka shows too, though the clubs were slightly bigger. Incredible.

Teengenerate's 1994 European tour started with two weeks of wild shows with Gaunt that ended with a full video camera of footage being lost forever when their van got broken into. But even that didn't shake

the band's spirit. Touring with Teengenerate was really refreshing because their outlook was so positive, aside from the feeling they gave you
that even halfway across the world you could find boon companions
who laughed at bad jokes and Dwarves songs. "We were really lucky,"
says Fifi. "We were just a small garage band, but we could go to the
States and Europe and play. No bad memories!"

After finishing off the 1995 U.S. tour through the West Coast, the
band broke up not long after they got home. By then, new Nippon
nutjobs like the Jet Boys and Titans were forming. Fifi has since fronted
his high-energy power-pop band, Firestarter, for nearly ten years now;
while Fink has his Raydios band turned on again. Teengenerated still,
and forever . . .

AROUND THE SAME time as Teengenerate were infecting the spazz-punk
bloodstream, another even more insanely trashy garage troupe from
Japan came cackling—Guitar Wolf. Well, "garage" if your garage is
occupied by a clanky old Toyota truck piled high with Ramones, Joan
Jett, and Link Wray records, half-empty pomade cans, grade-Z sci-fi
monster movie posters, rusted Erector sets, and tumbling fluorescent
lightbulbs, all soaked in gas and constantly reignited with comically
large matchsticks. Guitar Wolf was already a kind of papa to the new
breed Japanese punk bands. "When Teengenerate played with Guitar
Wolf for the first time," says Fifi, "I thought they were the worst band in
the world. They used to be an instrumental band then. Actually Seiji—
Guitar Wolf himself—couldn't play guitar then. "

Live, Guitar Wolf explode with a complete disregard for anything
resembling song structure, their songs only rarely wrung back into place
by a loud scream of "Lock 'n' loll! Lock 'n' loll!" Or if one of the three
sweat-soaked, leather-clad killers—looking like *'68 Comeback* Elvis just
dropped in from a vigorous arm-wagging flight from Saturn—stopped
to pull out a switchblade comb to fix their mile-high pompadours.
Then it's back to a continued vivisection of Link Wray's two most basic
chords, often played while Seiji is hanging upside down from a rafter
after giving his guitar (down to two strings) to an audience member to
slap at. And everything played so loud as if we're all deaf anyway, so
blast off! It was exciting and funny beyond belief, but something you'd
assume couldn't, or even shouldn't be captured on record. But . . .

Memphis-based Goner Records—started by Eric Friedl of the
Oblivians—unleashed the first Guitar Wolf album in America in 1994,

Goner Records ad, 1993.

the eardrum-decimating *Wolf Rock!*, that upon release seemed to make any more attempts at dumping hydrochloric acid on top of whatever was left of garage rock's bag of bones potentially pointless.

"I went up to Bellingham for a Garage Shock," Friedl recalls. "Guitar Wolf had invited themselves, and Crider let them play really early. They were amazing, inept, pretty much chaos and noise. The other more 'appropriate' garagers didn't really know what to do with them. Yoshiko [Fujiyama] from the 5.6.7.8's introduced us, and they came down to Memphis to play a Wednesday night at the Antenna Club. Turned out Seiji had been to Memphis before and had gotten robbed after being taken to see some 'real blues' with a local who took him to a drug den, ripped him off, and tried to beat him up. Despite all that, they loved Memphis. They played their show to maybe thirty people, then came back a week later and played for about 150. When they were leaving town, they left me with a cassette that blew me away. I

Fujiyama Attack! Guitar Wolf, Normal, IL, 1997. (Photo by Canderson)

faxed them a request to do a record. The first pressing was misplated so that everything was covered in an additional layer of grinding noise. I thought it worked for the record, and luckily the band liked it, too! So the Goner Records label was thus started on miscommunication and mistakes—and hasn't let up since!"

Guitar Wolf themselves went on for over ten albums and twenty years, in unending determination to convince us that the Ramones and a defective clone of Link Wray had a test-tube baby abortion in the back of a burning vinyl pants factory, and they called it Lock 'n' Loll.

"Seiji writes songs with song name first," Teengenerate singer/guitarist Fink explains. "They must be cool words to him, but most of them mean nothing at all. One night he called me on the phone at 4 A.M. He was so excited at an idea of a new song name, 'Reizoko Zero' (means 'Refrigerator Zero'). He asked me what I thought. I didn't understand what his brain produced, but I said, 'It's great.' He was happy with my answer and finally went to bed."

"Oh man, crazy," says Shane White, guitarist for masked San Francisco trash punks, the Rip Offs. "Seiji was an acid dude, Billy [aka Bass Wolf, Hideaki Sekiguchi] was a fucking speed freak, and the drummer [Toro] didn't do anything except smoke cigarettes. Seiji would fucking meditate before going onstage, really *become* the guy in the black leather jacket. He had this glass case, with his guitar and jacket in there, and records of Link Wray, Johnny Thunders, Joan Jett—and you couldn't touch it! The glass case was to bring energy into his guitar and his leather jacket. Those guys were stone fucking freaks!"

"By our second Japanese tour, they we huge over there," says Greg Cartwright of the Oblivians. "They were on a major label, playing to massive crowds. We were opening for them, playing the same rooms the Ramones would play! It was crazy."

One day while New Bomb Turks were on tour in Japan, Seiji insisted that we must go to this restaurant, we *must* go to this restaurant!! So he takes us there, we walk in, and it is a huge, interesting, converted warehouse. The food was good, and the sake flowed. But for the most part, we seemed to be missing something. So Seiji eventually says, "Go piss, go piss." Okay. So first Bret Lewis goes to the john, and comes back out with his jaw dropped and eyes wider than Tokyo. "You have to go take a piss." So I run over, stop at the bathroom door, take a deep breath, and walk in. Built around each urinal were these large, supercolorful, ceramic samurai warriors—their faces at about the same height as the average Japanese guy's mug. And as you commenced to leaking, the huge smiling mouth on the samurai would flap up and down while a loud "Yaarrrgghhaaa!!!!" came screaming out at you.

12.

HALF-ASSED, WILL TRAVEL

B Y 1996, NEW Bomb Turks had entered that inevitable phase where all the touring, girlfriend-losing, hometown-tiring, and not developing skills beyond rocking meant we kind of wanted to at least start

New Bomb Turks' version of "We cleaned up," at Bikini Test, La Chaux de Fond, Switzerland, 1993. (Photo by Pete Pfiffner)

Flier for *Information Highway Revisited* record release party. Columbus, OH, 1994. (Art by Arturo X)

making a little money at this. *!!Destroy-Oh-Boy!!* had sold about forty thousand copies or so; decent for an indie release at the time. Our second Crypt album, *Information Highway Revisited*, sold about the same. We'd been touring more, the alt-rock zeitgeist was still a-haunting, and music biz pals told us we could probably score good advance cash from some major label. And, crucially, Crypt had given us the okay to skedaddle.

"*!!Destroy-Oh-Boy!!* just did so well in the States," says Tim Warren. "You got that great *Maximumrocknroll* reveiew; and there's the fuckin' sound of that record. It's a fuckin' classic. But I understand why Sam Phillips sold Elvis to RCA—because there's demand. You've gotta keep repressing and repressing; distributors ordering a thousand, two thousand more. Great! But are they paying for them? Where was the money? Remember, you guys and I were talking about making a piss-take remix and video for "Mr. Suit" [from *!!Destroy-Oh-Boy!!*], where you guys were gonna wear spandex bicycle pants, lookin' like a rap-rock group! And we could've, and it would've sold so many copies in Europe!"

Aside from bicycle-pants-wearing videos, we were always told that getting a manager would've helped us get a bigger deal. I always figured it would've just hastened the end of the band. Also, anything a manager could do—besides having contacts to movie producers or Levi's ad men or something—we could do ourselves, and did. I won't claim that was the mutual opinion within the whole band. As it turned out, we never took tour support from any label either, never really needed it. Most bands with eyes widening around that time asked for tour support from their labels because they wanted to have cash on hand for rental vans, motels, and gas; only to blow it on dope by the second week of touring; or a thousand-dollar-a-day rock-star tour bus to make it look like someone gave a fuck. Since our first trip out west in 1993, we'd always made enough money to cover most costs, usually crashed at pals' pads, sometimes rented cheaper minivans for shorter tours (no matter how goofy it looked), and landed back in Cap City with dough in our dungarees. But being twenty-eight ain't twenty. You start accumulating things like self-esteem and gas shut-off notices.

A few offers trickled in, but nothing that sounded like anything more than the usual shell game that we were quite familiar with.

Enter Jim Guernot. Guernot was a nice guy who got in touch with us around 1995 to "have lunch." We met him at a beach in L.A. Just walked around the beach all afternoon; stopped at a cool lil' Mexican grub stand where Guernot bought us great fish tacos; and generally, he didn't come over like some shyster. Until he really started talking about signing the band, and his perfect white smile and baggy skater shorts started to look as foreign to us as an El Salvadoran contra's funeral attire.

He was the model of the alt-rock era "cool A&R guy." A preteen Social Distortion fanatic, he was soon asked to go on the road with them and sell T-shirts. Eventually he became their manager, which somehow led him up whatever ladder has Whitney Houston and Amy Grant video shoots at the top. He'd brought the mainstream punk Three Stooges—Green Day, Offspring, and Rancid—along for the ride, as he had managed them too. And now he'd recently turned down a big promotion to instead take start-up dough to "get back to his roots" and form his own new label. It was going to be called Time Bomb Recordings, which for a few minutes I took as a good omen. . . .

As the conversation progressed, Guernot sounded more and more like any other major-label guy: tour nine months out of the year, don't expect much advance money, but oh boy, the royalty rate will be better than those of most big labels (meaning like 4 percent rather than 3 percent after recoupables like posters and CDs, of course, which the label can then write off their taxes as "promotion"). I flatly told him that we

March 8, 1995

VIA FEDERAL EXPRESS

Eric Davidson

Re: **New Bomb Turks -w- Onion Records - Proposed Recording Agreement ("Agreement")**

Dear Eric:

At Johan Kugelberg's request, I am enclosing a "short form" draft of the Agreement. Please review the same with your advisors and give Johan and I the benefit of your thoughts. We all look forward to meeting you when you come to town.

Inasmuch as I am simultaneously forwarding a copy of the Agreement to those listed below, none of whom have had the opportunity to review the same, I must reserve their rights to request modifications.

Best.

Cordially,

Brian McPherson
ROSENFELD, MEYER & SUSMAN

BHM:hns
Encl.

cc: Rick Rubin (w/encl.)
     Johan Kugelberg (w/encl.)
     Mark Goldstein, Esq. (w/encl.)

Legal mumbo-jumbo from American Recordings, 1995.

only wanted to tour in no more than three-week clumps, preferably about four months a year total, with some Euro touring in between, since that's where the majority of our fans were. American labels care very little about "big in Belgium" boasts. And they like five- to seven-record deals too, another thing we weren't down with.

I could tell as we headed one way to our van and Guernot headed the other, with the sun setting behind us, that this wasn't going to go past that second round of fish tacos. He did send his friendly Boston-based assistant to a few of our East Coast shows, and she genuinely seemed to like us. But label heads themselves like to talk to managers or lawyers, not musicians. They assume you're dumbasses who can barely pronounce "perpetuity." Months later I'd heard from a biz pal that word was Guernot didn't think we would tour enough. So he signed Tenderloin instead, a perfectly powerful punkish boogie-woogie band we'd done some shows with. Great guys, road warriors no doubt, but a first-month intern at Merge could tell they weren't going to burn up the charts.

Time Bomb's initial offerings were Social Distortion reissues; next was No Knife, a bland Midwest indie rock band; then the Tenderloin contract that lasted for one album. The label had a minor hit with the techno-rock band Death in Vegas around 1998, but otherwise, Time Bomb Recordings didn't exactly blow up.

And then there was Brett Gurewitz and his Epitaph Records. One thing I liked about Gurewitz's pitch, thrown late 1995, was that he said, "We like to think we're a big label where you don't need a manager." Of course that means there's no one with biz clout on your side to badger their ass to work your record. But what I believe he genuinely meant was that rather than pawning off 25 percent or more to a manager, you could keep that cut, and that there were people you actually knew at the label who would work out the managerial specifics the band might be sketchy on. Their idea was that they take a little more of your publishing (which we bargained down), which was a somewhat smaller amount than paying a manager. Epitaph was still an independent label (save for Sony distribution in the Far East), and we were given assurances no major was going to swoop in, buy up the label, and toss out our contract (as was the trend back then).

Sure, Gurewitz took us up to his swanky Sunset Strip pad and showed off his gadgets; Epitaph's splashy new website (still an excitingly novel development at the time) was clearly confusing if cool looking; and within months, rumors of minor power struggles and divorces ran through the Epitaph halls. But hey, this is the music industry, not the usual American corporate enterprise where all economic activity is precise, honest, and lucrative.

"Our booking agent Julianne Andersen had talked to me at length about Brett's interest in the band," guitarist Jim Weber recalls of the grapevine Gurewitz traveled to Camp NBT. "She thought it was a good idea based on the experience that Gas Huffer had with the label. So his initial phone call was not a shock per se, but it was very weird. Gurewitz was impressed that I had 'Devo Corporate Anthem' on my answering machine at the time, which got him on the topic of the second Bad Religion record (*Into the Unknown*, 1983) which is all synthesizers and shit. Of course I had no idea what he was talking about because I'd never heard the fucking thing at the time. He was talking about how all the bands were doing really well on the label, and all I could think of was how much I hated all those bands. Yet that's where we wound up. It wasn't until after talking to the Gas Huffer guys and seeing the other kind of garage bands that they were signing (Cramps, Humpers, Red Aunts, Zeke) that I became somewhat comfortable with being there. Don't think I ever felt totally comfortable though . . ."

Epitaph's offices—located in a really cool renovated train station up on a hill in the then slowly gentrifying Silverlake area of L.A.— were fun to hang out at. Keith Morris (Circle Jerks) and Wayne Kramer (MC5) were often hanging around. The label gave us all the free shit we ever wanted (and let me tell you, in 1996 you could buy a hell of a lot of bagels with NOFX and Pulley CD trade-in cash). It was easy dealing with Epitaph. They basically did what they said they'd do, our distribution all over the world was much better, and the people who worked there were nice, if half of them didn't know their Real Kids from their Gay Dads. Thank God for staffers Jon Wahl (from Claw Hammer), Kim Chi, and Christina White Trash, a good-time rock of reality who was once a DJ at WCSB at Cleveland State University. She had conducted one of our first radio interviews in the early '90s. I took that as a good omen . . . for about six months.

We probably should've paid more attention when we were in L.A. mastering our Epitaph debut, *Scared Straight* (1996), while hanging among the cool old vintage doohickeys at the studio and pondering dumping beer on the fucking *Dark Side of the Moon* master reels that were lying around on the floor. But the next two Epitaph albums are our favorites, after *!!Destroy-Oh-Boy!!* Epitaph never asked us to change anything at all about anything (which, in the world of bigger labels, could mean they didn't *care* to ask us, and assumed from early on that we weren't going to sell tons). They kept our records in print for a bit after the contract ended in 2001, and kept us on the label website even longer. Overall, a positive experience.

There was one time when Epitaph tried a dive off a higher cliff. It was called the "Roadkill" campaign, launched around 1998, where they tried to take all their representatives from this gutter garage scene to a higher profile. There was a compilation CD, a mess of posters, and attempts to get those bands to tour together. It was an honest if fumbled attempt from a label that merely had to dump boxes of new Pennywise and Bad Religion records on the Pacific Coast Highway to sell three hundred thousand of them. They weren't really tuned into the swampy end of the punk landscape.

When I flew out to L.A. in March 2008, to try to get some interviews for this book, I hadn't seen or spoken to Gurewitz in nearly seven years. The swanky offices now had a little dust on the huge hot rod engine/ front desk, some crumpled boxes in corners, and scuffs on the framed neon Coop posters of yore, scattered amid the quieter din of an industry pulling the forces back, bloodied but unbowed. Gurewitz was back in the boss chair (after some personal problems around the time of our Epitaph end run), even back playing with Bad Religion sometimes, and still excited about new bands the label was hoping to sign. "When I look in the mirror," he said, "I look like the Crypt Keeper, but I still feel like a scared teenager all the time. I never outgrew it."

"The 'Roadkill' campaign was my idea," says Gurewitz. "When we first started up we were like many indie labels, we had a sound. So we had a bunch of bands that sounded like Bad Religion. But that's not all I listened to. I'd always liked garage music. In '85, I put out the Morlocks live album, I produced an album by the Primates, and I worked with a group called the Things. There was that whole garage scene then. I was into the Fuzztones, the Chesterfield Kings, that whole mid-'80s garage thing. So I was aware of that stuff, though my label didn't really reflect that. We became known for skate punk, but we wanted to branch out."

"We decided to sign with Epitaph," says Matt Wright of Gas Huffer, "because it was an opportunity to take all the hard work we were doing a little further in terms of distribution and resources. When we went down to meet with them the first time, they were still in the old office, and they showed us a video of 'Keep 'Em Separated' by the Offspring, which was just barely starting to hit. They were really nice folks, and the first few years were great. We always did tons of interviews, and on tour you'd see Epitaph-printed posters all over the place. Later on, we lost our ace support team. Add to that *Just Beautiful Music*, our third and final record for them—which was especially weird and probably difficult to market—and you've got a recipe for splitsville."

Drummer Joe Newton was a little more ardent in his reaction to splitsville. "On the last tour—six weeks around the U.S., then four more opening for the Cramps—they got us all of two interviews," says Newton. "That still offends me. It's like they just totally gave up. I mean, not even a fucking fanzine interview! Maybe people were less interested than before, but it seems hard to believe that ten weeks of touring on a new album can't render a bit more press than that for an established band. A lame ending for an otherwise favorable relationship with that label."

Nearly the same thing happened to New Bomb Turks with our last Epitaph release, *Nightmare Scenario* (2000). We had a fantastic new drummer, Sam Brown, and were really energized; the new album was produced by Detroit garage rock producer du jour Jim Diamond; and we did a lot of touring with labelmates Zeke. But by then, some staff had changed at Epitaph, the wave had long crested on the neo-punk trend; and while we got a decent amount of press and great crowds on those tours, the air had left the sails.

"I think some of that kind of garage scene probably wasn't happening in L.A. as much as other places," Gurewitz admits. "But the *Roadkill* comp was an attempt to tie all that together and explain to the kids who were Epitaph customers because of skate punk that, hey, here's a whole scene that has coherence. It never took a foothold. None of the garage bands I signed ever really caught on. What's interesting to me is that it's just a question of when that magic track is going to arrive. Because many years later, look what happened with that White Stripes. It did happen, later.

"There's no question that the music industry is in absolute turmoil, and the publishing industry too. Anything that can be digitized will be, and there's nothing anyone can do to stop it. It doesn't mean people won't buy a record for convenience or to get a little premium with it, like we still print vinyl. But it will never go back to being what it was."

MID-DECADE, THE POP-PUNKED Warped Tour was becoming a summer suburban teen institution, and the raw rash of early '90s punk
bands had either broken up (Gories, Devil Dogs, Teengenerate) or were
working the major-label route (Supersuckers, Reverend Horton Heat,
Rocket from the Crypt), and thus spit-shining their sounds. In contrast
to those developments was the next crop of punks who were stumbling
further into the other fidelity field. The lost '70s punk compilations
were starting to number in double figures; the lightbulb of four-track
home recording was at full wattage; and "lo-fi" was now a given goal
instead of a happy accident. The ol' Beatles/Rolling Stones/Kinks debates were now Electric Eels/Pagans/Saints squabbles. Tim Warren of
course had a denunciation for this latest bumpy bandwagon: "Killed by
Bloodstains Across Supercharger."

Perhaps the first to fully extol those ultratrashy rules, to almost pa-
rodic effect, were the Rip Offs and the Rip Off Records label, both
led by Greg Lowery, who'd helped kick in much of the predilection for
pissy production with Supercharger. He'd soon rope in a stable of little
lo-fi snots on singles that always had songs only on one side, in B&W-
only sleeves. The Rip Off label came before the band, when Supercharger was close to calling it a day in 1993.

"Supercharger was playing the Crocodile in Seattle, with the Supersuckers," says Lowery. "I met the Statics there. Me and Darin Raffaelli
[Supercharger singer/guitarist] had this pseudo stupid label, Radio X.
So I presented [the Statics' demo] to Darin, and he goes, 'I don't like it,
it sounds like bullshit.' So I said, Fuck it, I'll do it myself. And that's how
Rip Off Records started. Then when the Rip Offs started very soon
after the Supercharger Euro tour, I thought, Fuck it, why don't we do
another gimmick thing, like the Mummies. . . . I was not a huge fan of
the Mummies on record; I thought they were a great live animal. Most
gimmick bands do gimmicks because they suck. But I wanted to be a
gimmick band that was good."

Raffaelli went on to the quirk-garage band the Brentwoods, and
later was Svengali for the early days of future demi-stars, the Donnas.
Lowery could be his own kind of Svengali. "I started realizing in Supercharger that I was a control freak. It has to be my way. So the first person I called was Jon Von. He'd been kicked out of the Mr. T Experience
and was showing up at Supercharger shows. Jon Von said yes instantly.
Jason White was in the Fingers, so I asked him."

The Fingers are one of those bands described as legendary by all seventeen people who saw their infrequent gigs. "Oh shit, Ralph, their bass player, was insane," Lowery recalls. "He could vomit on cue on-stage. He was a vile human being, you just don't want to be around him." The Rip Offs were a logical extension of the wildest edges of that SF scene, meaning they'd look like they were fighting, but kept actual fisticuffs to a minimum.

"Yeah, our first practice, one of the first songs Jon wrote was about how it's okay to like Green Day. And I'm like, uh . . . ," Lowery says. "Then the problem with Jason White was that Jon Von went to MIT, and there was a weird class thing there."

"Looking back, we were pretty petty, to be honest," says the infamously abrasive Rip Offs guitarist, Shane White. "My brother Jason and I were from East L.A., welfare kids. Jon came from a well-off family, good school, making money we couldn't comprehend. I mean, he owned a house! It bummed me out. We got reviewed by Lawrence Livermore, from Lookout! Records—who became a mutlimillionaire himself, so he's one to talk—and he said, 'The Rip Offs guys aren't "budget rock" because of the money Jon Von has.' So fuck, I thought, Jon's giving the band a bad rep. But Livermore was a fucking shithead anyway. Look at the bands he promoted: Operation Ivy, Green Day, Lagwagon. He's a schlock-meister, but I knew he had influence. . . . And after a while, Jon and I got really tight. Jon Von is a great fucking guy, really nice; and he started bringing in all these great songs. But Greg was very competitive. His ego got huge. That eventually brought us to an end."

"Shane didn't want to join because of Jon, and he'd already started the Spoiled Brats," says Lowery. "So we had a meeting, and of course we get over there, and Jason doesn't say a motherfucking thing, and I've got to explain everything, like I'm the big asshole. . . . So I said, This is the way it's going to be—we're going to go on with the masks. And everyone agreed, but there was already some friction there. I was perceived as the boss, and nobody likes the boss."

The Rip Offs could seem like just like a larf at times, though their singles got progressively nastier, and stand up very well today, mainly due to Lowery's snotty vox, just-searing gits, and the band's catchy hooks. And their record covers are pretty hilarious, more meticulously planned (despite their cheap-ass aesthetic) than most mock-up jobs of that "budget rock" scene.

"The cover of the album [*Got a Record*, 1994] was done at the SF

"The second one from the right, officer. I'm sure of it!" The Rip Offs *Got a Record* LP cover shoot, 1994. (Photo by Jennifer Simpson)

police department," Lowery remembers. "It was actually a fan who worked for *MRR*. Her real job was at 911, and I told her about how it'd be great to get in a lineup. She said she could set it up. She knew one of the cops; he took us up the seventh floor of the building, like an auditorium. There was an old 1970s lineup bar, and he said, 'Whatever, stay up here as long as ya want.' Then a week later I had an idea for the back cover, like we're pissing on a police van. So we spent a couple hours running around SF until we found a police van. It was in this alley around from the Killowatt club, and we did it in ten minutes. I had a marker—I thought it was erasable; I was going to put 'The Rip Offs' on the white part of the van, and started writing it, then tried to quickly erase it to see, and it wouldn't erase! So I thought, No fuckin' way! We took our masks off, walked around the other side of the van, and there was a cop right there the whole time, talking to this old lady."

At the same time that most new underground punks were taking on this kind of crude, middle-finger fun-times approach, *Maximumrocknroll*—the West Coast punk bible that by the very beginning of the decade had become a kind of police force themselves, pointing judgmental index fingers at any bands who might've used the word *bitch* once in a while—was suddenly all snot 'n' swear words again, aesthetically. But politically, arguments railed among its pages about no longer reviewing anything on a major label or that utilized "corporate" distribution—which would include nearly every indie, if you followed the paper trails far enough. Yes, it was very silly.

"Shane and I were friends at the time," says Lowery. "Jason was quiet but turned out to be the craziest of them all. I felt I could handle Shane. He was very punk rock, very negative, he was writing for *MRR*, hanging out with Tim Yohannan all the time, which was kind of shocking because he used to rally against it, those people [and their rules]. . . . Right away, I never embraced that *MRR* crowd ever. I hate politics, especially in music. But then as soon as the Rip Offs started, they were championing us, right after our first single. I'm not stupid, I'm going to go for the publicity. But even in that first interview I asked, 'Why are you doing this?'"

"I had a magazine called *Pure Filth*," White replies, "at that time, the only vehicle many of these bands had. Of course we ragged on everyone, including *MRR*. One day, me and my girlfriend Elka were in a record shop, and Tim Yohannan was like, 'Hey man, I love your mag. How'd you like to like to write for *MRR*? I could use an obnoxious asshole.' I thought, Why not? Started hanging over there, and Tim was a pretty straight-up guy, different than I thought he'd be. Then I found out he was a real troublemaker—smoked, drank, fucked young blondes. And he smelled the whole garage thing from the get-go. So we got tight. I started reviewing, and he didn't give me any shit for fifteen years. I loved him. Since he died, SF has not been the same."

"You know, in any scene there's infighting and shit," says Lowery. "I'm sure every fucking band in Columbus was jealous of the New Bomb Turks because you got popular. It was all egos and problematic. I felt like I had to babysit these assholes. The good thing is, I thought we were writing good, catchy, simple songs, and we were all contributing. Everything was going swimmingly until we recorded *Got a Record*. Shane and Jason were lazy fucks who didn't want to come to the mixing sessions. So Jon and I would mix, then race twenty miles to San Fran from San Bruno to ask them what they thought. Shane would throw the tape and say, 'Ya can't hear the guitar!' Race back to San Bruno, etc."

"Greg may have done more of the driving," says Shane, "but it was a group effort definitely. That record came out, and we were all completely disappointed. I think Greg and I agree we wanted it a little bit more heavy, just stronger, not overproduced. We didn't want to sound like a lo-fi band."

"There was always a weird animosity toward me between Shane and Jason," Lowery says. "We'd do interviews in the Rip Offs, and everyone would want to talk about Supercharger, not about Mr. T or the Fingers."

"No," says White. "Greg got this weird trip that people are jealous of him. He's a good singer, he's got enthusiasm on stage. But he's a horrible bass guitarist, and not the best songwriter, and he uses other people as crutches. No one was jealous of Supercharger, because they couldn't play their way out of fucking paper bag!"

"For the Rip Offs, I was also very concerned about the live shows," Lowery says. "I wanted us to be as good or better than the Mummies. . . . Any crazy idea I had I tried to incorporate. I'd break beer bottles over our heads, but they were breakaway bottles! Shit like that . . . But I really wasn't much of a drinker. Shane would drink and smoke like a sailor, Jon did his share of drugs, Jason too."

"Well, my younger brother has a genuine mental condition," White explains. "He used to be a very heavy acid user, claims to have done acid over five hundred times. It jolted his chemicals, so he's bad bipolar, mild schizophrenia, and lot of times out of nowhere, he'd act really bizarre. Now he's got extreme psychological problems. Too bad, because he was the only Rip Off who was a real musician. Actually, that was one thing Greg and I bonded over, like, 'What are we going to do about Jason?'"

That odd bond didn't hold for long. "It was ugly," Lowery admits. "I did these T-shirts for the Japanese tour, and after we got back, the girl that did the photo I used on the tees called me, and in this like Linda Blair *Exorcist* voice yells, 'Who gave you the right to use my image on a T-shirt?!' What the fuck?! You don't tell me anything about my band, and that photo was my idea. And to be honest, I could've had a motherfuckin' monkey do it! Well, that was Shane's wife at the time. So they thought of the ultimate thing to piss me off. He put out a single of some practice songs, without me knowing. And he hands it to me at the Purple Onion club and says, 'Here's our latest record.' He called it *The Savage Middle Age Rip Offs*. It's utter horseshit. I said, 'Fuck you,' threw it in his face, and that was it, the band was over."

"I totally regret putting that out," White admits. "Total passive-aggressive bullshit." The band fit in one last show in 1995, in Green Bay, Wisconsin, set up by the inimitable Time Bomb Tom.

Seven inches of passive aggression, 1993.

*

NOW HERE WAS a cat who is, as they say, one of the good ones. Time Bomb Tom was manager of the great indie record store there, the Exclusive Company, and single-handedly—with much help from *MRR* scribe and all-around keen kook, Rev. Nørb—made Green Bay an unlikely but imperative tour destination for any punk band worth their cheese in the 1990s. Tom found an old gutted bowling alley in which to stage all-ages shows and called it the Concert Café (later, Rock 'n' Roll High School); and it sat right across an alley from a killer lil' dive called the Speakeasy.

When the Cleveland Browns moved to Baltimore in 1996, Rev. Nørb and some cheerleader-garbed girls held a surprise, pre–New Bomb Turks set ceremony honoring guitarist Jim Weber as an honorary Packers fan, cheesehead hat included, which Jim was able to balance on his head for a good three songs into another insanely bouncy Green

Bay bash. Another favorite (of many) gigs there was one with the very underrated Neckbones. Hailing from Mississippi and waving a good ol' boy banner stained with 1977 Bowery gutter slush, they were on par with Alabama's awesome Quadrajets for Southern punk slamming in the '90s. That particular night ended with one of the many charming, chubby Green Bay chicks rubbing Neckbones' singer Tyler Keith's half-haired dome and slurring, "I'd like to rub my pussy on your head. . . ."

Sometimes, at the tail end of the night, the Rhythm Chicken (a guy wearing a giant rabbit head and flailing away on a full drum kit) would show up across the street in the empty parking lot, performing for the heavens, the drunks, and the cops, who were kind enough to never show up—except once, and I think they were drunk too.

It was no different for the Rip Offs, even at their last show, with bad break-up vibes brewing in the wake of a canceled overseas tour. "Oh yeah, that last show in Green Bay was off the hook, totally insane" says Lowery. "It's hard to explain Green Bay to people, but the shows were always unbelievable. There are certain places that go over the top, and then they die, like all scenes. It was awesome, and we were lucky we hit it at the right time. If we went now, nobody would show up."

So, the Rip Offs were done, but the Rip Off record label was just starting. Lowery scoured the States for shrill thrillers like Loli & the Chones (L.A.); Kill-a-Watts (Milwaukee, Wisconsin); the Problematics (Indianapolis); the Motards (Austin, Texas); the Chinese Millionaires and the Metros (Detroit); and the Registrators from Japan. "The dirty little secret is I liked them more then Teengenerate," Lowery admits.

The label's near–cartoon craziness was codified in the Rip Off Rumbles, annual fests in San Francisco featuring Rip Off bands. "My next band, the Infections, played our first show at the first Rumble," Lowery explains. "I got a real pig head, and I threw it out in the audience, and it was bouncing around like a beach ball! After the show, the club owner goes, 'Get that fuckin' pig head outta here!' So I had to walk out with the pig head in my hands."

The Infections—whose one album, *Kill . . . the Infections* (Rip Off, 1997), arguably trumps all the Rip Offs' records—crumbled even quicker. "Same as the Rip Offs, Greg got too big for his britches," says Shane White, who went even wilder with his guitar slashings in the Infections. "We wanted a band to be like a gang. But Greg started sleeping in separate hotels with his girlfriend, riding in separate vehicles.

Anytime the bands got going good, Greg would break away from the gang. To this day, he doesn't understand it. He blames everyone else. Greg is a funny guy, and I do like him, but he's kind of a tyrant. Then I've got bad temper—punch first, ask questions later. Together we're like dynamite."

By 1997, THE sheer number of trash-punk bands that started multiplying like the monsters in *Night of the Lepus* could send the most poised accountant to a rubber room. And they were crawling out of unusual outposts.

Today, Austin, Texas, is the quirky model of new, overcredited, phony growth-spurt America. And college music heads make it their spring break every year at the ever-expanding South by Southwest music- and film-biz keister-kissing fest. But in the early '90s, though home to the second largest university in the country, it was still just your usual state capital town—albeit one with a music history as deep as any in America. Roky Erickson and his 13th Floor Elevators on up to 1980s hardcore heroes like the Dicks, Really Red, and the Big Boys, then post-'core fist art like Butthole Surfers and Scratch Acid—they were all some of the best of their genre, but also some of the weirdest, with a stew of sweaty, Southern-back-road burly fermented with open-minded lysergic loopiness that seemed to stop at that town's borders.

Once inside Austin's city limits, the fear of fat-ass, magnum-packing pigs was gone, replaced with worry that you might drink yourself to death for all the partying that town organically inspired. You could buy crappy frozen margaritas on the streets; happy hour seemed to measure in days; the little local bars you'd stumble into would usually have amazing jukeboxes and cool, neon-infused rock art on the walls, with giant flames, guns, and all that Sailor Jerry illustrative stuff. Coming from mid-Ohio—where a bar owner's idea of "ambience" was turning the game down and replacing the Archie Griffin poster with one of Eddie George—it was like entering psycho-rock Shangri-la.

"I think there was a slower, lazy way of life that prevailed there," says David Head, guitarist for the town's most notorious '90s skizz-punk lunatics, the Motards. "It was easy to squeak by on some shit job and have enough dough and free time to go crazy. They used to call it a great place for young people to retire."

While some may consider working at a record store as perpetual retirement, such was not the case when working at the overactive hub that was the awe- and guffaw-inspiring Sound Exchange in Austin. Miles of product, loads of in-store performances, broke collegiates hawking for deals, and the usual array of loony locals.

"One nice, ripe, hot summer day when I was working at Sound Exchange in the mid-'90s," says longtime record store proletarian Tim Hayes, "these crusty punks came in to cool off. One of them came up with a T-shirt and said, 'Dude, can I have this?' I said, 'Fuck no! Put it back.' Just then a woman came up asking me to help her, and when I came back, I found the empty hanger. So I bolted out the door, up the street, and saw the crusty dude. He took off into Captain Quackenbush's coffee shop. There was a hallway with glass doors at each end, and I had him trapped there. In a methlike frenzy, he turned around and started flailing his feet and fists at me. I grabbed him in a headlock, we were rolling around, bashing against the glass, then we flew out the front door. We both fell to the ground. He jumped up to make a getaway; I grabbed his feet, got him to the ground, and put my knee up against his head. I literally was grinding his cheeks into the cement. Cassettes, hot sauces, cigarette butts, and that damn T-shirt flew from his rotten army jacket.

"Dude wouldn't get up, so I dragged him by his feet, on his ass, down the sidewalk to the store. And as I was dragging him, he shit his pants. Then he reached down the back of his pants and tried to wipe his shit on us! Fuckin' crusty punks, man. I hate 'em! Two cop cars came, and the cops were arguing with each other about who was going to take the crusty in their car, because he had shit all over him. As I was walking out of the shop I looked at him in handcuffs, and I said, 'All for a fucking Butthole Surfers T-shirt.' He looked down and mumbled, 'I know. I know.'"

Great music haunts have come and gone in Austin. The biggie in the '90s—not just for Austin, but one of the most important rock clubs of the whole alternative rock era—was Emo's. Still standing strong, it's a soggy, dark complex of neon-lit rooms, cluttered bars, and an actual giant Frank Kozik painting on the wall that greeted you when you walked in: an S&M-gear-bedecked Wilma Flintstone and Betty Rubble. A stage is next to that wall, where they have nightly shows; and a bar with at least three bartenders at the ready.

Not enough working toilets, though; considering the thirsts Emo's engenders, the Hearst Castle would be wanting for enough porcelain to leak into. There's a sizable, open-air courtyard, perfect for convers-

**The Motards take a spill at Emo's, Austin, TX, 1993.
(Photo courtesy of Toby Marsh)**

ing away from the noise of the music or rushing your date out to puke. Then into the larger hall (about four hundred–plus capacity) where the big bands play. Half the ceiling covers the stage and the audience area, while the other half is open to the elements, save for some trees hanging overhead, growing right there in the room. Huge old rusty gas station signage wobbles on the walls, and a decent-size bar back is there too. Not much backstage room for the bands, but a closed stairwell up to the stage with an exit to book out of and onto the street, should you piss off the stray good ol' boy in the crowd, which is always a major possibility—one of the reminders that you are most certainly still in Texas.

"There weren't any punk bands in Austin in the early '90s," says Motards bassist Toby Marsh. "The underground trend was the whole Butthole Surfers/Scratch Acid acid-drenched 'There's something weird in the water down there' vibe. I used to go see those bands take a half hit of acid and drink all night." Such mind-altering hobbies led to the formation of the Motards in 1993.

In the shadow of the increasingly hyped alt-rock/SXSW situation, a good garage gaggle flourished, with bands like the Cryin' Out Louds, the Inhalants, and Jack O'Fire, featuring Tim Kerr—formerly of local legends Big Boys and Poison 13—who was starting to produce scrappy bands around town.

"But the Motards were fucking insane." says Greg Lowery. "Some bands on my label could stay at my place. But the Motards were one band I would not allow in my house. They were not right in the head." I personally felt the brunt of the Motards' skull-vacuuming vibe—and bespectacled wild-child singer John Wilson's tough love—when we played with Teengenerate at Emo's in 1995.

Teengenerate hit the stage last, and the place was like napalm in a hot-air popcorn maker. Wilson and I made our way to the "private suites"—that stairwell right next to the stage, watching the band from behind for a few songs. Suddenly Wilson says, "Come on, let's stage dive!"

"Nah."

"Oh, come on, this is amazing!"

It *was* amazing. I think Teengenerate's energy and the mood in the room could've convinced my mother to take a plunge. So John and I locked shoulders and went flying. . . .

The last thing I remember was seeing a bunch of raised hands. Our bodies slid right through the sweaty-gripped throng, I was nabbed by my ankles a millisecond too late and landed directly on my noggin, so I've been told. Matt Reber said he felt the concrete floor shake for a split second. As I came to, I was yelling at the ambulance attendant that I had to get back onstage: "Teengenerate wants me to sing 'Savage'!" Reber's standing there: "Eric, the show ended like ten minutes ago." The doc said, "Just take it easy, drink some water, and go get some sleep." An hour later, I was sipping keg beer at an Austin house party, flirting with some girl, and loving Austin all over again. . . .

THERE WAS AN Emo's in Houston too, though smaller, and it didn't last for long. We played there circa 1998. A few songs in, and I was doing my usual audience-razzing routine and mussed up the 'do of a perfectly arranged rockabilly cat. Now I usually have a good sixth sense for that stuff, but "usually" rarely applies in Texas. In one fluid motion, the flat-headed Shure mic slipped out of my hand and hit the floor; rockabilly cat swept it up in his right hand, then clocked me hard, right across my left eyebrow. Just as fluidly, I blacked out for a second, hit the ground in front of the stage, and as I quickly came to, Jim and Matt were already standing above the guy, pummeling him with the aid of some fans. They get me backstage, blood flowing, and as I'm given a towel to sop my brow, a fan tells me that the rockabilly cat was of the white power persuasion, just got out of prison that day, and was greeted with hugs by most of the bouncers in the club. Jim and Matt, having defended my silly ass, inform me that we'd only done about three songs, and the kids were going crazy, so we should probably go play more. Which we did, me holding that towel on my eye, for another half hour or so. Bill hooked me up with butterfly bandages that night (drummers are prepared motherfuckers), and the next morning as I slowly peeled them off, I looked at myself in the mirror and figured, for the first time since we began, there's got to be a better way to make seventy-eight dollars.

13
INSTANT HEADACHE

A S IS OFTEN the case, our neighbors to the north in Canada picked up on the trash-punk trend toot sweet, if in that traditionally friendlier manner. We did a few shows with the Spitfires from Vancouver, around the later '90s. While hanging at a party they informed us that they'd applied to the government for an arts grant, and that the Canadian government loves that spreading Canuck culture shit. Radio and TV stations are required by law to play 40 percent Canadian material, which means the Tragically Hip are like gods up there. The Spitfires, who at that point had one single out, got twenty thousand dollars from the government!

"Not sure it was that much," says Chad "CC Spitfire" Cornies. "These days those grants are next to impossible to get, but back then you basically just needed a label and distro in the region you were touring. We did get several grants to tour the States, Canada, and the UK. We used to blow American bands' minds—fly into town, get nice hotels, and eat good meals. Looked really rock star-like!" Plus, the Spitfires blew off three Chicago shows on three different tours so they could spend the day at the amazing roller-coaster capital, Cedar Point, in Sandusky, Ohio. Now that's what I call wise use of taxpayer money! If anyone deserved it, it was the Spitfires who, besides being great guys, really worked their fast-action rock—along with their equally black-dyed hair and dank dive–destroying street-punk pals, the Black Halos—up in a country where just getting people to leave their homes for the frigid weather is a chore.

Toronto and Montreal, though, had increasingly fruitful scenes. The hipsters recently slobbering over the King Khan & BBQ Show and their various offshoots probably have no idea who the Spaceshits were. In the latter '90s, they were ground zero degrees for gunk punk in the Great White North. Starting out around 1996 before their 'nads had finished descending, they quickly released singles full of Standells-swiped garage turned snowball-stung burn-punk.

The Spaceshits were an odd amalgamation of half greaser punks, half dudes who just wanted to rock, and a singer with a zipped hoodie and baseball cap yanked down like he just stormed out on his former hardcore band's practice next door but wanted to keep singing. And *could* he sing! What now is obvious about Mark Sultan (aka BBQ)—that he has a vocal timbre more Sam Cooke than Mike Maker—was just warming up then. And Arish Khan (aka King Khan)—himself a soul-shouter of some renown now—sat behind the Spaceshits drum kit at first. "I'd been in a violent punk band," Sultan confirms, "and they had seen some shows. I kinda knew them, so I volunteered to sing."

Canada is well known for its constant stream of comedy; but it's usually not of the salaciously aggressive bent the Spaceshits preferred. Dig their description of the other 'Shits:

"Dan Pedro Dorrito (aka Skid Marks, Casino, Chonks). Best drummer turned Tony Montana turned Bad Lieutenant. If drugs were a person, it would be Dan. Fantastic Mr. Fox (aka, Tongues, Mr. Shampoo) was a great guitarist turned enemy turned adult and great writer. He of course was a secret expert on exotic fruits. Oliy Chi (aka Cantons Finest Youth). He became my brother-in-law and was and still is one of the greatest painters ever. Chi was the genius behind songs like "Bacon Grease" and "Backseat Boogie," and put the rock back in the Chinese for us all. Donny Ciccarelli (aka the guy who can't wear shorts at the beach 'cause his legs are too muscular). Donny was a Spaceshit for a summer and now sports a moustache and helps breastfeed his wonder child. Stinky B—the only tragedy in the Spaceshits. We don know if it was acid or just schizophrenia, but whatever it was, it had three layers and the wrong prescription. Alex Fascination. Also a semitragedy . . . got his tongue ripped in half in Bethlehem, New York; gave up rock 'n' roll to become a suit."

The Spaceshits were apparently too unpredictable for their country's indie labels. So once again along came Long Gone John and his Sympathy label. Khan explains, "We sent him a demo called 'Beer Fueled Mayhem,' and he freaked out. He was like a lost grandfather of sorts. He once sent us ten thousand bucks in cash, stapled to loose-leaf paper." Crypt was also interested in the band for a spell. "I prank phone-called Tim Warren when he put out the Pagans record," Arish recalls, "and said that I had punched my dad in the face when I heard it, so it was his fault. He was always a buddy of ours, and to this day is a insane motherfucker."

The Spaceshits soon shared the scene with the amazing Hendrix-meets-Didjits-gone-glam trio, Danko Jones. Then came the Leather Uppers, Deadly Snakes, Los Sexareenos, Teen Crud Combo, Scat Rag Boosters, and Daylight Lovers; not to mention other funsters from far away and in between like Resin Scraper, the Smugglers, and the Von Zippers. Gonzoid journalist, national radio host, and nerd-rocker Nardwuar the Human Serviette and his band the Evaporators framed the scene in classic Canadian cutup style. And most of these bands often played or even ended up moving to Toronto, where Lee's Palace constantly hosted hyper hubbubs, and the fantabulous fanzine *Gravy* got it all down in ink and glitter glue. It was one of the few zines of that time I'd read cover to cover because of its fun slumber-party vibe that made like a vodka-stained *Tiger Beat* for the garage punk set. That's mostly due to *Gravy*'s femme editors, Kary Cousineau and Samia Canzonieri. They also booked numerous shows in Toronto, Kary eventually becoming one of the main booking agents of famed alt rock in eastern Canada; and Samia marrying Electric Frankenstein guitarist Sal Canzonieri.

CONTINUING ON OUR mid-'90s mess-rock map quest . . . about eight hours or so south in Cincinnati, Ohio—and eons apart from twenty-thousand-dollar government grants—a few knuckleheads knocked out some of the most spastic, nutty noise of that period. The Twerps, the Slobs, the Long Gones, and Archie & the Pukes can be seen as the beginning of a trend of bands just trying to ape their swelling *Killed by Death* piles with their own derided discs. And yes, maybe Andy Slob (of the, uh, Slobs)—who hit "record" for most of this sick little scene in his musty basement (for fifty dollars or two twelve-packs)—did wisely use Legionnaires Disease's 1979 song "Rather See You Dead" as a cranked-up template for the shaky teens who trod down into his den. But anyone who saw these bands live or heard their records knows this was no pose. These guys were very young, demented, and really bored.

Archie & the Pukes thought it a good idea to release an eight-track compilation of their singles . . . in 1996. We made an initial batch of three," says Slob. "We were ready to sell them at the same price as the record, if anyone ordered one." Matt from Archie & the Pukes (most of these guys don't really care to divulge their last names anymore) recalls a story that should sum up this Ohio basement show-sequestered scene:

Gravy zine, issue No. 3, 1996.

"It was posted in bold letters on both toilets upstairs: DO NOT FLUSH! But of course, someone did, and during the middle of our set, sewage began bubbling out of the floor drain beneath our feet, soaking our shoes and splashing up onto the bottoms of our pants. By the time we were done we found ourselves inch-deep in an unholy stew of other people's feces, urine, obscure strands of ejaculate, bile, parasites, and excretions of all the classical humors. It was glorious.

"At one point I looked over at [bassist] Jeff the Amish and saw vivid blue electric arcs jumping from the microphone to his mouth when he did background vocals. It hurt like a bastard, he later told me. I guess this happened because the microphone stand, the cord, and his feet were all resting in a puddle of noxious slush; or maybe because earlier, when the three-pronged PA plug would not fit into the two-prong wall socket, some skinhead used one of those Boy Scout pocket tools his type are fond of carrying to simply bust off the offending third prong.

"I think the Slobs headlined the cesspool show because 1) I remember them threatening to dismember this over-hyper Cincy-via-Detroit transplant who kept jumping in the muck and splashing it all up their legs; and 2) I don't recall any other band in town who could have gotten me excitable enough to spill a whole box of our recently released 7"s into the feculence. They were only two dollars [apiece], so if they came

Archie & the Pukes 8-track, 1996. (Courtesy of Matt Tribbe)

smeared with a little poo, who could complain?

"And to those of you in the Southwest and California, it's not your fault your part of the country doesn't have many basements, but it does help explain why most of your bands suck."

Flyer for a show at the infamous half laundromat/half smoky dive Sudsy Malone's, Cincinnati, 1998. (Courtesy of Andy Slob)

14.
TALENT IS A CRIME

THIS ROCKING AVALANCHE of ramalama rolled across Europe too. The proof of that pudding was a booming scene in that historically important hotbed of great rock 'n' roll . . . *France*? Oui!

The No-Talents, from Paris, were fronted by two luscious ladies—one, Cecilia Meneau, who squealed along like a bride of Frankenstein of every 1979 punk gal yalper; and the other, Lili Zeller, a shit-hot guitarist whose long curly red locks were always in danger of catching fire from her rowdy riffs. A bass player, Iwan Lozac'h, so tall and stern-faced you'd think they imported him from Austria, only his klutzy playing was nowhere near Austrian anal. And a drummer, Laurent Bigot, stone-still and suave-as-fuck French except for his flailing arms. The sound that shot out was sprung from the snottiest edges of the first few *Killed by Death* comps, knocked across the head with a baguette of Franco silly-sexy, and layered with lyrics that played the classic punk-poetry pamphlet like it was a knock-knock-joke anthology.

Lili already had another garage band, the Splash Four, who, like the No-Talents, would soon have records out on American labels like Estrus and Dionysus, and as far away as Japan's 1+2 Records. She even ran her own fine trash-rock imprint, Royal Records. And Cecilia had already established herself as the main punk booking agent for France, and also later started her own cool label (with then boy-toy Lozac'h) Wild Wild Records, doing singles with Teengenerate, Thee Headcoats, the Blacks, and more; and releasing the No-Talents' first album, *100% No Talent* (1996).

Via e-mail, Lili and Cécilia claimed ownership of every answer, and this two-headed approach fit the combination oi! salute and Martin/Lewis act of their stage shows.

The No-Talents floating on fumes in their garage, Paris, 1996.
(Photo by Isabelle Soulier)

Lili & Cécilia: "The idea was to quickly form a band so that three days later we could play a private party with two cover songs. That was for the French Independence Day party in July 1995, in Cecilia and Iwan's giant garage at that time. Our name was a statement against laborious musicianship, endless guitar solos, and everything stale and ugly that goes with it. We liked to do everything very fast."

The band was—as was most of the Euro garage-punk scene by mid-decade—steeped in the strata of lost late-'70s punk, adding a layer of regional pride by unearthing more than just all those great skuzz-punks from Indiana. The Euro volumes of *Killed by Death* and *Bloodstains* soon overtook Yankee ones, and more comps came, centering on regions of Denmark and such.

At the beginning of the '90s, though, there wasn't much of a regional scene in France, but the American slobs were starting to flow through like Beaujolais in the fall. Lili & Cécilia: "Yes, because of Crypt

Records! Crypt was in all ways one of the main actors in the garage punk scene in Europe. Other influential people were Billy Miller and Miriam Linna (*Kicks* mag, Norton Records), Billy Childish, Mike Lucas (the SF scene), Mike Stax (*Ugly Things* mag), and of course Lux [Interior] and [Poison] Ivy [of the Cramps]."

Needless to say, two cute girls fronting a kitschy, sizzling punk band that could pack illegal schoolhouse parties on the outskirts of Paris was going to get attention. Once the No-Talents made their way to the U.S. West Coast, quick friendships were struck with the usual Left Coast trash-punk ignobles like Estrus, who released the band's second album. "I was working for Air France," says Cecilia, "so that actually helped us a lot to save money on the flights when we toured the States. That was pretty funny when the gang was picking me up after work for a gig, and I was changing in the airport's restrooms, trading my blue uniform for my rocker outfit!"

The No-Talents and much of the Euro scene's appropriation of late-'70s punk iconography was almost charming in its razor-slashed style. But their crass was au courant.

Lili & Cécilia: "Even if all garage punk bands were definitely inspired by old rock 'n' roll, you can't reduce it to just a retro thing. There were lots of original sounds, and new, funny aesthetics. But most of all it was the new kind of DIY culture that changed everything. It was terribly exciting! That's almost impossible to figure out for today's MySpace kid generation, after punk rock became horribly fashionable again in the early 2000s."

QUAINT FRENCH HAMLETS like Perpignan and Eugene didn't exactly scream "wild punk rock party" when you drove up to them. But the avidly sauced citizenry that showed up at gigs there were as insane as any fans on the globe. And other groups like Greedy Guts, the Blue Devils, Deche dans Face, Steve & the Jerks, and the Beach Bitches were particularly punchy in their pursuit of a sound born decades ago and thousands of miles away from their fine French food and femmes. But the most vicious of all Franco-fuckheads were the T.V. Killers. Their crazed live sound—featuring smashed TV sets adding crash-boom-bang to their blazing, transistor Radio Birdman bash-up—was further slapped with song titles like "Babyboomers Motherfuckers," "The Beach Sucks," and "Stinky Smile." They told stories of France not found on the Travel Channel.

While even the oft-artistically dour Germany spewed out some surprisingly fun spazz-punk—like the Steve McQueens, Jet Bumpers, and
the Cellophane Suckers—the usually on-the-ball United Kingdom offered up little in the way of this mini-movement of mess-ups. But the
best one, the X-Rays, more than made up for it. "Formed in a popular
drinking hole in Nottingham, England, in February 1994," says glee-
fully spazz-eyed bassist Coop, the band displayed the kind of sauced-
by-3-PM, never washed, and general noisy, stairs-fall fuck-all that will
garner enough paragraphs from the British press to equal the number
of times bangers and mash appear on a Parisian café menu. "At the
time the rest of the UK was immersed in Britpop, and we just wanted
to be the antithesis to all that lame shit," says Coop.

But the band had a pub-pal punter heart endemic to the best British rock 'n' roll. "A special mention should go out to Blake Wright from
Empty Records," says Coop, "who put out the first two albums. I took it
upon myself to fly three thousand miles over to Boston, then drove the
other three thousand miles to Seattle to meet Blake in person, and hand
him our first demo tape. You can't trust the postal service!" Shakey Lee,
owner of UK indie, Sonic Dirt Recordings, has his own tipsy tale:

"My first exposure to the X-Rays live experience remains the most
memorable. Having taken full advantage of a local boozer's cheap

Just a couple of the many great European garage zines of the 1990s.

whiskey offer since lunchtime, the boys had managed to get into the kind of state that would have made Oliver Reed proud. Seconds into the first song, G-Man [guitarist]was on his back, playing out the rest of the night staring at the ceiling. Two songs in and Charger [drummer] had lapped the rest of the band, having pounded out a fifteen-minute set in two minutes flat. By the fourth song it was carnage. Coop was prowling the audience hammering his bass and shouting at anyone who would listen, his cord dragging feebly behind him, unplugged. No one even noticed Gary [singer] throwing a tantrum, ripping off his shirt and slinging it to the floor before storming off into the cold night air to the soundtrack of four different X-Rays songs all being played at the same time. Thirty years earlier and the night would have been hailed as visionary. Three bottles of whiskey later, and it could have been forgettable. Genius."

"And," Coop concludes, "I didn't even get 'round to telling y'all 'bout wrestling with the Motards in Missoula, Montana; getting fucked with the Fumes in Spokane; arrested in Groningen; and getting drunk in every single town we played!"

WELL, IF ENGLAND wasn't allowing a lot of garage bands onto their shores in the '90s, they could always ship the dregs to the friendly, drunken arms of Australia, where, of course, amazing punk was not exactly an anomaly. The Onyas were Australia's prime addition to '90s nut-crunching punk.

The east coast of Australia, where all the bigger cities are, has beaches and is hot in climate—but in spirit, more L.A. Spicoli than Miami Scarface. Onyas singer John "Mad Macka" McKeering was a perfect example. A star swimmer in high school, he would go hit the road with his power trio, amass a beer gut, then come back and lifeguard it all off in a few weeks. Sonically, the Onyas might've sounded like the wise-ass little brothers of the Cosmic Psychos, but they left even their big bros' partying habits in the rearview mirror.

"Bands that we felt akin to included you guys, Lazy Cowgirls, Billy Childish etc.," says McKeering. "In Australia we loved Bored, Splatterheads, Freeloaders, Cosmic Psychos, Kim Salmon & the Surrealists, the Powder Monkeys, and we loved the Hard-Ons." Onstage, the Onyas would pummel away like a metronome that had gotten gum stuck to it—hoisting good hooks that, given the level of sobriety, would wobble back and forth within the always forward shove. Then, during the day,

the blokes—due to hangovers or weed-whacked wooziness—would offer comical lowlights. We'd been hanging in Sydney for a few days in
the beginning of our Aussie tour with them in 1999, and were finally
making our way out of the big busy city, then blocked up at every turn
due to construction connected to the oncoming Olympics. Just as we
finally get on the highway, the car starts sputtering, and bassist Richard Stanley keeps starting up again. Grumbles of, "Oh fuck, we're not
gonna make the next show, what do we do now, oh fuck!" Then Jim
Weber says, "Uh, Richie, did you check the gas meter?"

"Oh, ha, we're like out of gas or something. Ha ha."

When in Melbourne, a swanky modeling center of the world, the
less-than-glamorous boozing the Onyas brought with them led opening one-man band, Bob Log III, to puke into his motorcycle helmet/
microphone contraption, the bile dripping out the rest of the set. The
three models in attendance were less than amused.

"By the time we actually started to play live a bit more," McKeering
says, "grunge or whatever you call it was in full swing. I know Richard
saw the first Mudhoney show in Brisbane; and the Nirvana show in
Melbourne with Cosmic Psychos. There was a period when we liked it
just like the next twenty-one-year old, but we were definitely not into
the bands that were aping that sound in our scene in Brisbane."

The Aussie '90s scene was aided immeasurably by indie imprints like
Au-Go-Go, Giant Claw, Lance Rock, and Shock Distribution. Dave
Laing had run Melbourne-based Grown Up Wrong records in the '80s,
releasing regional raw rock bands and distributing the Lazy Cowgirls
early Aussie releases. When contacted for this book, Laing expressed a
strong belief—shared by most Australian rock fanatics—that the country, because of location and sustained mystery, gets short-changed in
most rock recounts.

"As the label went along, while I was trying to work with local bands
that excited me, I was always looking to do records with overseas bands
that I thought were great too, many from L.A., like Claw Hammer,"
says Lainge. "This was before Sympathy for the Record Industry was
around." His signing of Bored in the very late '80s sparked success
for them Down Under that Lainge relates to Mudhoney's influence in
America's underground at that time. Grown Up Wrong begat his Dog
Meat imprint, which became a conduit for not just the latest raw Aussie
bands, but a lifeline for bands from In the Red, Sympathy, Crypt, et all
looking for some Down Under action.

"So the first three Dog Meat releases were albums by Antiseen, the Jeff Dahl group, and Don Waller's mid-'70s L.A. band, the Imperial Dogs; and there were loads of other releases from the likes of Johnny & the Jumper Cables, the Barracudas, Thee Headcoats, Devil Dogs, Dead Moon, and even New Bomb Turks right there at the end. And doing the Troggs and Scientists tribute albums was a great way to work with even more bands I dug."

COMPILATIONS WERE ALL the indie label rage in the early '90s: tributes (Sonics, Rolling Stones, Kinks, Shonen Knife); the soundtrack to the garage punk cult flick *The Sore Losers*; the *Cheapo Crypt Samplers*; and the numerous comps that came with the amazing Greek magazine *The Thing* are just a few. I even released my own in 1997, called *Half-Assed, Will Travel*, a collection of trash-punk bands I'd come across while touring around. Then in 2002, Gearhead Records ponied up and entrusted me to compile *Greaseball Melodrama*.

Mike LaVella, Gearhead Records' Oakland-based founder, came into the New Bomb Turks transom way back in 1993, on our first trip out west. He'd already started *Gearhead*, a cool music-and-muscle-cars mag that featured split-singles from some garage bands of the day. We didn't even realize until years later that this hilarious guy was in the '80s Pittsburgh Mohawk-core crew Half Life, but had since made Ed "Big Daddy" Roth his spiritual guide.

"The first concert I ever saw was the Banana Splits," says LaVella. "I saw them with Arthur Godfrey in 1970 at the Pennsylvania State Fair. I was five, front row, and freaking out. The costumes were dirty and the fingertips were cut out for playing guitar." Aside from being a bottomless pit of distant details (his memories of Starbuck on *The Mike Douglas Show* were a personal fave), LaVella is also chattier than a seventeen-year-old girl textless and in line at a mall cell phone store.

"As soon as I heard hardcore, everything else paled in comparison," says LaVella. "From there, every moment of my life was about booking shows, doing a fanzine, starting a label." A move to Pittsburgh proper in January 1982, led to more wanderlust. "My stepbrother lived in DC, and once, over a three-day period, we saw the Cramps, the Gun Club, the Necros, the Faith, and the Meatmen. I saw the Cramps March 27, and by April 20 my band had written a set and played out. Eight days later we opened for Hüsker Dü, and two days after that we opened for Flipper. This was 1983. . . . I saw the Pagans in '83 open for the Ra-

Dog Meat ad, 1996.

mones at the Agora in Cleveland. I can't stress it enough—1981, I'm at Styx; 1983, I'm at the Pagans!"

The character of the '90s vintage-clad cad with a pinstriped-over hardcore past was becoming common back then, only most of those kinds of guys became more and more ensconced in their tiki-festooned apartments. But LaVella kept going to shows, and going, and going. His garage lean had started leaning when he met the Cynics. "Me and Greg (Kostelich, guitarist) worked at the same record store. He made me tapes of 13th Floor Elevators and stuff. I would never have met Dee Dee Ramone if I hadn't been roadie-ing for them."

The move to San Francisco in 1988 had LaVella sharpening his getting-up-in-grill skills, and he was soon writing for *Thrasher* and *Maximumrocknroll*. "The night I moved here," he recalls, like an eight-year-old rattling off what he got for Christmas yesterday, "Die Kreuzen and the Lyres were playing, the next night Fang, the next night the Damned. Later, Nirvana playing to ten people. That's when I started writing for *MRR*. I was working at this record store, Frankie Fixx walked in, and I interviewed him—that article on Crime was the first thing I wrote for *MRR*."

Soon enough, frustrations with the skate-punk world of the mags he wrote for started to set him off: "At that time they were listening to Sore Throat. Huh?! I thought it was retarded. It was suddenly a big me-versus-them thing. You could like Fugazi, but you couldn't like *actual* funk. They had weird restrictions there. I'm interviewing Mudhoney and the Sub Pop guys, who were a full-on phenomenon at that point . . . and *MRR* puts Capitol Punishment on the cover! When are we going to hep the kids to the good shit?!"

Despite any differences of purpose though, there was no denying MRR editor, Tim Yohannan. "How his mind works is God's own fucking mystery. He had a wonderful laugh and enjoyed the company of people, but only on his terms. I never met anyone like him before or since. When nobody was there but me and him, he'd talk about the Cramps and buying all these old R&B records; he would play Andre Williams for me. He was so fucking hip, but also, he could never break out of that rigid comfort zone of what *MRR* was.

"The way *Gearhead* got started," LaVella continues, "is that I knew I was gonna start my own magazine, and I also loved muscle cars. Out here people had cool cars. Every chick had a '62 Comet or a '74 Fairlane or Dart. My '68 Charger I got for two thousand dollars, and now it's worth like a quarter of a million dollars. Anyway, a lot of new garage bands didn't necessarily make it out here for whatever reasons the New Bomb Turks did, and that was a big turning point. It's very weird. It was like you knew something new was going on. The Mummies were happening, and Supercharger, the Trashwomen, Untamed Youth, and the Phantom Surfers. And because I had a background in garage being a roadie for the Cynics, I took to it like a fly to shit. But I still had waist-length hair. Man, did I stand out at those shows! Then overnight, in 1992, I got my Michael Corleone haircut, and it was the gas station jacket and the chain wallet. Everybody looked like Joe Newton. But I was still friendly with all the hardcore dudes. I roadied for Samhain and Government Issue; Brian Brannon from JFA is the one who created the *Gearhead* logo with the racing flags. And no magazine was covering that mix of shit. I'd lay it out like a vintage car mag to make it unique."

A few other cool national indie magazines, like *Brutarian*, *Fiz*, *Motorbooty*, *Carbon 14*, *Ugly Things*, and *Your Flesh*, offered exposure to the furious fumes coming from the trash-punk carport. And of course numerous regional zines shed some light onto the scene too, like *Black to Comm* (Sharon, Pennsylvania), *Chunklet* (Athens, Georgia), *Noise for Heroes* (San Diego, California), *Suburban Voice* (Lynn, Massachusetts), and *Ten*

Things Jesus Wants You to Know (Seattle). But Lavella's gazette catered most acutely to the retro-forward contingent, and also included cool split singles with neo-garage bands like the Red Aunts, Fastbacks, and Claw Hammer.

At this point, LaVella's infectious excitement got the better of him, as he went on to claim revisionist ownership of Ed Roth and Von Dutch, when Estrus had been shining that chrome too. "I knew I *had* to reintroduce these guy," says LaVella, "because they weren't going to be around forever. It was the one good idea I had in my life. There was *Speed Kills* magazine too, but that was indie rock—like, the cars of the Dischord employees. Peter Bagge did the cover for *Gearhead* No. 2. Frank Kozik moved up from Texas. He loved *Gearhead* and gave me seventy-five posters. When we did No. 3, we moved into Mans Ruin's office, and they hired me to help with the label.

Frank Kozik had established himself as the preeminent rock poster artist of the era—a new golden age of rock poster art—and decided to parlay that into his musical interests with his Man's Ruin label, which leaned heavily into the burgeoning stoner rock trend of the time

Mark Arm (Mudhoney) gets cheeky with Mike LaVella, San Francisco, 1989. (Photo courtesy of Mike LaVella)

(Kyuss, Melvins, the Desert Sessions) but released hot-rodded garage punk too (Dwarves, Gaza Strippers, Nomads, Electric Frankenstein, Hellacopters). The label also put together a benefit compilation (*Flaming Burnout*) to raise money for Estrus label head Dave Crider after his tragic fire in 1996. "People made the assumption that I was rich," says Kozik, "which I was not! But I initially put a hell of a lot of my own money into Man's Ruin, which turned into a lot more."

LaVella claims, "By the time I was doing *Gearhead* No.10 with the Robert Williams cover, I was selling thirteen thousand copies. Then the Gearhead label has started, and I couldn't concentrate on the magazine as much."

"Mike LaVella and I met in 1990 when we were both writing for *MRR*," says Gearhead Records cofounder Michelle Haunold. "I was making a living working at Reckless Records, as the buyer for all rare punk and garage vinyl. Mike and I became friends. He left *MRR* to start *Gearhead* magazine, and I continued to write for *MRR* until 1996. I left Reckless in 1994 to go work for Mordam Records. Mike had hooked up with Frank Kozik at some point in there, and when Frank started Man's Ruin, he came to Mordam for distribution. Then Mike and Frank agreed to distribute the Gearhead magazine through Man's Ruin too. There was a staff meeting to debate this move, as Mordam wanted to keep it out because it had advertisements for motor oil and "big business" stuff inside. Long story short, we won, *Gearhead* magazine was brought in through Man's Ruin, and Mike continued to sporadically do the mag while working for Lookout! Records.

"Mike didn't know the business side of his record label ambitions," Haunold continues. "All he knew were the bands. And since I knew sales, distribution, and finances, we became partners. We agreed to call it Gearhead Records. We went out to dinner to celebrate, at the behest of Frank Kozik. He took us out for steaks and then stuck me with the bill, since neither he nor Mike had any money. I should have seen this as foreshadowing. . . . By December 1999, we started on the first record, a collection of singles from the magazine called *Runnin' on Fumes*. Mike handled finding the bands and getting artwork together; I did the sales and, with the help of the Mordam staff, the promotion, the production, etc."

Gearhead Records was the first label to really expose the new Swedish garage rock scene (the Hives, Hellacopters, Mensen, "Demons," Puffball) in America—which of course soon led to legal troubles.

Gearhead No. 2, 1994, featuring Peter Bagge (*Hate* comics) cover art.

Essentially, the Hives' Euro label, Burning Heart, licensed Hives records to Gearhead; when the Hives started getting more popular, Burning Heart worked out a distro deal with Epitaph in America; and then Warner Brothers worked another deal to sign the Hives world-wide, which led to more contractual skirmishes, legally landing Gear-head in a tug-of-war with three much larger labels. The Hellacopters—different labels, same complications.

"Plus, with Man's Ruin," Kozik says, "Mordam started saying, 'Oh, you do, like, heavy metal music, and we don't want to distribute *that* stuff.'" That's an interesting reminder that in the '90s, record distribu-tors thought they could afford to be discriminating. After some legal wrangling, Kozik got himself extricated from Mordam, which resulted in him being able to walk away with only a screen-print machine. A truckload of Man's Ruin releases—most of which are today incred-ibly collectible, if mostly for Kozik's cool screen-printed sleeves—were thrown into a landfill.

By the time LaVella came to ask New Bomb Turks if Gearhead could release what turned out to be our last album (*The Night Before the Day the Earth Stood Still*, 2002), his lid still flipped feverishly, just not 24-7 anymore. Haunold was slowly taking over the day-to-day, and LaVella was thinking about getting out of the record game and back into the mag more seriously again. Today, Haunold is the sole owner and presi-dent of Gearhead Records.

The Gearhead milieu begat a more manly strain that started to spring from the space-age-bachelor-padded cells of the neo–garage rock nuthouse, favoring ol' Chevy and chest-heavy Coop imagery, early '60s men's mag graphics, martinis, pomade, and clothing like Dad used to don at backyard BBQs back in 1962.

"Yeah, and ya know what? We got blamed for that," says Andy Gortler of the Devil Dogs. "A lot of people said, 'I hate the Devil Dogs now, I hate all that Fonzie shit.' But what you actually hate are all the bands that copied us. That's not my fault! All I was trying to do was play rock 'n' roll the way I thought it was supposed to be played. If it's real, it's rock 'n' roll. If it's not, then it's relegated to some sort of de-cade dump." The corniest tail to the Gearhead heads was the mid-'90s swing trend, whose zoot suit was sagging six months before the Cherry Poppin' Daddies, Big Bad Voodoo Daddy, et al were getting major play.

Then labels like Scooch Pooch and Junk took the most brawny

Speed Kills magazine, 1992.

byways of the garage interstate by seeking out bands that could violently one-up the last lot of punk bloodletters.

In only about three years of existence, Junk—begun in 1996 by L.A. scene vet Katon W. De Pena—released thirty-plus records. The Weaklings, Stallions, B-Movie Rats, and Electric Frankenstein were the better second-tier tough guys Junk unleashed. "A lot of the releases were 7" singles," says De Pena, "and we were doing at least one to two thousand, depending on the band—and you don't make money on those. . . . The worst thing we did was merge with another label, Nitro, headed by Dexter Holland, singer of the Offspring. Basically, he had money to spend and wanted a tax write-off. Then we put out a River City Rapists album with a picture of a pregnant woman drinking a big bottle of booze, and the album and group got banned. It cost us money because we pressed a whole bunch of them. And for Dexter Holland, it's too much because he was doing this poppy punk label, and we're doing the dirtiest rock 'n' roll records in the world. I didn't realize that some people would take it so seriously. You'd have to be a moron to think that I support rapists! Or that I would support a pregnant lady drinking whiskey! I got to put out some bands that I loved, but after that, I just washed my hands of it."

De Pena is as excited and experienced as LaVella. He's also a black guy, and the lead singer of a hyper-metal band (Hirax) for years—both rare traits for this scene. I assumed hanging around such vicious bands and fans, he must've had run-ins with racist assholes. "Well, I wasn't stupid to the fact that I was black, so I was careful where I went, but it kind of sucks that you have to be like that. Sometimes a band, even if they're cool, they attract idiots. . . . A lot of those kinds of bands though are disrespectful to alternative lifestyles, women, people of a different color. It's kind of a fine line to walk because you like the energy of the music, but you don't like some of the people who go to the shows. . . . Still, to this day I don't see a ton of black kids at metal or punk shows, but that never deterred me from liking it."

Lisa Kekaula is also African American, and a woman to boot. Her band, the BellRays—begun in 1995 in Riverside, California, but not really hitting the road hard until the end of the decade—were on the other end of the macho instinct scale from Junk's fight club. The Bell-Rays promoted the soulful, sexy '60s city-sway side of the MC5 guitar army–like invasion advancing through the garage punk milieu. "I know too well since we started this band that people listen with their eyes first," says Kekaula. "It's an obstacle I'm used to, but I won't condone it."

The BellRays rise up, Beachland Tavern, Cleveland, 2000.
(Photo by Jay Brown)

*

CONCURRENT TO THE louder, faster flexing on one end of the garage playground, there were diametrically stripped-down duos forming elsewhere, intrinsically humbled if just as pissed.

Don Howland had set the stage with his post–Gibson Brothers act, the Bassholes, who created the template of disillusioned garage rockers metaphorically driving a rusty pickup down south to exhume the plywood coffins of lost bluesmen and force-feed them '77 7"s, washed down with whiskey. Then Doo Rag dumped out a buzz-igniting batch of singles early in the '90s before breaking up and into the one-man bozo, Bob Log III. Chet Weise of the Quadrajets had formed his Southern-fried Immortal Lee County Killers. And in 1996, Crypt signed a dynamite duo from Lansing, Michigan—Bantam Rooster—who could distill the Crypt ethos via just skins and guitarist Tom Jackson Potter's desperate screech that made like an old Elisha Cook Jr. character finally blowing up at all those deceitful molls.

Potter was just out of his first band, Kill Devil Hill (which included future Wolf Eyes members), and grabbed fellow B-flick fan Eric Cook to drum. The two had the looks of hungover substitute teachers but the physical whomp of a closeted Catholic-school nun with a new ruler. Jackson's taste went from Touch and Go then back to the *Graves*, but really flipped when '68 Comeback came through town in 1994.

"Really, we were just trying to reproduce the sound on Guitar Wolf's *Wolf Rock!* LP," says Potter. "We figured if we had to sound shitty, then let's make it jump off the tape like that did. Plus it covers up a lot of mistakes. . . . But shit, man, none of the prewar blues guys even needed a fuckin' drummer to get the folks dancing. I loved the Bassholes, and I recall seeing the Flat Duo Jets open for New Bomb Turks at St. Andrews in Detroit. Honestly, Eric and I started as a two-piece out of necessity. By the time we thought about adding a bass player or whatever, we'd already been writing songs that worked as a two-piece, so who needs the extra baggage? Any bass player who was even mildly cool knew better than to offer. So it would always be the mulleted guy with the Rush T-shirt offering to 'dial in our tones on my eight-string Feinheimer,' or whatever. And of course there'd be the 'What do you have against bass players?' dudes. To which we'd usually reply, 'Why, nothing, in fact we've got a retarded monkey we're training to play bass right now.' I actually love bass, by the way . . . and am especially fond of retarded monkeys—even dated a few.'"

15.
THE EVIL POWERS
OF ROCK'N' ROLL

A S "ALTERNATIVE ROCK" became profitable, it was inevitable that some of these groups would get courted by major labels. Logical, since this stuff at its core was fairly traditional. But the leap to major labels was also another affront to a standard, misconstrued tenant of punk rock—that bands should pursue willful obscurity. Actually, most of these bands would've loved to have hits, to hear fun catchy songs on the radio again, and to finally make some money at it.

AFTER PUSSY GALORE fell apart around 1990, leader Jon Spencer soon formed the trio the Jon Spencer Blues Explosion, who proceeded to spend a couple years working their butts off on tour, releasing records on In the Red, Crypt, and Matador incrementally adding accessible layers of melody, dance-flavored production, and hip guests and producers to their root-garage racket.

"When I named the band," says Spencer, "I thought, I'll do this ridiculous obnoxious name, sort of making fun that usual thing: 'Oh, now this guy's moving on to his solo project.' But the Blues Explosion was much more about embracing some traditional rock 'n' roll and showmanship. A high-energy, James Brown sort of soul revue." The Blues Explosion took two savage steps forward for every rearview influence they'd twisted, and by 1994's *Orange*, they'd become a now-sound all their own.

"When the Blues Explosion first came to Detroit," says Mick Collins, there were about twelve people there, at Paychecks. It became a sort of house party. They'd bash out some songs, we'd hand them some beers, bash out a couple more songs, joke, then do a couple more songs.

It was a really cool show. Then the next time I saw them, it was on the *Orange* tour (the Blues Explosion's fourth album, 1994), at a big place, Clutch Cargo, and it was a whole different deal. Two thousand frat boys, a light show . . . and I thought, What the fuck happened? But I have to admit, it was a great show!"

As the Blues Explosion exploded, the band wisely retained their publishing rights by licensing their records throughout the world on various labels, which got them a larger percentage of what they earned. But that next level of mall-rat fame remained elusive with no huge label behind them—though they never chased that carrot too hard. "We toured with the Beastie Boys and the Roots in '94, '95," Spencer recalls. "Stadiums, arenas—it was weird. I kept waiting for someone to say, 'Okay, you can go home now.' But as a band, we were really clicking, there was no stopping us."

Spencer was also involved in another successful band in the '90s, Boss Hog, co-created with his wife Cristina Martinez. The pair were based in NYC and well connected at this point; Spencer's rare combo

Jon Spencer Blues Explosion, 1994. (Photo courtesy of Jon Spencer Blues Explosion)

of street and music-industry cred, combined with Cristina's looks and incongruously marauding stage presence—not to mention their sound, a potentially more accessible Ike & Tina Turner–meet-grunge thing— seemed like a lock for some kind of crossover fame. After solid indie efforts on Amphetamine Reptile, a move to Geffen in 1997 proved pointless.

"Well," says Spencer, "it was a feeding frenzy at the time; you could make some money. I kind of regret it. The first Boss Hog record on Geffen was the only record in my post–Pussy Galore career that I didn't license—and now that's unavailable. We did demos for the second record, *Whiteout*, with Jerry Teel at Funhouse. Geffen passed on it, but we were free to get a deal with someone else, and we still got a good chunk of the advance." (*Whiteout* eventually came out on In the Red in 2000.)

"I still need to fill that psychological hole—performing on record and on stage, which is the best." Spencer most frequently does that these days with his bentabilly combo Heavy Trash; while the Blues Explosion's amazing guitarist Judah Bauer tours with Cat Power. . . . If you plan on remaining a working musician with Charlie Feathers and the Electric Eels as your main musical inspirations, one would be hard-pressed to find a wiser way to do it than the way Jon Spencer has.

THE SUPERSUCKERS WERE a quintessential example of the '90s major-label-machine practice of casually juggling band fortunes before all the pieces end up getting fumbled to the curb. Mind you, I would never call the 'Suckers "victims." By the mid-'90s, the stories of working-class rock dudes getting starry-eyed and ripped off mercilessly at the hands of evil corporate giants was a tale as old as that of Icarus. So in my opinion, if you were a young band who signed a bad contract or let some manager rip you off, you either hadn't studied your rock history (which encompasses the PhD-level workload of reading the occasional issue of *Rolling Stone* and watching a few VH1 *Behind the Music* episodes); or you just plain wanted lots more money and/or wanted to be a big star—which is fine, but this is the music biz in America, and even your grandmammy knows the percentages are stacked against that bet.

The 'Suckers knew their history but made the decision to play the game anyway. It's important to mention again that there really were loads of (or at least the *speculation* of loads of) dollars floating around the music industry at the time. Subsidiary "incubator" labels were popping up monthly (Imago, Onion, Almo Sounds, etc.). A&R guys were

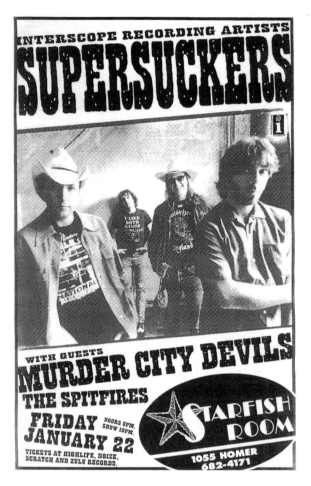

The Supersuckers take umbrage with that iffy "Interscope Recording Artists" tag, Vancouver, BC, 1999. (Courtesy of Chad Cornies)

still glad-handing goons, but they were goons who knew what "DIY" meant, had maybe read *Motorbooty*, and might actually go to a dank bar to check out your band, label gold card in pocket. So the feeling was the inmates were getting internships at the asylum.

"Our second Sub Pop record, *La Mano Cornuda* (1994), had been out for like a month, and they told us we had to go in and make another one," says singer/bassist Eddie Spaghetti. "Someone at Sub Pop said, 'Ah, no one's listening to that punk rock stuff.' Then Green Day's *Dookie* blows up, and they thought, 'Hey wait, we've got our own *Dookie* right here!'" So a load was dumped on their fourth long-player, *The Sacrilicious Sounds of the Supersuckers* (Sub Pop, 2005), the first 'Suckers album without original lead guitarist Ron Heathman, who'd been ably replaced by the great Rick Sims (ex-Didjits). The album featured a shmancy gatefold LP sleeve, a hologram in the CD, and a pricey video for the single "Born with a Tail" (that featured *Exorcist* star Linda Blair as a lil' she-demon).

"That was kind of cool—posters everywhere, had a billboard on Sunset Boulevard," says Spaghetti. "That video was fun! Linda Blair was really nice, but we didn't see her very long. Maybe like two hours total for her. So I think they spent like three hundred thousand dollars on that record. That's where we went into debt with Sub Pop. But the record didn't do what they hoped."

Plus, the band had reined in Paul Leary to produce *Sacrilicious*. Leary, guitarist for veteran experi-poonks the Butthole Surfers, had by then become a go-to knob twiddler (Meat Puppets, Sublime, Weezer, and more). It's still kind of amazing to think that the Butthole Surfers had a couple minor "hits" and that Leary survived such an insane band and actually became a guy who could command a hundred grand to do, well, anything. But that's how the music biz was rolling, mid-'90s.

The CD sales boom and radio and MTV's sudden reception to somewhat louder, punk-festered sounds added up to a fairly lengthy period (in pop music standards) of heightened hope for rock bands of all stripes to be able to pay the rent on this hunch. That boom stretched from about 1992 to 1997, and its height of purse-strings loosening was 1995, right when the 'Suckers decided to sign to a major.

"We chose Tom Werman to produce the Interscope record," Spaghetti says. "He did all those amazing Cheap Trick records, [Mötley Crüe's] *Shout at the Devil*, etc. So we thought we had a big-time producer; he thought we were his comeback too. It didn't end up happening for either of us. The nail in the coffin was driven by the musical climate at the time, with the Limp Bizkit and Korn shit starting up."

And it's not just the impatience of pop music press and fandom that must be breached, it's band momentum too. As far as the incremental development of a rock band can go, the 'Suckers had cleared every hurdle up to that point. They started with a solid, fresh sound that nabbed fanatics; were based out of the hottest music city of the day, Seattle; and had a not too complicated "brand" as a cool-looking cowpoked gang who could project their act to the back rows of a bigger theater if need be (and it be, by then). And whatever your opinion

of their fun show/hokey shtick, their work ethic could never be ques-
tioned. (Though whether music fans still want hardworking bands or
myth-propping flashes in the pan is still up for debate.)

The 'Suckers kept on gamely touring and released the country record *Must've Been High* as their last Sub Pop album, in 1997. They finally
did finish up the Interscope debut—at a ridiculous cost in money and
time. In an anecdote that became as familiar in the '90s as a Bill-Clin-
ton-cheating rumor, the excited people at Interscope who pushed to get
the band signed had been canned. Interscope dropped the band, said it
owned the tapes, and shelved the album, reminding the band that they
were not even allowed to have the long-gestating recordings to farm out
to another label. Even the eventual "dirtier" redux of the Interscope
record, *The Evil Powers of Rock 'n' Roll*, that came out on Koch in 1999,
cost the band a hundred grand in preproduction.

"It was really depressing, took a while to get over," says Spaghetti.
"I don't know where the original master tapes of the Interscope album
are now. In an office at Universal, I guess. But we had a CD-reference
copy, and that's what we used to release some of it over the years on fan
club singles and stuff. We're not allowed to, we just did, because we are
the masters of our own destiny. We've always been of the mind that it's
easier to ask forgiveness than to ask permission."

SIMILARLY SHOT OUT of the tired-of-hardcore-canon cannon circa
1990, Rocket from the Crypt jump-started a moribund San Diego
scene. Formed from the debris of post-'core band Pitchfork, RFTC soldered cheeky, sequined, showbiz tailfins to a locomotive, horn-blasted,
gang-punk revue that soon garnered them a huge following and countless releases on cool indies like Sympathy, Sub Pop, and Merge. Fanatical audience debacles were the norm, and often spilled onto the stage,
though front man John "Speedo" Reis was always able to sling his pompadour back into place.

"At one show," says Reis, "someone brought a German shepherd
into a party and sicced him on me while we were playing. I got bit on
the arm. We were playing up against a wall where there was a window
behind us, and I fell back, tripped over my amp, and went right through
the window. But it was on the first floor, and I landed on the ground
with broken glass all around me." Of course they finished the set.
Their rabid following led to many fans falling hard for a band lark. They
suggested in early interviews that if you got a tattoo of their rocket logo,

you'd get into their shows free for life. "It was just an accidental thing that happened," says Reis. "It was never a design to try and get people to emblazon our logo on themselves. It just kept going. . . ."

All this action assured major-label interest would stick like pomade to Reis's jet-black pompadour. RFTC eventually signed to Interscope Records in 1994. The subsequent album, *Scream, Dracula, Scream!* (1995), was a rare instance where a major label nabs a rock band at its height. The record got some MTV play and a couple of catchy, near-hit songs. And RFTC's brother band, the more angular Drive Like Jehu (who shared some members), broadened Rocket's base. "Both bands had garnered interest from pretty much everybody," Reis states. "Some labels were into one more than the other, but they all kind of realized that they had to do business with both bands to make it work."

RFTC was a band that needed the support a major label can offer, given their nonstop tour habits, and that available horn players sometimes expanded the band to seven or eight members. Reis, being a fan of early-'70s mega-glam like Wizzard, Slade, and the Sweet, really wanted to make a go at bigger and better matching getups. And the band's big sound lent itself to the huge-room-studio trickanery of major-label dreams.

"Yeah, it was odd," says Reis. "The budget to make a record before was maybe six thousand dollars for everything; then just to make a post-card mail-out was suddenly six thousand dollars. The waste was pretty crazy, but we never got any royalties anyway, so we knew the accountability just wouldn't be there no matter what. So these guys will give us a big chunk of money, and we can go and use the same studio that the Beach Boys used, and get self-absorbed and just marinate in our weird ideas of what we think is cool. That just sounded like a lot of fun; and if we can go on the road, do a tour for free because the label is going to pick up the tab . . . Well, we just looked at it like the label was an enabler for all our stupid ideas. It wasn't, 'Let's get rich and famous.' It wasn't, 'Hey, we made it!' It was like, 'Here's the beginning—let's start doing everything we've been talking about.'"

Mind you, this comes from a guy who also loves the Gories, and has released gunk-fi gaga like Demolition Doll Rods, Crime, and CPC Gangbangs records on his cool label, Swami. And his band took their name from the legendary Cleveland proto-punks Rocket from the Tombs. "Ah," Reis admits, "we figured no one knew who the hell they were back then, certainly not in California!" Once RFTC's ball started

Must listen to Rocket from the Crypt, must listen to Rocket from the Crypt . . .
Interscope promo photo, 1997. (Photo by Michael Halsband)

rolling, they were in a unique position for a band of raw rock lovers to hit their other roots hard.

"By that time, we'd done countless tours on our own across the country. Now go on tour with Foo Fighters or whatever, maybe play to some new people. But the Soundgarden tour was terrible. The band were all very nice and genuinely into us, but they were at the end of their run, and I don't think they were digging each other all that much. And the crowds were terrible, throwing change at us a lot and booing. But thinking about it later, it made sense because in the middle of America by that time, the Soundgarden crowd was kind of a mainstream rock crowd. But we weren't thinking that way—we saw a band on Sub Pop and didn't think it was too removed from where we were."

Then the usual label staff shifts occurred, along with the loss of time and inspiration. "That was right around '98," says Reis, "when our last record for Interscope, *RFTC*, came out. We recorded that record with this guy Kevin Shirley, but the label thought we should go with someone a bit more 'hip.' They didn't want us using this guy who had recorded Journey and Aerosmith. But we decided we wanted to do something different after recording eight records on our own. You know, now's the time, that's what the money is there for. We had a recording budget, and we couldn't really take it home with us anyway, because of how our deal was structured."

That is always an odd thing to relate to people; hell, it's hard for bands to understand. But basically, you don't get the hundred thousand dollars, spend two grand recording, then pocket the rest. Managers and lawyers get their cut. And the label structures contracts so that you have to spend all that money—then they use it as a tax deduction. "Yeah," Reis agrees, "you might as well just burn it. Or at least use it as an opportunity to try something new. We all liked the way *RFTC* came out. All the riffs came out of the back of the tour bus; it was a real party record, really simple. So I don't know, the label didn't push it or they didn't like it.

"Plus, it seemed like we were beating a dead horse. We were separated from one of the best parts of being in a band—the creative part. We didn't have the time to stop and incorporate any new ideas because we were just touring the same songs. We kind of had to—the only way to pay the rent on your house is to be gone from it all the time. We also just felt that if you're in a band and you want to be a good band, the only way that works is that you play live and prove you're a good band. But that kind of ran its course."

But as befits a guy who continues making music to this day with his new band, the Night Marchers, and has his Swami label going, Reis harbors little bitterness about the whole Interscope experience. "We actually ended up getting validated—it just wasn't here," says Reis. "In England, we played on *Top of the Pops* a couple of times, we had a song that was on the same pop charts as fucking Wham, you know? Photo shoots with live tigers, stuff like that. It was fun."

Then, after some finagling and a promise not to sign to another major, Rocket extricated themselves from Interscope. "The times were changing and we weren't interested in changing with them whatsoever," Reis says. "If anything, our music was going in a more primitive direction." They found willing fans at the indie Vagrant for another couple albums. "The Vagrant guys were roughly our age and big fans of Rocket. It was a revitalization, and I think we made our best record with *Group Sounds* [2001]."

Rocket from the Crypt released a great, catchy album on a major label immediately following the neo-punk green days, toured nonstop, and *still* got dropped fairly quickly—a confounding, but ultimately not surprising example that the mainstream's tolerance for more explosive, noisy pop music had hit its ceiling.

MAYBE THE MOST confounding '90s story of a garage-parked band inching out of the driveway into major-label land was that of the Muffs. Here was a band made up of connected L.A. rock vets like drummer Roy McDonald, who was in Redd Kross, and singer Kim Shattuck who'd spent the late '80s in a fairly successful retro-'60s group, the Pandoras. Besides being a good guitar churner, Shattuck's a total looker loaded with extremely catchy tunes like they fell off the vintage toy shelf above her bed and hit her in the head when she grumpily rolled over in the morning.

The Muffs mugging, Los Angeles, 1998. (Photo courtesy of Kim Shattuck)

I met with Shattuck and bassist Ronnie Barnett in March 2008, in L.A. at a cheap Mexican joint, where they rattled off stories and finished each other's sentences—as much like brother and sister as former frequently fighting couple. Shattuck has the air of a bubble-gum-smacking, besmirched Valley girl. Within minutes, she was rattling off the info: Their first show was January 25, 1991; the first single came out seven months later; they did a West Coast tour five months into the band's career; Sympathy and Au Go Go singles came out at the same time; already talking to Warner Brothers by year's end; by the time of the Sub Pop single, they were signed. Whew! How'd they fit in practice?

"Oh, we practiced," says Shattuck. "We practiced beating each other up!" Shattuck always had a hard time reining in her scalp-ripping bridge screams, and was known to punch her bandmates on stage. "We always played loud," says Shattuck, with a mama's pride. "We'd hit people with instruments. I kicked a girl in the chest because she was being obnoxious. Hit a promoter in the head with a highball glass. Hey, he was grabbing my ass! We were aggressive, but it was always from the heart." That cutesy killer instinct made their shows unpredictable, and their records crackle with just enough punk energy to have piqued the attention of scruffy garage indies like Estrus. Yet the Muffs had sharp hooks aplenty to have Reprise/Warner Brothers release their first three albums.

"Our A&R was a young guy, Dave Katznelson," Barnett explains. "He'd just signed Mudhoney, and we were next. When we signed we had no manager, no agent, didn't even have a demo." They toured fairly frequently. New Bomb Turks played with them in Philadelphia in 1994, with the Didjits and the Devil Dogs—and the Muffs were as sweat-slinging and audience-berating as any band on that bill. I remember hanging backstage right before the Muffs went on, and Shattuck running in yelling, "Does anyone have any underwear? Oh, fuck it!" Later, she swung the mic stand like an axe right into Bartlett's nuts as he crowd-surfed, then stormed off the stage.

The band's self-titled 1993 debut was hard candy; their second, *Blonder and Blonder* (Warner Bros., 1995), was leaner, catchier. There was even a swell video for the single "Sad Tomorrow," one of the most affecting pop songs of the decade. And a Muffs song got on a national Fruitopia TV commercial too. So what happened?

"Well," says Barnett, "first Katznelson brought up another A&R

guy, Rob Cavallo. Our debut was the first record he produced. He signed the Metal Blade label for distribution. He went on to produce then manage Green Day. Then when *Dookie* got big, they took all our businesspeople and said, 'Oh, those guys are all too busy now.' Katznelson had dropped out once we split with Melanie [Vammen, lead guitarist], in 1995, because he romanticized the original lineup. . . . I mean, when Green Day blew up, our second album did get a bit of a push. That 'Sad Tomorrow' video cost sixty thousand dollars; same director as Green Day."

"We just didn't play the game the way it's normally played," Shattuck states. "We wanted to do our own thing. We were told we couldn't come to the Warner Brothers offices anymore, because every time we'd go there, they'd say we're wrecking the place. Like, wow, everyone had rubber-band balls, and I'd be throwing them around. Big deal! You guys are boring! We were pretty mean—but nursery-rhyme mean. We were playing a show the day Kurt Cobain shot himself, and I dedicated our song 'I Need a Face' to him. I couldn't help it. But it was like crickets in the crowd."

Even still, the classic pop sound and look of the band sure seemed like it should've taken off. Of course that's what they said about the Shoes, Marshall Crenshaw, the Smithereens, and many others from the previous decade. Obviously, classic pop wasn't classic anymore. "I always thought," Barnett says, "that if people could just hear us, how could they not like us? We're so infectious! Then we went on the Warped Tour, and that's when we realized, wow, weird. The audience just kind of stared. The last show at Asbury Park, we were on at three o'clock between Anti-Flag and Longbeach. So we're watching Anti-Flag—full circle mosh, 'Fuck the government,' blah blah. And then it's like, 'Hey, here are the Muffs!' Well, all the *bands* watched us, but the mall punk crowd—"

"Ah, bunch o' poseurs," Shattuck interjects. "Of course Anti-Flag got on their big bus after that, wearing their new free Vans shoes. . . ."

"Like when we signed to Honest Don's (a subsidiary of pop-punk powerhouse Fat Wreck Chords)," Barnett recalls, "we did a pop record like always, and [Fat Wreck Chords boss] Fat Mike was like, 'Oh, I thought you guys were going to make a fast record.'" "We never made a fast record!" Shattuck shoots back. "And he never came by while we were recording or anything. He's essentially a cool enough guy, but he has this cookie-cutter thing, a name brand."

"We never heard any criticisms like that from Warner Brothers," says Barnett. "I was talking to [singer/songwriter] Mark Eitzel once, and we were both saying that Warner Brothers was the best time of our careers. No one told us how to do anything. But indie labels, they do sometimes." After their third Warner Brothers LP, *Happy Birthday to Me* (which Shattuck said is her favorite), their contract was up.

"For better or worse, we made the records we wanted to make," Barnett says. "They just didn't promote them much. . . . It was cool because it was post-Nirvana, so they let bands like us do their thing. Looking back, it was the last of the big-money major-label careers. We got dropped in 1997, and the business has been downsizing ever since. . . . But hey, we made it on some Rhino '90s box set, on the same disc as 'Whoop! There It Is'!"

"We did this Aaron Spelling TV show pilot, *Crosstown Traffic*, in 1995 that never got picked up," Shattuck says. "We were actually on it! The plot revolved around somebody stalking me, with my real name. It was this million-dollar cop show, super corny. Tone Loc is in it playing a cop, and he's like, 'He's stalking Kim Shattuck of the Muffs. That's right, you heard me, THE MUFFS!' And they make fun of the name!"

"And," Barnett responds, "we were also in this movie *Father's Day* with Billy Crystal and Robin Williams, where we were also 'the Muffs.' I get about twelve bucks quarterly for that! And we were the first song on the *Clueless* soundtrack, had a gold record with that."

"You know, those things are just like spray-painted vinyl records," says Shattuck. "But they wouldn't give one to us unless we paid them to get one made. Oh, and Dee Dee Ramone told us our first two albums got him through rehab in '95. And now he's dead. Oh well."

As POP CULTURE trends were turning all "to the extreme"—X Games, energy drinks, and all that crap—maybe the Muffs' "aw shucks" aggressiveness was a detriment. That was definitely not the case for Nashville Pussy.

Fronted by stompin' 'n' screamin' former Nine Pound Hammer guitarist Blaine Cartwright, Nashville Pussy was the Village People of neo–garage punk—a stage-storming act that came along just when everyone figured the trend had crested, bearing a delirious consolidation of the genre's most crowd-pleasing characteristics but retaining some genuine pow of the base sound. Make no mistake, once Nashville Pussy got going, the year of their debut, *Let Them Eat Pussy* (The

Enclave, 1998), they were an amazing band. Trailer-park birthed, shit-kicking AC/DC–Motörhead worship, phenomenally fired by the cave-man strumming of Cartwright and his wife, lead guitarist Ruyter Suys, who shredded with the best of them. That collided with the baseball bat drumming of Jeremy Thompson, and the murderous three chords of 6'3" bassist Corey Parks (sister of NBA center Cherokee Parks). She could not only stomp around the stage in 6" heels, but at the show's sweaty heights, she would breath fire, even in the tiniest clubs they started out in. Did I mention both ladies were *Hustler* hot, and Cartwright barked out songs sore-throated as if the more fit femmes in the group had forced him into an extra thirty minutes of pie-diving aerobics the night before?

Cartwright had already beat himself to death in Nine Pound Ham-mer, with relentless Euro touring, but he didn't have much to show for it, income-wise. When New Bomb Turks had dinner with Cartwright and Parks in their hometown of Atlanta in 1995, he regaled us with his new vaginal vision.

"That's Corey. She's playing bass. She can't play bass for shit right now. But I gave her *!!Destroy-Oh-Boy!!*, and I told her, You play bass like Matt Reber right there. You strum the shit out of it! No pickin'!" Corey meekly smiled over at us and went back to her meal. She was a shy, untattooed lady.

"Blaine and I met in Chapel Hill, North Carolina, at the 1994 Sleaze-fest, when he was still playing with Nine Pound Hammer. We hung out one day and I took them for some good Southern BBQ. Later on that night I was telling Blaine that I wanted to do an all-girl band. Maybe about six months later, I got a call from Blaine saying that he and Ruyter were doing a band and looking for a bass player. I took a seventeen-hour bus ride up to Kentucky to jam with them. If I didn't know how to breathe fire, I'm not sure if I would've made it in the band."

Fast-forward a year, and we see Nashville Pussy for the first time. Festooned in leather and flames, the band was a fully formed, boogie-eating animal, an X-rated cartoon of white-trash wigout. And there was Corey, hair colored a few different shades, thigh-high boots, an "Eat Me" tattoo (among many) right above her, uh, big belt buckle; and she and Suys making like the vengeful ex who was going to get back at Gene Simmons for all that condescending shit he talks about girls. "I was an unpredictable drug addict who was handling a flame thrower," says Parks. "So basically I brought a danger element to the show. We were all drowning in a sea of indie rock, cargo-short-wearing shoegaz-ers who sang songs about how they weren't getting laid. I think Ruyter was really the mindblower for us, because she was technically so fuckin' good on lead guitar. I don't think anyone had ever seen anything like her ever!"

A *Penthouse* interview, an MTV feature, indie labels tripping over themselves to do a single, more mag stories with loads of pictures, a bidding war—it was all falling into place. . . .

Once again, ladies and germs, Andy Slob, Cincinnati punk pro-doucher: "Nothing like deep-fried hamburgers, coffee, and highlight-ing your hair. But most of all, I'll never forget watching Blaine record vocals in his underwear, keeping time with his foot, while his member is starting to work its way out. Should I stop the take? Urgh! No, *never* stop the take!"

Getting more metal every day, the assumption would be that paddy-wagon loads of lonely, drunken dudes were lining up stage left to grope the Pussy. "There is always 'that guy' in the audience," says Parks, "just begging to be made an example of. He'd usually be in the front row trying to touch my bass or move his hands up my legs to see how far he could get. When we moved to bigger venues that had security goons lining the front of the stage and barriers five feet high, we would fight to get them removed. Clubs simply didn't understand that we sort of had this unspoken understanding with our crowd. All except 'that guy.' That's when the fire comes in handy.

"I always jumped into the crowd for the second or third fireball. Most people knew to get the fuck out of the way—you can feel the heat from five rows back! But I swear to God, it would be like the parting of the Red Sea, and there, still standing dead center, would be that fuck-ing guy! I would scream, 'MOVE!' but he would remain—and I aim to please! I'm sure there are quite a few boys who could say they lost their eyebrows at our show."

Nashville Pussy tried to go a smart route with a "cool" incubator label or two; Cartwright and Suys had a terrible fire at their home and actually lived in their tour bus for a spell. They kept touring relentlessly, but the fickle mainstream attention moved on. As did the band—away from Parks.

"It's so hard for me to remember. I guess you could say I wasn't ex-actly in my right mind for most of the '90s. There was only one thing I loved more than playing rock 'n' roll, and it wasn't my bass. I didn't

Corey Parks (Nashville Pussy) heating up, Normal, IL, 1998.
(Photo by Canderson)

realize what a fucking annoying, gross, nightmare bore I'd become. Especially that last year, around 1999, it was pretty dark. Blaming everyone else for your unhappiness and trying to stay high so you don't feel it. After a while, people just get tired of being around it."

Nashville Pussy kept on truckin', though, releasing six albums in ten-plus years and going through a few bassists to date, still kicking shit and taking promoters' names. Parks lives in L.A., separated from street punk skateboard legend and fellow former fuck-up Duane Peters. "People who've met me over the last eight years would describe a very different woman than people who knew me when I was with Nashville Pussy. That girl was selfish and self-centered and driven by a hundred forms of fear. In truth, I'm a really good mom and a really good friend. I just started a new band, Chelsea Girls. It's an all female supergroup doing all covers. . . . And my son, Clash, just turned four in November. He's such a funny kid, flippin' huge like me, with long blond hair, tight jeans, a constant dirt beard. His favorite saying is 'Rock and roll, fuck you,' of course. I've been working with the Center for Nonviolent Education and Parenting here in L.A. for over two years, helping parents to have a better understanding of what it is to love a child unconditionally."

THE CULTURAL ARBITERS had dubbed 1998, "The Year of Electronica," goofs like the Prodigy were getting multimillion-dollar deals, downloading was rearing its head, and the economy was showing signs of crashing from the dot-com high. Major labels were not just reverting to the usual cutthroat business bullshit (boy bands) but were totally freaking out, especially on all those alt-rock contracts they were previously doling out like grungy flannels at the Gap.

Way at the other end of that spectrum was the porn/punk rag *Horizontal Action*. Based in Chicago and named after, you guessed it, a *Killed by Death* track, Todd Novak's ink-smear smut-rock rag was no *Maxim*. Running for fifteen issues from 1996 to 2005, it covered the latest, most raw and head-splitting garage punk, like the Reatards, Piranhas, and Clone Defects. Its pages were flecked with fourth-generation photocopied poon 'n' boobs so close-up and pixelated that it almost reached the level of abstraction. Almost. The porn star interviews/reviews were hardly abstract.

New Bomb Turks first met Novak as "Todd Killings," a friendly, forehead-furrowed skatecore kid at our frequent Chicago gigs. But he

Horizontal Action, issue No. 1, 1997.

first gained his appreciation for stab-rock from his years living in the minuscule town of Normal, Illinois, right next to that other booming metropolis, Bloomington. I always remember the first time New Bomb Turks played Normal—as you drive up the main street, intermittently dappled with lame craft stores, a cheap Mexican eatery, and maybe a bar or two, jumping right out of the middle of the lane, a giant, blinking neon movie theater sign: "Normal."

"[Cofounder] Brett Cross and I both were raised in Kankakee, Illinois, about fifty-seven miles south of Chicago," Novak explains. "Skateboarding was the key, especially *Thrasher* magazine. But in college I gravitated toward Mother Murphy's [an amazing record store] in Normal, and that's where I really discovered '60s/'70s punk, before crossing over into the really obscure." And eventually, the *Killed by Death* comps slithered under Mother Murphy's doors. "Man, they were a really massive influence," says Novak, "just reinforcing the thrill of listening to obscure music that was actually great. It's hard to conceptualize to someone who isn't interested, but the whole series of compilations in *KBD*'s orbit was really a major milestone of '90s music."

Horizontal Action's jones for the most mental punk sounds of the millennial switch made for fine bathroom reading for the new noisy garage scenes that were creeping up in the Windy City, Memphis, and Detroit. "We just thought zines were too politically correct at the time," says Novak. "And we used to just laugh about how funny it would be to get officially incorporated—which we did really early on—and write off porn rentals and rubbers along with records and magazines as all 'business expenses.' It seemed like it was too funny to really work."

MEANWHILE, BACK AT Crypt HQ, Tim released the Dirtys and Los Ass-Draggers debut records around 1996 for Crypt: "But they were just like too-fast noise to me," says Micha Warren. "They're great, crazy records for sure, but it just felt like maybe Tim was trying to find the fastest thing to be faster than the last band." Crypt was starting to feel the pinch of unmet expectations, and Tim was finding it a better idea to maybe look around his backyard for new Crypt acts (Los Ass-Draggers from Oviedo, Spain; DM Bob & the Deficits from Hamburg, Germany); or get back to a new volume of *Back from the Grave*. By that time, he and Micha had settled into a nice house in Hamburg, but the seeds of moving back to America were sprouting. . . .

Crypt Records ad, 1996.

16.
HATE TO SAY
I TOLD YOU SO

AUGUST 2000, LAS Vegas: Sauced swarms of trash-rock fans from around the globe filled the crumbling old Gold Coast Hotel & Casino for a weekend of gonzo punk rock action called the Las Vegas Shakedown. The band list was a veritable who's who (Dead Moon, Bantam Rooster, Wayne Kramer, Necessary Evils, Donnas, Holly Golightly, Leaving Trains, the Dragons, Cheater Slicks, and many more). The amazing Raunch Hands reunion reintroduced them to a younger crowd. The Weaklings singer bled enough for four punk fests. Illicit substances piled up in the suites like the help was on strike. Frazzled security guys were rubbernecking. And stories of little old lady tourists watching elevator doors open to see a greasy punk couple in midscrew made the rounds. Before Sunday night hit, the hotel management was already crying, "We'll never do this again!" A total ball!

But it also felt like a kind of last gasp, gunk punk's Woodstock and Altamont all in one. What would be considered "classic" '90s garage punk records had come out by 1997. The main fests of the era (Garage Shock, Rip Off Rumble, Sleazefest, etc.) seemed to be on hiatus. And the gigantic expulsion of sweat, puke, and energy of that Shakedown weekend left the departing trips back Monday morning feeling like returning home from a really fun wake. . . .

So it was beyond bizarre to see in the mainstream music press that fall that "garage rock is back!" The Strokes' recordings were being described as "raw" based on the fact that you could hear a guitar. That girl in the Yeah Yeah Yeahs screams. Those White Stripes don't have a bass player. Even weirder, the Hives like the Rolling Stones! Mainstream music critics went from convincing themselves they really dug

Yours truly getting a knuckle sandwich at the Las Vegas Shakedown, 2000. (Photo by Keith Marlowe)

the Chemical Brothers to slavishly covering this "neo–garage rock thing." Nineties garage vets would've laughed if they weren't so pooped from all the partying.

But the party hit a second wind in Detroit. Locals had been eating up their hometown gyros, the Gories, and spitting out their own takes on that kind of greasy roots-digestion. While Bantam Rooster may have been the last of the great Crypt *"groupes moderne,"* the duo themselves were at the forefront of the Detroit garage revival that became the bridge from the early decade's detonation into the Hot Topic topic of the early 2000s. . . .

"Most definitely there was a scene," says Tom Potter of Bantam Rooster. "Not necessarily a 'garage rock' scene, more so that everyone kind of knew everyone else. You had the Demolition Doll Rods and Hentchmen; the Detroit Cobras were getting some action from their first couple singles. Rocket 455 was still going. Mick had done the first couple Dirtbombs singles. The Witches were going, the Wildbunch (later renamed the Electric Six). We came in from Lansing and the Dirtys moved down from Port Huron. His Name Is Alive and their various offshoots. Plus, there was the Zoot's coffeehouse scene with poppier bands like Godzuki and Outrageous Cherry. The Gold Dollar, Magic Stick, and the Old Miami became the ground zeros.

"Soon after that time you had the White Stripes, the Clone Defects—all of whom had been doing crazy-ass shit already—the Go . . . The Starlite Desperation even moved here from California, which was weird because no one moved *to* Detroit. And the Crypt/Estrus types always drew a good amount of people. The whole Detroit thing was very 'rootsy' without being retro lame. It was more about revving up an old Irma Thomas song than it is about trying to create some 'new sound.'

"Detroit was really the wild west back then. Timmy Vulgar from Clone Defects and I were at a party standing on the dining room table stopping the ceiling fan with our tongues. I then offered to wrestle girls in the backyard and got my ass kicked. No one got pulled over for drunk driving ever. Joe Dirty got pulled over once for going sixty-five down Cass Avenue. The cop didn't even get out of the car, just got on the loudspeaker and asked Joe, "Do you know what day it is today?" Joe thought a moment and almost said Monday, but after a moment replied, 'Martin Luther King Day?'

"'That's right,' said the cop. 'Now get on home.'"

The Clone Defects in another tight spot, 2000. (Photo by Canderson)

*

IT WAS NEATO in a way to see big mags like *Rolling Stone*, *Spin*, etc. mentioning bands like the Sonics and the Stooges in articles about the trend. But once the wave really crested around late 2001, a natural knee-jerk response among gutter-rock fans was to feel exasperated. Rarely was there a mention of all the previous bands and scenes that these hyped acts came from. (Not the bands' faults of course—the Hives and White Stripes dropped Oblivians and Billy Childish references as much as nods to the Kinks.) And the editorial attitude was a not-so hidden implication that this "simple stuff" was all just a fad.

Garage punk bands of the early '90s—whether owing to their desire to distance themselves from '80s hair metal, or the thrift store anti-style influence of beloved '80s antecedents (Replacements, Hüsker Dü, etc.), or simply because they had no cash—rarely displayed a penchant for concocting a splashy look. The British press especially—the ones who really kicked in the hype for the trend—are seemingly incapable of writing about a band unless they have an attendant, obvious image.

ONE CAN ASSUME that the guy most put off by all the "neo-garage" press chatter was Jim Diamond, sometime member of the Dirtbombs and longtime studio fizz-wiz of the Detroit garage rock scene. New Bomb Turks met him at a Detroit party in 1998, loved the sound of the Bantam Rooster and Dirtys stuff he recorded, and ended up making our last Epitaph album, *Nightmare Scenario*, with him at his Ghetto Recorders studio in October 1999. "So Jim, what other bands have you been recording lately? Anything good?" He handed me the first White Stripes CD that had just come out on Sympathy. "I recorded this one. These guys are all right."

"I found myself at age thirty in 1995," says Diamond, "living with my parents in south Detroit, doing the morning shift at a steel-fabricating plant and freelance sessions at a studio in the suburbs. My friend John Linardos had a space in downtown Detroit, and I started doing sessions at his space. Bantam Rooster comes in and I do their first record, *Deal Me In*, for Crypt. That was fall of 1996." Diamond's "sound" was set as he became the go-to growl, producing the White Stripes, Mooney Suzuki, Compulsive Gamblers, the Hentchmen, the Go, Clone Defects, the Sights, and many of the best new garage thumpers.

If you've recorded with Diamond, there is simply no denying that he definitely puts his stamp on the recording, as does the rare, amazing two-inch tape machine he usually uses. And if there's a more easygoing studio engineer to work with, New Bomb Turks haven't met him or her. But not everyone saw it that way. "The White Stripes were assholes," says Diamond. "Not at the time, but later. And another band called the Wildbunch, who became the Electric Six. Of course, most everyone was my best friend while we were recording; they would just show their true colors after they made a little money."

Obviously, of all the 1999–2001 "neo–garage rock" ballyhoo, the White Stripes have had the largest mainstream impact. Leader Jack White assembled the seminal scene compilation *The Sympathetic Sounds of Detroit* (Sympathy for the Record Industry, 2001), and name-dropped neglected heroes like Billy Childish and the Gories in major magazine articles. Though they certainly weren't the first, the White Stripes made a stripped-down, two-man concept palatable to a mainstream audience still stuck with glitzy boy bands or bloated nü-metal, and whose previous notions of "raw 'n' rootsy" were John Cougar at best. And White's famed duo has released many actually good, lasting songs—something that rarely goes hand-in-hand with hype-heaved success.

But these sorts of stories often lead to inevitable clichés. Once the White Stripes' third Sympathy album, *White Blood Cells* (2001), really broke big and the majors came calling, White's relationship with his patron pal Long Gone John was forever severed. And White wanted full production credit on the first two White Stripes albums, while Jim Diamond wanted to be paid in kind. No one is ever a perfect angel or perfect devil in these kinds of spats, but it's hard not to side with a guy who was then charging thirty-five dollars an hour to record in a studio that burped out a million seller.

"Jack White is the greatest megalomaniacal rock-star cliché on the earth," says Diamond. "I told him when we did that debut album that I should get a production credit, and he readily agreed. Of course, back then everyone was your friend, so you didn't even think about legal paperwork or stuff like that. I made a mistake in trying to be a nice guy and waited too long to actually take him to court over royalties. I lost on the statute of limitations.

"The White Stripes then sued me, saying I had defamed their name by claiming to have been involved with their sound. Well, assholes, what does it say on the record cover? At least I didn't lie under oath. Jack said shit on the stand like the only reason he came to me was because he didn't have gas money to get to another studio. And the reason they

White Stripes, Pat's in the Flats, Cleveland, 1998. (Photo by Jay Brown)

recorded their second record at home and had me mix it was that it was an experiment in the Dutch art movement of minimalism or some bullshit. That second record, let me tell you, that guy is no engineer! I had to pull out every fucking trick in the book to make that thing sound good. I busted my ass. Jack actually told me that they did it at home to save money because Meg took too many hours of studio time getting one good drum take. I have a phone recording of Jack yelling at me, pretty funny stuff, like how I must be crazy if I think I would be anything without him. . . . Of course, having done the first two White Stripes albums definitely helped my career. But no way is it the only good thing I've ever done.

"I also took some poor legal advice from my lawyers, but hey, how did I know? They did some things I didn't want them to. After I lost, since I'd sued Jack, he could go after damages. He told my lawyers, 'Give me the name Ghetto Recorders, and I'll leave him alone.' I told him to fuck off! Then he said, 'Give me fifty thousand dollars and I'll leave you alone.' Again, fuck off. The judge basically told him to go away and never come back. The one good thing that did come of it is that Jack had to show his legal bills when he wanted the judge to go after me for money. He spent well over five hundred thousand dollars fighting me for what would have been fifty thousand in royalties. I hope he needs that half a million someday. To go to those lengths just to make sure I am not given any credit as 'coproducer.' That guy must have been touched in the 'no-no spot' as a kid or something.

"After I sued the White Stripes, I was on a TV show called *Entertainment Justice*, and their 'legal analyst' said I was a worm crawling out of the woodwork trying to steal their money, and that I was 'probably a guy hanging around the studio one day.' That stuff hurt for a year or two because some people actually believed it. My career now is much more diversified. I've done songs for movies, written a couple jingle things, and made money. And I work with international bands a lot more. But I look at that lawsuit as the last coffin nail pounded into Detroit garage rock."

IN RESPONSE TO an interview request and comments made in this book about him, Jack White only sent this witty, if metaphorically invalid retort, taken from an unknown text:

"The day Edgar Allan Poe was buried, a long obituary appeared in the *New York Tribune* signed 'Ludwig.' It was soon published throughout the country. The piece began, 'Edgar Allan Poe is dead. He died in Baltimore the day before yesterday. This announcement will startle many, but few will be grieved by it.' Ludwig was soon identified as Rufus Wilmot Griswold, an editor, critic, and anthologist who had borne a grudge against Poe since 1842. Griswold somehow became Poe's literary executor and attempted to destroy his enemy's reputation after his death.

"Rufus Griswold wrote a biographical article of Poe called 'Memoir of the Author.' which he included in an 1850 volume of the collected works. Griswold depicted Poe as a depraved, drunk, drug-addled madman, and included Poe's letters as evidence. Many of his claims were either outright lies or distorted half-truths. For example, it is now known that Poe was not a drug addict. Griswold's book was denounced by those who knew Poe well, but it became a popularly accepted one. This occurred in part because it was the only full biography available and was widely reprinted, and in part because readers thrilled at the thought of reading works by an 'evil' man. Letters that Griswold presented as proof of this depiction of Poe were later revealed as forgeries."

"EH, IT'S HYPE," says Tom Potter. "I suppose it's annoying, but that's the mainstream music business for you. I was friends with the White Stripes. I liked the band and figured they'd do pretty well. When I was in the Dirtbombs, our merch table sign read: Records, $8.00. T-shirts, $10.00. Questions about the White Stripes, $15.00."

ASIDE FROM THE White Stripes/Jim Diamond flap, the Detroit scene stayed fairly cordial. There was a similar familial scene at the time in Stockholm, Sweden. And the band that led the charge was formed, oddly enough, by the drummer of death metal band the Entombed, Nicke Andersson, who became the singer/guitarist for the Hellacopters.

Already tiring of where Euro metal was going, gobbling down the older Detroit rock influence, and digging on Crypt-style punk, Andersson and his friend Dregen decided to form a new band. "Union Carbide Productions was a huge influence too," says Andersson. "I was told if I liked them, I should check out the Stooges and MC5. At first I thought both of the bands were a little lame compared to Union Carbide, but I wised up soon after!" By late '95, the Hellacopters were churning out raw, electrifying glam-punk singles faster than ABBA went through platforms; culminating in their monster debut, *Supershitty to the Max* (White Jazz, 1996).

The influence of the Hellacopters on the whole European rock scene was enormous. In 1997, New Bomb Turks toured Scandinavia for the first time, and the Hellacopters already had side projects, like

A characteristically boss Hellacopters flier, 1999.

Turbonegro shove it where the sun does shine, 1997.
(Photo courtesy of Aaron Lefkove)

guitarist Dregen's Backyard Babies and the Sewergrooves, fronted by
Hellacopters drummer Robert Eriksson. We saw strong brother bands
like the A-Bombs, Gluecifer, and the Robots. And there were gangs of
kids at shows with long hair, flames on their pants, and MC5 patches on
their jean vests. By the next time we came through in 1998, it seemed
every other opening act was a Hellacopters copycat.

Turbonegro had been around since before the Hellacopters, but it
wasn't until their legendary third LP, *Apocalypse Dudes* (Boomba, 1998),
that they really took off as superstars in Europe. Creating a Godzilla
tail-swipe of hilarious arena cock rock played with punk fury by a bunch
of skinny dudes in Tom of Finland garb and a near-naked singer with
a murderous gaze and gut, they've since amassed a worldwide cult, the
Turbojugend. Soon came "Demons," the Flamin' Sideburns, Mensen,

and many more Scandinavian groups who slung two-gits as if Radio Birdman were the only rock 'n' roll band to ever exist.

THEN, FROM A much smaller burg outside of Stockholm—Fagersta— came five dapper lads ramming gunk-punk power and some new-wave chop into hard-candy hooks, dubbed the Hives.

"There was a hardcore scene but also some pop bands in Fagersta," says Nicholaus Arson, the Hives' lead guitarist. "We were a bit younger and would play everywhere we could. Howlin' Pelle [Almqvist, Nicholaus' brother and hyper-suave singer of the Hives] always refers to when Dad said the old blues guys that went off to Chicago only became better with doing more shows. I think we have played around thirty different places in Fagersta alone."

New Bomb Turks first played with the Hives at a cool little festival in Denmark, early 2000, at a site with some small old WWI bunkers. The Hives went on right before us, trying to keep their rickety cardboard and lightbulbs "Hives" sign tacked up while zipping through their tunes. I recalled meeting them as teens a couple years earlier. They'd given me their debut, *Barely Legal*, that was a good, crunchy pop-punk thing, but this was much better.

"At age twelve, thirteen, we started finding bands that the skateboarders listened to, bands like Misfits, the Damned, NOFX, Rancid," says Nicholaus. "At the same time, however, we were listening to '50s and '60s compilations that we would buy at the bookstore because they were cheaper. We thought some of those recordings were a lot cooler than the '80s manner that some of the bands were sporting. We would also buy *Maximumrocknroll* from the guy who had the Burning Heart record label in Fagersta. From then on we were hooked on NBT, the Oblivians, Electric Frankenstein, the Saints, and stuff like that."

"Also, a friend of ours found a record with the Sonics," says Pelle. "He was into psychedelic music and thought since it was called *Psychosonic* it would be psychedelic, so he gave it to me. This was life-changing for me. We all felt like we had then found our band."

The teen-punk tuneage met a skitzier sound on the band's breakout, *Veni, Vidi, Vicious* (Burning Heart, 2000), and by early 2001, stories about the Hives started to appear in national American mags. Surefire publicity hooks—like the matching outfits, zany stage names (including Vigilante Carlstroem, Chris Dangerous, and Dr. Matt Destruction), cocky interview quotes, and the mysterious Randy Fitzsimmons Sven-

The Hives, Stockholm, Sweden, 1998. (Photo by Ove Wilksten)

gali—were all in place, while the Hives had been busy doing age-old musician work like writing songs and touring like crazy. Slacker-hewn American indie fans often scrunched their noses at the Hives' shtick. But if there's one thing we learned while spending time with Swedish bands, it's that they're very pragmatic at zeroing in on their idea, not just the look but the musicianship too. It used to be called "forming a band."

"We saw Turbonegro for the first time in Ludvika," says Nicholaus, "a town with maybe three thousand inhabitants, in the fall of 1996. Thirty paying customers in the basement of Folkets Hus ("the people's house," a socialist idea). Offstage, Turbonegro looked exactly like the factory workers back in Fagersta; slightly tubby, with mustaches that were out of date fifteen years ago. But when they came on to play, they had all that seaman gear and denim gay-style leather caps and vests. They looked like complete freaks! Their songs were brilliant, like a more rock 'n' roll Poison Idea, just ripping the whole place apart with their fifteen-thousand-seat arena show in a place as small as a one-room apartment! After the show, some of the Turbo guys started to come out into the crowd dressed in sweatpants and worn-out T-shirts for the local cement factory. That was the first time I'd seen a band so shamelessly use stage outfits. We loved that transformation. I think that might still be the best rock 'n' roll show I have ever seen."

When told of Johan Kugelberg's assessment that Swedish people are incapable of original thought, but that they have a huge hunger and can quickly follow others' leads, Pelle admits, "Johan has a point. But it is often that the original thought is not the most successful, but the slight improvement on said thought. It may suck justice-wise, but it's the way of the world."

Producer Pelle Gunnerfeldt was at his best on *Veni, Vidi, Vicious*," says Nicholaus. "Very experimental and persuasive, miking guitars through synthesizers, using delays, envelope filters, and just tweaking sounds, but not in a way that sucks."

"The first attempt to record it was a disaster though," Pelle adds. "We then went back a few months later and recorded in Gunnerfeldt's new unfinished studio, with a skateboard half-pipe in the middle, where we put the drums. We also played some shows in Stockholm during the ten-day recording. Hectic. This was right before Christmas 1999, and then we went back and remixed four songs on New Year's Day 2000. It was probably the first record finished in the new millennium. Dare I say, still one of the best."

But it was actually the UK Poptones label compilation, *Your Favourite New Band*—featuring early material with some *Veni, Vidi, Vicious* tunes—that started to get the Hives notice in trend-hungry England. "We had played Alan McGee's club in London," Nicholaus recalls, "and all the Poptones staff were there and loved it. So Poptones decided to do a comp. And yes, that record got us all the UK hype. We would be there constantly playing, and Alan would say, 'If you do well on this TV show, we will sell fifty thousand records by next week.' And he was right. . . . We toured *VVV* near three years as it blew up in the UK and Europe, and started doing good in the U.S. a little too."

Once the Hives got their huge deal with Universal around 2002, they used most of it to make their next two records and open up a nice recording studio with attached apartments in their hometown, so bands could come there to record cheaply.

As usual, fame didn't come easy. "Yeah, we were sold to Warner Brothers against our will, [Gearhead and Epitaph got dragged in], a mess" says Nicholaus. "We later signed with Interscope because they seemed the best out of the big ones," Nicholaus recalls, "and we needed loads of money so that we could fight Burning Heart and Epitaph in court. . . . The day we got sold, I called Pelle up and said, This is it. I am quitting the band tonight. He convinced me not to quit and instead fight for our rights. And as always, my little brother was right.

"Suddenly, we had everything," Nicholaus continues. "It was weird. Chased by screaming girls down corridors of TV buildings, hanging out at posh private clubs with race car drivers. Ridiculous. We knew it would be a phase more or less. On the other hand, I really thought we were one of the best bands around, so becoming famous made complete sense to me as well, but was a bit unexpected. I think we really knew how to appreciate it too, because we got what all our band friends wanted, but didn't always get."

"We always knew our survival strategy was of the Ramones, AC/DC, Cramps type," Pelle says. "Just stick to your guns, keep working, and everything will be fine. The UK success always was great fun, but it seemed more like a chance to study herd behavior in an anthropological way. We *still* have great packed shows in the UK. One long-haired older guy said he hadn't liked a band since Guns N' Roses, and now here we were. That felt great."

ALL THE SWEDISH groups did well in their country, and some of them got signed for stateside action by Gearhead Records. "I was putting out the Hives and Hellacopters, but we were struggling to sell two thousand!" says Gearhead's Mike LaVella. "It became so frustrating, and someone had to be held accountable, and I didn't want to be that person. I apologized to them later. All your money is in it, and whenever you go see a band you just think of them in terms of if I should sign them or not. After the Hives, people started treating me different. I didn't like any of that phoniness. There was no joy in it anymore. Then there was this band called the Pink Swords. We put out their record, but they'd broken up and didn't tell us. I just spent thirty thousand dollars making your album, CDs, full color posters, and you don't even have the balls to tell me! And the label is always wrong; the bands are never the assholes. But let me tell you, some of them are. The joy I had being a little kid seeing Sparks on *Midnight Special* to seeing the Hives in Sweden, I was always that person, but somehow I became cynical. It took two years after I stopped putting out records until I could get the joy back."

*

LaVella's end point was just the start of perhaps the last, big, major-label signing frenzy. Jet, the Donnas, Mooney Suzuki, Kings of Leon, Sahara Hotnights, Star Spangles, Black Rebel Motorcycle Club, the Datsuns, Greenhornes, Division of Laura Lee . . . Even Crypt Records, now based back in New Jersey, jumped in with the cool NYC trash trio, the Little Killers.

"I remember back then," says Andy Gortler of the Devil Dogs, "when Nardwuar interviewed the Strokes, and he asked them if they had grown up in NYC listening to bands from the early '90s, like the 'late, great Devil Dogs.' And the reply was, 'Dude, like, I was only eleven then!' So how old was he when the first Velvet Underground record came out, huh?"

It should be noted that some of this hyped music was pretty good, or at least preferable to the rote boy bands or rap-rock that had been robotically marching out the radio/MTV dial by that time. "I really liked the Donnas' and the White Stripes' early stuff," says Todd Novak of *Horizontal Action*, "It was great that White Stripes first 'big' national tour had the Clone Defects as the opening act. And I guess it kind of 'legitimized' the oddly underground concept of 'garage music' to the point that my parents would even ask me about it, after reading the term in *Time*, *Newsweek*, etc."

Best Rip Off Records single? 1997.

Whether any of that hype translated to the slightly older bands that fomented these sudden proclivities toward raw roots sounds is anyone's guess. "Maybe it helped," says the Oblivians' Greg Cartwright. "But two things were colliding. There was this second wave of bands that were talking up a lot of the '90s garage stuff. But at right about the same time, free downloading and CD burning really kicked in. So maybe new fans thought, 'Well that older stuff's kind of cool, but I'll only actually spend my money on the new Hives record.' So the real amount of sales increase for us was not much."

But, like when Levi's become periodically popular, they'll soon enough be shoved to the back of the fashion mags again. None of these newer bands, save for the Strokes and White Stripes, consistently cracked the Top 40; the Strokes backlash could've put Shaquille O'Neal in traction; the Australian band Jet had an omnipresent 2003 hit with the uber-derivative "Are You Gonna Be My Girl," that exemplified the "jump the shark" moment for the trend; and the Hives soon got the stepchild treatment (at least in America). I remember seeing them at their second *Conan O'Brien* appearance in late 2004, then meeting up with them at a side door of Rockefeller Center. Pelle Almqvist told me, chuckling, "Last time, there were a bunch of girls waiting for autographs. We were popular then."

DURING THAT POPULAR new garage wave, the new decade newbies who grew up with the Crypt/In the Red/Estrus/*Killed by Death* blood flowing through their veins were in no mood for resigned acceptance. First came the Detroit/Chicago/Memphis axis of angst around 1999: Clone Defects, Piranhas, Reatards, and the Brides, among many; leading to the infamously intoxicated Blackout Fests in Chicago.

Inspired by the devolved dirt-kicking of their hometown Oblivians, the Reatards set a new standard for nix-fi production and backfiring pawn-shop pistol riffs, not to mention the band's notoriously rancorous gigs, replete with lead teen spazzo Jay Reatard's riot-baiting mood swings.

Mother Jones photo editor and former *Maximumrocknroll* editor Mark "icki" Murrmann, was a camera-wielding fixture on the San Francisco slop-rock scene back around Y2K. "The Reatards show was on November 19, 1999, at the Boomerang, a shitty place to see shows. It was right on Haight Street, across from the giant Amoeba record store that had just opened. I don't think any of the thirty or forty people there

The Reatards wreck the Boomerang, San Francisco, 1999.
(Photo by Mark "icki" Murrmann)

knew what to expect, but Jay and Co. delivered beyond anything antici-
pated. Some people sneered, 'How could such a young person have so
much to be pissed about?' Jay threw himself around the stage, wrapped
the mic cord around his head, hurled empty beer bottles at the walls,
then just started chucking the bottles into the crowd. And the people
egged him on, leaving empties on the front of the stage for ammuni-
tion. Jay swung the mic stand around, kicked the monitors. I'd seen
these sorts of antics before, but this time it all felt real. It was one of the
best shows I will ever get to see. Later, seeing Jay, it felt much more like
he had to *become* Jay Reatard, and live up to the legend he created on
that first West Coast tour."

The former trailer park denizen would eventually instigate just as
many side projects as onstage fisticuffs, unleash piles of singles, and get
signed as a solo act to Matador Records in 2008, becoming the most
prolific punk of that era. Reatard's nervous energy was sadly stopped
cold on January 13, 2010.

*

THEN AROUND 2001, from all over, came the Spits, the Baseball Furies, Black Lips, the Hunches, the Ponys, Functional Blackouts, Starvations, the Blowtops, and more. Imprints like Goner, Italy, Flying Bomb, Big Neck, Criminal IQ, Die Slaughterhaus, Florida's Dying, and others followed dirty suit. As Clone Defects singer Timmy Vulgar says about these vicious acts: "Yeah, we don't like being pretty. We're predators of rock 'n' roll, and the trend bands were the prey."

"But," says In the Red's Larry Hardy, "it's gotten to a point where if a band would actually use that term, 'Killed by Death,' to describe themselves, they're probably not going to be very good. It's weird for me, dealing with younger bands that grew up on this whole scene. I remember talking to the Hunches about the Damned, and they were like, 'Ew, we never listened to them.' Yet they're all into Crime and the *Killed by Death* bands. Those bands wouldn't have existed without the Damned or the Sex Pistols. It's all kind of like learning to fly before you learned how to drive."

So "art damaged" post-punk of the late '70s (Teenage Jesus & the Jerks, DNA, the Screamers, Wire) was the next forgotten exhumable sound, as the latest combos mixed cheap synths, angled beats, and charred couture into the garage grease. Jay Reatard's post-Reatards band, the Lost Sounds, led that pissed pack, jabbing out of a revived Memphis scene. Alicja Trout, keyboardist of Lost Sounds and leader of her own fine bands like Mouserocket and River City Tanlines, now has a child, and the perspective that comes with it:

"Here in Memphis in the late '90s," Trout says, "it was a total blast, and everyone was always dancing their asses off to the bands, just partying and fun and balls to the wall! But speaking solely for me and my part in Lost Sounds, I wished I could've made something basic like the Oblivians; I tried for Ramones simplicity, heart, and melody. But the Lost Sounds catalogue is what I got. I am very proud of the productivity, and I got to experiment a lot. But I'm still not sure what to make of the stuff, though I like a lot of it."

Of course it's no longer print zines but websites like Victim of Time, the Goner Records message board, and Terminal Boredom that cover the crunch for the kids these days. And circa 2007, those sites were crashing with loads of posts buzzing over imminent reunion shows from old faves like Teengenerate, the Gories, the Oblivians, the Mummies, the Rip Offs; and even older surprises like the Zero Boys and the Zeros. But those sites also crash when online loners unload their litany of nitpicky bitch rants about all of these bands and labels whose best shot at any sort of recognition is usually in the big-toe region. We, it seems, will never learn.

"A lot of the fun was tainted by anger," says Trout. "We drank a lot, broke lots of shit, used crappy amps and guitars, our keyboards got bloody and broken, and we never had a proper PA. We did sell tons of T-shirts and actually made some money. Eventually, everyone fought a lot. I don't know what could've been driving us to deal with so much misery. The end is a blur, but I know it involved violence and fear and giving up, probably right about the time we were getting really good."

Lost Sounds, Chicago, 1999. (Photo by Canderson)

Epilogue
THE LONG GOODBYE

F OR THOSE WHO know Long Gone John or are fans of his Sympathy for the Record Industry enterprise, the news that he was moving from L.A. to a cabin in the woods outside Olympia, Washington, was like hearing that Castro would be heading off to Dallas to manage a Starbucks. But then Long Gone, not unlike the Cuban leader, could probably use a rest after all these years . . . especially after having to move his countless collectibles like Iggy Pop's tiger jacket from the back of *Raw Power*, Ed Wood's original hand-notated script for *Plan 9 from Outer Space*, the Mummies' tour hearse, Sid Vicious's gold record for *Never Mind the Bollocks*, a huge fireplace mantelpiece carved from one piece of wood, and more than a hundred thousand records . . .

LONG GONE JOHN: I'm looking at a minimum of thirty thousand dollars to move. It's been estimated at seventy thousand pounds and two semis with an overflow. The [estimator] said he has never seen anything like this in ten years of work.

ERIC DAVIDSON: Rumor has it you're thinking of selling off a lot of your stuff.

LG: No. Well, I said facetiously that when I move I'll sell all my extra copies of everything. With records, I used to buy two of everything when they came out, with this ludicrous mentality that one day I would use them as trade—and of course I never did that. I just kept buying and buying. Things like all the original hand-silk-screened Residents singles, all the Misfits singles, I used to buy them every time I'd see them. Everything is mint 'cause I was always so anal.

ED: Is there anything you'd sell if you absolutely had to?

LG: Well, I have a lot of things I would never part with: a Manson family jacket—I used to live with Squeaky, Brenda, and a few of the other girls; the *Plan 9* script; the complete works of Edward Gorey; Sid Vicious's gold record; an original papier-mâché sculpture by Dr. Seuss, and I just bought this raccoon coat in auction a few weeks ago in Cape Cod. Fortunately, I've never been in that position to have to sell things. I feel very badly for people who've had to sell their stuff because of hard times. It's nice to know that if something came up, I suppose I can do that. I have paintings that I paid forty thousand dollars for that are worth five hundred thousand dollars that I could sell tomorrow. But then you don't have the painting anymore.

ED: *How did you get into the toy business with Necessaries Toy Foundation?*

LG: It's the same path as records. The toy figures are something I've always been into, and I went from being a fanatical over-the-top collector to one day saying, Fuck, I wanna do this myself. As far as the record label, right now I have no releases planned. I've been hit so horribly with returns, people going out of business. I do have a compilation I've got to get finished someday. I just went through my catalog pulling out all the totally weird shit: Savage Pencil, Satin Chickens, Smegma, all that. The record's called *The Longer the Drool, the Stranger the Brew, My Dear*. Maybe I'll only do it as a fuckin' LP, 'cause no one's going to really want it anyway.

Union Carbide Productions looking for kicks, Radium Club, Gothenburg, Sweden, 1987. (Photo by Carl Abrahamsson)

ACKNOWLEDGMENTS

B OTTOMLESS THANKS TO all the bands and individuals who chimed in with their memories and time. I originally handed in this tome at nearly twice the requested length, so very sincere regrets to all those who kindly contributed stories and/or interviews that sadly ended up as victims of the brutal infinity of the "delete" key. Kudos, too, to the many good folks who dirtied their mitts digging through old shoe boxes for cool pictures and other ephemera. (And listen up, people, scan those old faxes now, because they fade quicker than a Kate Hudson romantic comedy. . . .) I often scoured these websites for info: All Music Guide, ClePunk, CollectorScum, Grunnen Rocks, MySpace, and Trouser Press, among many others, of course. And finally, the friends and acquaintances who have helped along the way are too many to mention, but here are the primos:

The Davidson family; the cities of Cleveland and Columbus, Ohio, and Brooklyn, New York; Maria Asher; Gilles Bonnel; Jay Brown; Jessica Burr; CMJ Network, Inc.; Byron Coley; Stanley Crouch; Sherri Cullison; Valerie Dickson; Mike Edison; James Englebeck; Hal Leonard Corp.; Jodi Ham; Larry Hardy; Tim Hayes; Jay Hinman; Jean-Luc Jousse; Lesley Kunikis; Aaron Lefkove; Steve Lowenthal; Keith Marlowe; Erin McDermott; Cliff Mott; Mark "icki" Murrmann; New Bomb Turks (Jim Weber, Matt Reber, Sam Brown, Bill Randt); Henry Owings; Rev. Moose; Stephen Slaybaugh; Paul Sommerstein; Kim Toback; Alicja Trout; Steve Wainstead; Michaela Warren; Tim Warren; Polly Watson . . . and Baked, Coffee Den; Dub Pies; Naidre's; One Girl Cookies; Ozzie's; and any other java joint that let me sit there for five hours and spend like three bucks for infinite refills. . . . Oh, and

watch out for www.WeNeverLearnBook.com, where I will be periodically posting some of the punchy print and pix that got sluiced through
the editorial plumbing. . . .

GREAT UNDERGUT CUTS: 1988-2001

Yᴇᴀʜ, ʏᴏᴜ ᴋɴᴏᴡ the score with these list things. Impossible, presumptuous, maddening in general—but whatever. They make for ace icebreakers. I left off best-ofs, live albums, reissues, and compilations. Kept it alphabetical for obvious reasons (though "Teenage Love Bomb" is the best single) . . . So dig and dispute at will!

SINGLES (50)

Action Swingers—"Bum My Trip"/"Kicked in the Head"
    (Noiseville, 1990)
American Soul Spiders—"Lazy Cowgirls"/"Shot by Bad Nurse"
    (Sympathy for the Record Industry, 1991)
Archie & the Pukes—S/T EP
    (Centsless, 1996)
Bikini Kill—"New Radio" EP
    (Kill Rock Stars, 1993)
Brides—"Pushed Around"/"Get to You"
    (Rip Off, 1997)
Candy Snatchers—"Pinto Pony"/"Buzzsaw," "My Sleaze"
    (Sounds Like Shit, 1993)
Cheater Slicks—"I'm Grounded"/"Can It Be"
    (In the Red, 1991)
Chinese Millionaires—"Juvenile Justice" EP
    (Flying Bomb, 1996)
Clone Defects—"Bottled Women"/"Cheetah Eyes"
    (Tom Perkins, 1999)

Dead Moon—"Fire in the Western World"/"Room 213"
     (Tombstone, 1992)
Derelicts—"Misery Maker"/"Wash"
     (Sub Pop, 1990)
Detroit Cobras—"Village of Love"/"Maria Christina"
     (Human Fly, 1996)
Devil Dogs—"Get on Your Knees"/"Long Gone"
     (Sympathy for the Record Industry, 1991)
Dirtbombs/Whites Stripes split 7"
     (Extra Ball, 2000)
Dirty Lovers—"Teenage Lovebomb"/"All I Want"
     (In the Red, 1992)
Doo Rag—"Hussy Bowler"/"Grease & All"
     (Westworld, 1993)
Drags—"Anxiety" EP
     (Empty, 1995)
Dummies—"I'm Going to Hell"/"Runnin' Around"
     (Bag of Hammers, 1993)
Dwarves—"Drug Store," "Detention Girl"/
"Astro Boy," "Motherfucker"
     (Sub Pop, 1990)
Electric Frankenstein—"EF Theme"/"Fast & Furious"
     (Mint Tone, 1994)
Estrus *Gearbox*—3 x 7" box set
     (Estrus, 1992)
Fireworks—"Untrue"/"She's a Tornado"
     (In the Red, 1993)
Gas Huffer—"Hot Cakes!"/"Beer Drinking Caveman from Mars"
     (Sub Pop, 1992)
Gaunt—"Jim Motherfucker"/"Spine"
     (Datapanik/Anyway, 1991)
Gibson Brothers—"Emulsified"/"Broke Down Engine"
     (Siltbreeze, 1990)
Gories—"Telepathic"/"Hate"
     (In the Red, 1991)
Guilty Pleasures—"Trash Bag"/"Cruel and Unusual"
     (Sack o' Shit, 2000)

Thee Headcoats—"Hatred, Ridicule & Contempt"/
"Neither Fish Nor Foul"
   (Sympathy for the Record Industry, 1991)
Homewreckers—"I Want More"/"Built to Last"
   (007, 1998)
Lazy Cowgirls—"Teenage Frankenstein"/"Intellectual Baby"
   (Sympathy for the Record Industry, 1992)
Thee Mighty Caesars—"Cowboys are Square"/"Ain't Got None"
   (Get Hip, 1990)
Mooney Suzuki—"Turn My Blue Sky Black" EP
   (Telstar, 1999)
Motards—"I'm a Criminal"/"The Fast Song"/"My Love is Bad"
   (Scuz, 1994)
Motorcycle Boy—"Feel It"/"One Punch"
   (Flipside, 1991)
Mudhoney w/ Billy Childish—"You're Gone" EP
   (Sub Pop, 1990)
Mummies—"Shitsville" EP
   (Regal Select, 1990)
New Bomb Turks/Gaunt split 7" EP
   (Datapanik, 1991)
Nights and Days—"These Days"/"Lookin'"
   (Regal Select, 1989)
Oblivians—"Strong Come On" EP
   (Crypt, 1996)
Reatards—"Get Real Stupid" EP
   (Goner, 1997)
Rocket 455—"Bum Ticker"/"Scabby"
   (Mutt Jr., 1994)
Sinister Six—"Get Outta My Way"/"Deloused"
   (Bag of Hammers, 1993)
Slobs—"Goin' Nowhere Fast" EP
   (Centsless, 1993)
Spaceshits—"Fullfisted Action" EP
   (Sympathy for the Record Industry, 1996)
STP—"Smoke 'Em" EP
   (Circuit, 1990)
Superchunk—"Slack Motherfucker"/"Night Creatures"
   (Merge, 1989)

Supersuckers—"Like a Big Fuckin' Train" EP
   (Sub Pop, 1991)
Teengenerate—"Get Me Back"/"Get Stuffed"/"One Way Ticket"
   (Wallabies, 1993)
Thomas Jefferson Slave Apartments/
Monster Truck Five split 7" EP
   (Datapanik, 1991)
Various Artists *BrainBlo* —3 x 7" box set
   (Casting Couch, 1992)

ALBUMS (100)

'68 Comeback—*Golden Rogues Collection*
   (Sympathy for the Record Industry, 1994)
A-Bones—*The Life of Riley*
   (Norton, 1991)
Action Swingers—S/T
   (Primo Scree, 1991)
Bantam Rooster—*Deal Me In*
   (Crypt, 1997)
Baseball Furies—*All American Psycho*
   (Flying Bomb, 1999)
Bassholes—*Blue Roots*
   (Revenant, 1992)
BellRays—*Let It Blast*
   (Vital Gesture, 1999)
Beguiled—*Blue Dirge*
   (Crypt, 1995)
Blacktop—*I've Got a Baaad Feeling About This*
   (In the Red, 1995)
Boss Hog—*Drinkin' Lechin' & Lyin'*
   (Amphetamine Reptile, 1989)
Boys from Nowhere—*The Bridal Album*
   (Skyclad, 1991)
Candy Snatchers—S/T
   (Safe House, 1996)
Cheater Slicks—*Don't Like You*
   (In the Red, 1995)

Chrome Cranks—S/T
(PCP, 1995)
Claw Hammer—*Q: Are We Not Men? A: We Are Not Devo*
(Sympathy for the Record Industry, 1991)
Clone Defects—*Blood on Jupiter*
(Tom Perkins, 2001)
Compulsive Gamblers—*Bluff City*
(Sympathy for the Record Industry, 1999)
Cosmic Psychos—*Go the Hack*
(Sub Pop, 1990)
Country Teasers—*Satan Is Real Again or Feeling Good About Bad Thoughts*
(Crypt, 1996)
Cynics—*Rock 'n' Roll*
(Get Hip, 1989)
Danko Jones—*I'm Alive and on Fire*
(Bad Taste, 2001)
Dead Moon—*Unknown Passage*
(Tombstone, 1989)
Death of Samantha—*Where the Women Wear the Glory
and the Men Wear the Pants*
(Homestead, 1988)
Detroit Cobras—*Mink Rat or Rabbit*
(Sympathy for the Record Industry, 1998)
Devil Dogs—*Saturday Night Fever*
(Crypt, 1994)
Didjits—*Hornet Pinata*
(Touch and Go, 1990)
Dirtbombs—*Ultraglide in Black*
(In the Red, 2001)
Dirtys—*You Should Be Sinnin'*
(Crypt, 1997)
Donnas—*American Teenage Rock 'n' Roll Machine*
(Lookout, 1998)
Dwarves—*Blood, Guts & Pussy*
(Sub Pop, 1990)
Fall-Outs—*Sleep*
(Super-Electro, 1994)
Fells—*Amped 10"*
(Westworld, 1994)

Fluid—*Glue*
(Sub Pop, 1990)
Gaunt—*I Can See Your Mom from Here*
(Thrill Jockey/Crypt, 1995)
Gibson Brothers—*Big Pine Boogie*
(Okra, 1988)
Gories—*House Rockin'*
(Wanghead with Lips, 1999)
Guitar Wolf—*Wolf Rock!*
(Goner, 1995)
Halo of Flies—*Music for Insect Minds*
(Amphetamine Reptile, 1991)
Thee Headcoats—*Heavens to Murgatroid Even! It's . . .*
(Sub Pop, 1991)
Hellacopters—*Supershitty to the Max*
(White Jazz, 1996)
Hives—*Veni, Vidi, Vicious*
(Burning Heart, 2000)
Humpers—*Positively Sick on 4th St.*
(Sympathy for the Record Industry, 1992)
Infections—*Kill . . .*
(Rip Off, 1997)
Jon Spencer Blues Explosion—*Orange*
(Matador, 1994)
LaDonnas—*Rock You All Night Long*
(Scooch Pooch, 1998)
Lazy Cowgirls—*Ragged Soul*
(Crypt, 1995)
Long Gones—*Prepare to Burn*
(Shake It, 1998)
Lost Sounds—*Black Wave*
(Empty, 2001)
Magnolias—*Dime Store Dream*
(Twin/Tone, 1989)
Makers—*S/T*
(Estrus, 1996)
Make-Up—*Destination: Love—Live! At Cold Rice*
(Dischord, 1996)

Mono Men—*Stop Draggin' Me Down*
(Estrus, 1990)
Motorcycle Boy—*Popsicle*
(Triple X, 1989)
Muffs—*Blonder and Blonder*
(Warner Bros., 1995)
Mummies—*Never Been Caught*
(Telstar, 1992)
Murder City Devils—S/T
(Die Young Stay Pretty, 1997)
Naked Raygun—*Jettison*
(Caroline, 1988)
Nashville Pussy—*Let Them Eat Pussy*
(Amphetamine Reptile, 1998)
Nation of Ulysses—*13-Point Plan to Destroy America*
(Dischord, 1991)
Necessary Evils—*Spider Fingers*
(In the Red, 1997)
Neckbones—*Souls on Fire*
(Fat Possum, 1997)
New Bomb Turks—*!!Destroy-Oh-Boy!!*
(Crypt, 1992)
Night Kings—*Increasing Our High*
(Super-Electro, 1992)
Nine Pound Hammer—*Smokin' Taters*
(Crypt, 1992)
No-Talents—*100% No Talent*
(Wild Wild, 1996)
Oblivians—*Soul Food*
(Crypt, 1995)
Piranhas—S/T
(On/On Switch, 2001)
Prisonshake—*A Girl Called Yes*
(Rubber, 1990)
Problematics—*The Kids All Suck*
(Rip Off, 1998)
Pussy Galore—*Dial M for Motherfucker*
(Matador, 1989)

Quadrajets—*Pay the Deuce*
(Estrus, 1998)
Raunch Hands—*Have a Swig*
(Crypt, 1990)
Reatards—*Teenage Hate*
(Goner, 1998)
Red Aunts—*#1 Chicken*
(Epitaph, 1995)
Registrators—*Terminal Boredom*
(Rip Off, 1996)
Rip Offs—*Got a Record*
(Rip Off, 1994)
Rocket from the Crypt—*Scream, Dracula, Scream!*
(Headhunter/Interscope, 1995)
Scrawl—*He's Drunk*
(No Other, 1988)
Showcase Showdown—*Appetite of Kings*
(Elevator Music, 1996)
Soul Asylum—*Hang Time*
(A&M, 1988)
Sons of Hercules—*Hits for the Misses*
(Unclean, 1996)
Spits—*S/T*
(Nickel & Dime, 2000)
Splash Four—*Kicks in Style*
(Estrus, 1997)
Starlite Desperation—*Show You What a Baby Won't*
(GSL, 1998)
Starvations—*One Long Night* EP
(Kapow, 2001)
Strokes—*Is This It*
(RCA, 2001)
Subsonics—*Everything Is Falling Apart*
(Get Hip, 1996)
Supercharger—*Goes Way Out*!
(Estrus, 1993)
Supersnazz—*Superstupid*
(Sub Pop, 1993)

Supersuckers—*La Mano Cornuda*
(Sub Pop, 1994)
Teengenerate—*Get Action!*
(Crypt, 1994)
Thomas Jefferson Slave Apartments—*Bait and Switch*
(Onion/American, 1995)
T-Model Ford—*Pee-Wee Get My Gun*
(Fat Possum, 1997)
Turbonegro—*Apocalypse Dudes*
(Boomba, 1998)
TV Killers—*Fuckin' Frenchies*
(Radio Blast Recordings, 1998)
Union Carbide Productions—*In the Air Tonight*
(Radium, 1988)
White Stripes—*White Blood Cells*
(Sympathy for the Record Industry, 2001)
Andre Williams—*Silky*
(In the Red, 1998)
X-Rays—*Speed Kills*
(Lowlife, 1995)
Zeke—*Flat Tracker*
(Scooch Pooch, 1996)

INDEX

We Never Learn

The Soundtrack

USE THE UNIQUE download code printed on the card included with this book to redeem your free MP3s, the soundtrack to these sordid tales. Just go to www.weneverlearnbook.com and follow the instructions. It's so easy even a punk can do it! Then crank the stereo dial clockwise and become the blight of your neighborhood.

1. Death of Samantha — "Savior City"
2. Cynics — "You Got the Love" (live) *
3. Raunch Hands — "Your Fat Friend"
4. Thee Headcoats — "Girl from '62"
5. Dwarves — "Throw That Girl Away" (alternate take) *
6. Didjits — "Gold Eldorado"
7. Gories — "There But for the Grace of God Go I"
8. A-Bones — "Button Nose"
9. Devil Dogs — "Big Fuckin' Party"
10. Cheater Slicks — "Spanish Rose" (demo) *
11. New Bomb Turks — "Slut" (live)
12. Mummies — "Mashi"
13. Supercharger — "Buzz Off"
14. Oblivians — "Memphis Creep"
15. Candy Snatchers — "Sympathy Trip"
16. Rip Offs — "She Said Yeah"
17. Archie & the Pukes — "I Got Worms"
18. No-Talents — "Blondes Have More Guns" (demo) *
19. Hives — "Barely Homosapien"
20. Clone Defects — "Cheetah Eyes"

*Previously unreleased

"Savior City"—Death of Samantha (1988; written by John Petkovic; from the album *Where the Women Wear the Glory and the Men Wear the Pants*; courtesy of Homestead Records)

"You Got the Love" (live)—Cynics (1991; written by the Cynics; courtesy of Michael Kastelic)

"Your Fat Friend"—Raunch Hands (1993; written by Chandler/Mariconda; from the album *Fuck Me Stupid*; courtesy of Crypt Records)

"Girl from '62"—Thee Headcoats (1991; written by Billy Childish; courtesy of Regal Select Records)

"Throw That Girl Away" (alternate take)—Dwarves (1996; written by Blag Dahlia; courtesy of the Dwarves)

"Gold Eldorado"—Didjits (1990; written by the Didjits; from the album *Hornet Pinata*; courtesy of Touch and Go Records and Rick Sims)

"There But for the Grace of God Go I"—Gories (1992; written by the Gories; from the album *Outta Here*; courtesy of Crypt Records)

"Button Nose"—A-Bones (1991; written by Benny Joy; courtesy of Norton Records; www.nortonrecords.com)

"Big Fuckin' Party"—Devil Dogs (1992; written by A. Gortler; from the album *Saturday Night Fever*; courtesy of Crypt Records)

"Spanish Rose" (demo)—Cheater Slicks (1994; written by Shannon/Shannon/Hatch; courtesy of In the Red Records)

"Slut" (live)—New Bomb Turks (1992; written by Scrawl; from the compilation *Living in Fear*; courtesy of New Bomb Turks)

"Mashi"—Mummies (1991; written by Ormsby/Morrill/Burk; courtesy of Budgetrock Global Talent, LLC; www.mummies.com)

"Buzz Off"—Supercharger (1992; written by Supercharger; from the album *Goes Way Out*; courtesy of Estrus Records and Supercharger; ripoffrecords@hotmail.com)

"Memphis Creep"—Oblivians (1996; written by Eric Friedl/Oblivians; courtesy of Oblivians; www.gonerrecords.com)

"Sympathy Trip"—Candy Snatchers (1997; written by the Candy Snatchers; from the compilation *Half-Assed, Will Travel*; courtesy of Perineum Recordings/Anyway Records)

"She Said Yeah"—Rip Offs (1994; written by Jon Von/Rip Offs; from the album *Got a Record*; courtesy of Rip Off Records; ripoffrecords@hotmail.com)

"I Got Worms"—Archie & the Pukes (1996; written by Archie &
     the Pukes; courtesy of Centsless Records)
"Blondes Have More Guns" (demo)—No-Talents (1995; written by
     C. Meneau/L. Zeller; courtesy of the No-Talents)
"Barely Homosapien"—Hives (1999; written by the Hives; from
     the compilation *Instant Assholes*; courtesy of Anger Factory
     and the band)
"Cheetah Eyes"—Clone Defects (1999; written by Clone Defects;
     courtesy of Tom Perkins and In the Red Records)